Somerset and the Defence of the Bristol Channel in the Second World War

Somerset and the Defence of the Bristol Channel in the Second World War

David Dawson, David Hunt
and Chris J Webster

Somerset Archaeological and Natural History Society
2011

Published by
Somerset Archaeological and Natural History Society
Somerset Heritage Centre, Brunel Way, Taunton, TA2 6SF
2011

© Somerset Archaeological and Natural History Society and the authors

ISBN-10: 0 902152 23 8
ISBN-13: 978 0 902152 23 6

Front Cover: 'Fortified islands in the Bristol Channel. 6" Naval gun emplacement, Gallipoli Gun, Steepholm.' By Ray Howard-Jones 1943. Imperial War Museum. ART LD 3525. All rights reserved.

Typeset by CJW using LaTeX.

Contents

List of Figures	vii
Preface and Acknowledgements	ix
Abbreviations and Glossary	xi
1 Introduction	1
2 Naval activities	5
3 Anti-invasion defences	19
4 Coast Artillery	47
5 Air defence of the Bristol Channel	57
6 Other military uses of the Somerset coast	77
7 Conclusion	95
Sources	97
Bibliography	99
Index	103

List of Figures

1.1	Somerset ports in 1939	2
2.1	Command areas 1939/40	6
2.2	Walton signal station	7
2.3	Forces in the Bristol Channel 1940	8
2.4	The sinking of SS *Carare*	8
2.5	The tug *John King*	9
2.6	British and German force dispositions 1941	10
2.7	The ketch *Garlandstone*	11
2.8	Forces in the Bristol Channel 1942	13
2.9	Minefields laid in 1941	14
2.10	The Langbury Hotel, Blue Anchor	15
2.11	The invasion of Normandy	16
2.12	RNAS Henstridge from the air	17
3.1	The perceived German threat	20
3.2	Stop lines and anti-tank islands	22
3.3	Junkers Ju 52 landing obstructions	25
3.4	Aircraft landing obstructions on Black Down	26
3.5	Slit trenches on Brent Knoll	29
3.6	The Pink Area	31
3.7	Williton Police Station defaced sign	31
3.8	The Emergency Licence	32
3.9	Anti-invasion defences on the Somerset Coast	33
3.10	Pillboxes at Dunster Beach	34
3.11	Section post at Blue Anchor Bay	34
3.12	Pillbox at Roadwater	35
3.13	The exposed sands at Berrow Flats	38
3.14	Pillbox at Uphill beach	39
3.15	Army states of readiness	40
3.16	The AU SD wireless network	43
3.17	The use of carrier pigeons	44
4.1	Minehead Coast Artillery battery from the air	47
4.2	The local defences of Minehead Coast Artillery battery	49
4.3	Artillery defences of the Bristol Channel	50
4.4	Gun emplacement on Brean Down	52
4.5	Coast Artillery searchlight on Steep Holm	54
4.6	Plastic armour roof on Steep Holm	55

4.7	The 3-inch AA gun	56
5.1	The 4.5-inch AA gun	58
5.2	Barrage balloon sites at Weston-super-Mare	59
5.3	Fighter Command organisation 1940	60
5.4	Fighter Command organisation 1941	60
5.5	The V1 threat to the South West	61
5.6	Searchlight deployment in the Coastal Defence Zone	62
5.7	Searchlight Cluster deployment 1941	63
5.8	Searchlights in the Fighter Box deployment 1942	64
5.9	Typical searchlight battery layout	65
5.10	Coverage of the GL radar 'carpet'	66
5.11	Coverage of GCI radars	67
5.12	Coverage of CD/CHL radars	68
5.13	*Luftwaffe* Bomber Navigation Systems	70
5.14	Washford Cross radio station	73
5.15	Norton Supply Reserve Depot from the air	75
6.1	The bath house at Dunster Beach camp	78
6.2	The Doniford AA range	80
6.3	The 'Queen Bee' at Doniford	81
6.4	Doniford Camp	82
6.5	Comparison of tank ranges at Kilton and North Hill, Minehead	83
6.6	Firing ranges in the Bristol Channel	84
6.7	Lilstock range target arrow	85
6.8	Birnbeck Pier, Weston-super-Mare	86
6.9	Experimental rails at Brean Down	87
6.10	The balloon hanger at Pawlett	89
6.11	RAF DF sites at Alstone from the air	92
6.12	Unidentified structures on Brean beach	93

Preface

Viewed from the Somerset coast, the Bristol Channel looks very empty. The odd boat fishing and perhaps one ocean-going ship may be all that is visible. This appearance belies an important maritime highway – 12m tonnes were handled at Bristol alone in 2007. Eighty-five years ago the scene was very different. Ocean-going vessels were much smaller and carried cargoes in man-sized units, so-called break bulk. Coal was king – the export of coal from south Wales to supply bunkering stations all over the maritime world was still a significant trade. Colliers supplying the power stations and gasworks at places like Portishead and Bristol, as well as London and the south coast, were among the myriad of smaller vessels, some still under sail, employed in the coasting trade. Their employment has either disappeared entirely or has been taken over by the modern articulated lorry. With the outbreak of the Second World War, it became increasingly obvious that Somerset was in a key location to ensure the forward and coastal defence of this waterway and its associated ports and industries and to offer facilities that furthered the prosecution of the maritime war.

The Somerset Archaeological and Natural History Society has embraced the need to address this period of the county's archaeology and history and trusts that this volume will appeal to the growing popular interest in these relatively recent times. It was originally solicited as a contribution to the Society's series, The Maritime History of Somerset, but later it was felt that it would be better produced as a freestanding book of its own. As far as the authors are aware, amongst all that has been written there has been no other study examining the evidence for the response to the maritime challenges that involved the county from 1939 to 1945.

This volume is very much a statement of work in progress. It is a summary, which it is intended will serve as the basis for further more detailed studies to be published in future. Some of the ideas and evidence presented will be familiar to all who attended the symposium on the subject of the *Archaeology and History of Somerset in the Second World War* organised by the Society's Archaeology Committee at Wells and Mendip Museum on 20 November 2010. Over the preceding five years the three authors had come to realise that their skills, experience and research complemented each other's so well that a published collaboration would be valuable and productive. This grew out of their participation in the preparation of contributions to the post-medieval to modern sections of *The Archaeology of South West England* (Webster 2007) in which the scope of studies of the 20th and 21st centuries is explored. The research is based on the premise that examination of all sources of historical data including archaeological evidence, can result in a more coherent view of what happened and why, despite the inevitable problems of survival and reconciling different kinds of evidence. David Hunt has done the bulk of the work searching out and sifting the records in the National Archives and all three authors have visited most of the sites on the ground to discuss their siting, construction and use, bringing to bear their extensive knowledge of Somerset: David Dawson and Chris Webster as archaeologists who have worked in the county for over twenty years and David Hunt as a Somerset man who knows the county well and sees it through the eyes of a retired senior Army officer with well over thirty years' service in command, staff, technical and regimental posts.

Acknowledgements

Many people have helped us over the years to increase our knowledge of the Second World War in Somerset and in the Bristol Channel. These have included landowners, who were usually more than willing to allow access to sites on their land, other researchers who found sites by patient detective work and specialists in fields such as electronic warfare who provided information on Somerset aspects of that work. It would be impossible to list them all here but many are recorded as contributors to the Somerset Historic Environment Record. For the present volume we are particularly grateful to John Penny for access to his extensive unpublished researches; to Vernon Stone, Harbourmaster for Watchet and Minehead, for sharing his local knowledge of these harbours, their defences, the Blue Anchor gun site and the ranges to the east of Watchet; and Tim Wray for sharing his knowledge of Auxiliary Units and access to his unpublished research. We would also like to thank Stan Ames, Don Brown, Roger JC Thomas of English Heritage and Jeffrey Wilson for their patience in answering our queries.

We would like to thank the Imperial War Museum for permission to reproduce Ray Howard-Jones's painting of the Steep Holm gun emplacement on the cover; English Heritage for figures 2.12 and 4.1; Ilfracombe and North Devon Aqua Club for figure 2.4; the UK Hydrographic Office for figure 2.9; Somerset Historic Environment Record for figures 3.5, 4.4, 5.14 and 6.12; Somerset Studies Library for figures 3.4, 6.7 and 6.11; The National Archive for figures 4.2 and 5.15; Tim Dawson for figure 3.10 and Vernon Stone for figures 4.7, 5.1, 6.2, 6.3 and 6.4.

The production of maps and diagrams and the design and typesetting were by Chris Webster. We are grateful to Nicholas Dawson, Peter Ellis, Terry Hunt, Captain Hugh May RN, Mike Osborne, Jane Porter, Bill Stebbing and Adrian Webb who commented on, and thereby improved, earlier drafts. Any errors that remain are the authors'.

Abbreviations and glossary

The military definitions provided are only those current in the context of Somerset and the South West at the time of the Second World War.

8 Corps (or VIII Corps) The Army formation responsible, between July 1940 and January 1943, for the area of Somerset, Devon and Cornwall.

AA Anti-Aircraft.

Action Stations Army alert measure ordered when there was an immediate threat of invasion to bring the Army and Home Guard to the highest state of readiness.

ADGB Air Defence of Great Britain. This included RAF Fighter and Balloon Commands, the Observer Corps and the Army's AA Command.

Admiralty The executive Department of State responsible for Royal Naval and Marine Forces.

Aerodrome A term used by the RAF in both World Wars to describe an airfield or airbase.

AFV Armoured Fighting Vehicle (eg tank or armoured car).

AI Aircraft Interception. Radar mounted in an aircraft to direct it to intercept a nearby enemy aircraft once the two had been brought together by GCI.

Air Ministry The executive Department of State responsible for the Royal Air Force.

Anti-Aircraft Command An Army organisation, administered by the War Office and under operational control of RAF Fighter Command, controlling all AA guns and searchlights in the UK.

Anti-tank island A town or route centre provided with all round defences to deny the use of the routes and town to an invader.

Army Class Men (in a given age bracket) conscripted into the Army under the National Service Act.

ARP Air Raid Precautions for civilians; which later became Civil Defence. The military term was Passive Air Defence (PAD).

Aspirin Radio Counter Measures against Headache (*Knickebein*).

ATDU Aircraft Torpedo Development Unit.

Atlantic Wall The anglicised German name for their coastal defences from the North Cape in Norway to the Franco-Spanish border including the Occupied Channel Islands. The most intensively defended stretches were along the English Channel and southern North Sea coasts.

ATS Auxiliary Territorial Service, the women's service organisation supporting the Army.

AU Auxiliary Units, the deliberately misleading (plural) name given to the GHQ Auxiliary Units which consisted of two parts; the Operations Branch of selected men (primarily from the Home Guard) who were trained to attack German forces after an invasion from concealed bases (OB) and the Special Duties Branch that was set up to provided a network of civilian spies with wireless communications within any coastal area occupied by the Germans.

Auxiliary patrol In 1939, an anti-submarine and minesweeping service formed from requisitioned sea-going fishing vessels. Crews were drawn from the Royal Naval Patrol Service. During and after the evacuation of Dunkirk, the Auxiliary Patrol was considerably expanded by requisitioning inshore craft to assist in the evacuation and to serve as anti-invasion patrols.

Baedeker raids German bombing campaign in 1942 against historic British cities listed in a pre-war guide book of that name. The first attacks were on Exeter in April 1942 followed by Bath and later Weston-super-Mare. Attacks were also expected at Taunton, Glastonbury and Wells.

Balloon barrage The deployment of a number of barrage balloons in one of more rings around a factory or aerodrome to make it difficult for enemy aircraft to attack it from low level.

Bareback Operation Bareback, the use of the BBC Washford and Brookman's Park (Hertfordshire) transmitters to jam German instructions to bombers.

Battery The smallest permanent unit of the Royal Artillery. In Coast Artillery, one or more guns emplaced in the same area under a battery command post. In AA searchlights, an organisation with 24 searchlights normally deployed onto 24 single sites or 8 cluster sites.

BBC British Broadcasting Corporation, the government broadcasting monopoly in Britain.

Beach barrage Fire from Coast Artillery along a beach rather than at a specific target.

Beach defence gun A static gun with the role of engaging enemy transports, landing craft or other targets on landing beaches but without the fire control facilities to engage shipping at sea.

Beetle A wireless system to broadcast immediate warnings of a German invasion to all units and formations using normal civilian wireless receivers.

BEF British Expeditionary Force, the British Army and RAF assistance to French forces defending the eastern borders of France.

Benito British name for the *Luftwaffe Y-Gerät* bomber navigation system.

Benjamin Radio Counter Measures against the *Luftwaffe Y-Gerät* navigation system for bombers.

BL Breech loading (gun).

Black out A wartime measure requiring outside lighting and street lamps to be switched off, light from inside buildings to be completely masked between dusk and dawn, and restricting vehicle lighting, all to make it difficult for enemy bombers to navigate at night.

Bletchley Park The headquarters of the Government Code and Cypher School, actually Britain's main decryption centre.

BCP Battery Command Post from where the guns of a battery were commanded.

Bofors A 40mm light anti-aircraft gun later know as the L40/70.

Bolero The plan to build up American strength in Britain.

BOP Battery Observation Post, the place where the observers and range finder of a battery were sited. In a small battery, the BOP might include the BCP.

Bookrest A hose filled with plastic explosive as a device for clearing beach minefield

BRO British Resistance Organisation, an entirely modern term referring to the GHQ Home Forces Auxiliary Units.

Bromide Radio Counter Measures against Ruffian, the *Luftwaffe Y-Gerät* beam navigation system for bombers.

Bubble breakwater A system to break up waves in heavy seas using pipes with air jets.

Cased petrol Filled petrol cans in a case or crate (normally two four-gallon tins in a wooden case).

CCMA Commander Corps Medium Artillery, a brigadier at a Corps HQ responsible primarily for Coast Artillery.

CD/CHL Coast Defence/Chain Home Low, a type of radar used to detect shipping and low-flying aircraft over the sea.

CH Chain Home, the earliest type of radar giving early warning of high-flying aircraft approaching Britain.

CHL Chain Home Low, radar that could detect low-flying aircraft over the sea.

Cluster A grouping of three anti-aircraft searchlights on the same site. Also used for three or four interconnected Observer Corps posts in an area.

Abbreviations and Glossary

Coast Artillery Part of the Royal Artillery, providing anti-shipping gunfire from forts and batteries.

Coast defence zone The area of responsibility of the commander of the coastal defence zone running inland for five to 10 miles from the shore.

Coast searcher Part time civilians working for the Coastguards checking beaches for signs of enemy agents landing.

Coast watcher Civilians used by the Coastguard service to maintain a seaward watch, particularly at night.

Coaster The strict legal definition is any vessel running a cargo between ports within the UK. In practice this type of vessel plied cargo anywhere between the seaports of north-west Europe.

Coastguard An Admiralty service whose duties included the prevention of smuggling, the protection of shipwrecked property, assisting distressed vessels, providing storm warnings and assisting in coast defence.

Collier A vessel used exclusively in carrying coals, usually from ports near coal mining districts to major cities and other ports and direct to plant such as gasworks and electricity power stations.

Cold War The continuing state of political conflict, military tension, proxy wars, and economic competition existing after the Second World War, primarily between the Soviet Union and its satellite states, and the powers of the Western world, particularly the United States.

COXE Combined Operations Experimental Establishment, Appledore.

Cromwell The code word used in 1940 to bring Army units (but not the Home Guard) to the highest star of readiness to repel an invasion.

CW Chemical Warfare, the use of chemical substances (gases or liquids) to cause casualties, to harass or delay the enemy or to render ground dangerous to occupy. The term also included the protection of friendly troops against such use by the enemy.

D-Day The day on which an operation begins or is due to begin. In this book, it refers to the first day of Operation Overlord – the invasion of Normandy on 6 June 1944.

Darkie The wireless system used by certain Observer Corps posts allowing communications to assist aircraft who did not know their position.

Defile The portion of a route that troops can only pass on a narrow front (eg a mountain pass or bridge).

Degaussing vessels Vessels specially equipped to reduce the magnetic signature of an iron or steel hulled ship and confer a degree of immunity to magnetic mines.

Denial measures Measures taken to prevent the enemy from capturing transport, fuel or rations or from using ports, harbours or other similar facilities.

DF Direction Finding of radio transmissions to establish the bearing of the transmitter.

DMWD Royal Navy Department of Miscellaneous Weapons Development.

Domino Radio Counter Measures against Benito the *Luftwaffe Y-Gerät* beam navigation system for bombers.

Dual role guns AA guns capable of firing against air targets and shipping.

E-boat A British term which was often initially used for German light naval forces in general. Later it became equated with the heavy fast motor-torpedo boats that the Germans called *Schnellboote* or *S-boote*.

Eire The name of Ireland (the nation state) in Irish, also used in English during the Second World War and later to prevent confusion with Northern Ireland.

EL Emergency Licence to permit certain key civilian vehicles to move during invasion alerts.

Emergency battery A Coast Artillery battery constructed in 1940 using old naval guns to guard the approach channels to ports, landing places and beaches against armed merchant vessels, transports, armoured fighting vehicle (AFV) carriers and similar craft.

Examination battery A Coast Artillery battery specially designated to cover vessels undergoing checks by the Examination Service and be able to fire on the vessel if found to be hostile.

Examination service The port entry service organised by the Royal Navy 'to identify and ascertain the character and intentions of vessels (excepting war vessels) seeking entrance in order that the defences may have warning of the attempted entry of suspicious or unfriendly ships.'

ExHER Exmoor National Park Historic Environment Record.

Expendable Noise-Maker A ship-borne device intended to confuse acoustic-homing torpedoes.

Field Service Regulations The War Office publication which laid down the organisation, administration and conduct of operations by the Army in war.

Fifth Column A network of agents or Nazi sympathisers, which was (wrongly) believed to have been set up in Britain to carry out acts of sabotage or, in the event of an invasion, cause confusion and panic in the population.

Fighter box A layout of anti-aircraft searchlights designed to enable night fighters to be directed towards enemy aircraft.

Fighter Command RAF formation responsible for the air defence of Britain, which was organised into Fighter Groups each with a territorial area of responsibility.

Fighting Vehicle Proving Establishment A military research establishment responsible for testing and developing armoured fighting vehicles.

Fire control predictor Equipment that calculated the future position of an enemy aircraft to enable AA guns or rockets to fire at it.

Fixed defences An Army term used to describe Coast Artillery defences.

Fixer stations Directional finding (DF) stations working with other DF stations to take bearings on aircraft radio transmissions and thus 'fix' the position of the friendly aircraft.

Flag Officer An executive officer of the Royal Navy with a rank superior to that of a captain and who is entitled to fly a distinguishing flag of his rank.

Fleet Air Arm (FAA) The aviation branch of the Royal Navy.

Fliegekorps A *Luftwaffe* operational formation within a *Luftflotte* (air fleet) which consisted of a number of *Geschwader* (each equivalent to an RAF Group).

FOIC Royal Naval Flag Officer in Command.

Fort Record Book A book containing the records and plans of coastal fortresses.

GCI Ground Controlled Interception, use of ground-based radar with associated ground-air radio communications to direct a fighter aircraft equipped with AI radar towards a target.

GDA Gun Defended Area, an area protected by anti-aircraft guns or rockets.

GHQ General Headquarters (in this book GHQ Home Forces).

GL Gun Laying, a radar used to direct the fire of anti-aircraft guns or rockets onto their target.

GPO General Post Office, the government organisation with a monopoly for the provision of postal and telecommunications services in Britain.

Granite Flares used by the Observer Corps in bad weather to warn friendly aircraft of nearby high ground.

Ground watcher stations RAF Radio Counter Measures stations searching for German navigation beam transmissions.

Group (Coast Artillery) A HQ commanding and administering a number of Coast Artillery batteries.

Group (Observer Corps) An RAF organisation responsible for some 30 to 40 observer posts for tracking aircraft with a HQ to receive, process and distribute the reports from its posts.

Group (RAF) An RAF Group controlled a number of fighter wings and the airfields on which they were based within a geographical area.

Abbreviations and Glossary

Group (Royal Navy) The Royal Navy organised its Patrol Service into Groups of minesweepers and anti-submarine vessels, usually between three and ten vessels who acted under the command of a single officer in charge.

GWR Great Western Railway, the commercial railway company that operated the majority of railways systems in Somerset and along the South Wales coast.

HAA Heavy Anti-Aircraft, AA guns of 3-in calibre or greater used against high-flying aircraft.

Haslar A mobile smoke generator used to make smoke screens to conceal important installations like ports from air attack.

Hajile Retarding rockets designed to enable air-dropped vehicles to land softly after parachute descent.

HDU RAF Home Defence Units intercepting and monitoring *Luftwaffe* VHF air and ground-air communications.

HE High explosive.

Headache British name for the *Luftwaffe Knickebein* beam navigation system for bombers.

Hedgehog Forward firing shipboard anti-submarine mortar throwing a salvo of bombs in a pattern above the suspected position of a submarine.

Hedgerow A mortar designed to fire salvoes of bombs from a landing craft to clear beaches of mines.

HM His Majesty's.

HMS His Majesty's Ship, a commissioned Royal Naval war vessel or shore establishment.

HMT His Majesty's Trawler, a fishing vessel commissioned in the Royal Naval Auxiliary Patrol.

Home Forces Sometimes abbreviated as HF or HFOR, Home Forces, with its own Commander-in-Chief and its own GHQ, comprised all Army field forces in the UK (but not Anti-Aircraft Command and certain War Office controlled units) and was responsible for the ground defence of the British Isles.

HQ Headquarters, the organisation that supports a commander and enables him to carry out his command functions.

Hydrographic Department The branch of the Admiralty responsible for the compilation and correction of charts, tide tables, and light lists for many parts of the world and control of the Navy estimate for surveys, observations and chronometers.

IFF Identification Friend or Foe, a device fitted to RAF and allied aircraft to return a distinctive signal to a radar station distinguishing them from enemy forces.

Immobilisation parks A park used by civilian police under invasion conditions to impound vehicles moving without an EL (emergency licence) to enforce the 'stand firm' policy and keep roads free for troops to repel an invasion, also called Civilian Car Parks.

Infantry section post A linear pillbox covering a limited arc designed to take an infantry section of about 6 to 12 men with loopholes for each weapon.

INTSUM Army abbreviation for an Intelligence Summary.

Jamming The deliberate transmission or re-transmission of radio or radar signals with the object of impairing the use of radio or radar devices by the enemy.

Ju Official German air ministry abbreviation for Junkers aircraft (eg Ju 52).

KG *Kampfgeschwader*, a *Luftwaffe* formation roughly equivalent to an RAF group.

Killer zone The zone in a 'fighter box' deployments of searchlights where the night fighter would be directed towards the raider to destroy it.

Knickebein The first generation of *Luftwaffe* beam navigation systems for bombers using the Lorenz blind landing system.

LAA Light Anti-Aircraft, normally guns under 40mm barrel diameter used against low flying aircraft.

Landing When referring to enemy forces, the term may refer to landing troops from vessels over beaches or in harbours, by parachute, gliders or from powered aircraft landing on beaches, roads, open ground or aerodromes.

LMG Light machine-gun, carriable by a single person (eg Bren or Lewis guns).

Lorenz A blind landing system used by German bombers, manufactured by Lorenz.

Lowered his flag A naval term used when a senior officer leaves his command.

Luftwaffe German air force.

Magnetic mine A sea mine fired by the magnetic influence of a steel or iron vessel coming close.

Marconi Adcock aerial A direction finding (DF) station using four vertical aerials set in a square with the DF equipment in a hut in the centre.

Materiel A term, originally French, covering military equipment, stores, supplies and spares.

Meacon A British system for 'masking' *Luftwaffe* Medium Frequency navigation beacons by retransmitting their signals. Meacon is a contraction of 'masking of beacons'.

MFDF Medium Frequency Direction Finding. An RAF organisation that provided radio navigation services.

MI5 The British security service dealing with counter-espionage within the UK. Originally a branch of Military Intelligence.

MI6 The British security service dealing with overseas espionage.

MMG Medium machine-gun (eg the Vickers 0.303 MMG) which is capable of accurate sustained fire over a long period.

MOD battalion An ad hoc battalion formed within training establishments for anti-invasion purposes. Possibly named from a contraction of Mobile Defence.

MOI Ministry of Information, wartime government department dealing with news and press censorship, home and overseas publicity/propaganda and the assessment of civilian morale.

Molotov cocktail An improvised anti-tank weapon consisting of a bottle filled with an inflammable mixture which burst into flames when broken.

Mulberry harbour Harbours constructed on the Normandy invasion beaches using floating components constructed in England and towed across the English Channel.

Navy List A periodic publication authorised by the Admiralty listing all commissioned officers then currently serving in the Royal Navy, including those of the Royal Naval Reserve (RNR), Royal Naval Volunteer Reserve (RNVR), Royal Marines (RM), Queen Alexandra's Royal Naval Nursing Service (QARNNS), and Women's Royal Naval Service (WRNS).

NCO Non-commissioned officer in the Army or RAF (eg corporal or sergeant).

NOIC Naval Officer in Charge (often the senior RN officer in charge of a port).

Neptune The naval deployment to deliver and support Operation Overlord.

OB Operational Base, a deliberately misleading name given to the concealed bases of the operational patrols of GHQ Home Forces Auxiliary Units.

Observer Corps A civilian organisation, working under RAF Fighter Command, which tracked aircraft both friendly and hostile over the UK. In April 1941 it became the Royal Observer Corps (ROC).

ORB Operation Record Book, the RAF equivalent of a war-diary for an aerodrome or other unit.

Orbit point searchlight A searchlight within the 'fighter box' deployment with a vertical beam around which night fighters would orbit waiting for enemy raiders to enter the killer zone.

Overlord The code name for the operation to invade north-west Europe in 1944, which took place on D-Day, 6 June.

OpO Army abbreviation for Operation Order.

PAC Parachute and Cable rocket, an experimental AA weapon.

Abbreviations and Glossary

PBA Port of Bristol Authority, then owned by the City and County of Bristol and consisting of the City Docks, Avonmouth Docks and Portishead Dock.

Pdr Pounder, normally the weight in pounds of the projectile fired by a gun.

Permitted lighting A low level of lighting permitted during wartime blackout to facilitate essential nighttime work in railway yards, docks, depots and other important factories.

Persistent gas Gas vapour or droplets of chemicals that cause severe irritation or blistering to unprotected troops which do not readily disperse.

Petroleum Board The wartime government organisation responsible for petrol supplies in Britain which controlled commercial fuel depots.

Pink area The area where the threat of invasion was considered to be significantly higher and special additional measures were required to safeguard petrol stocks.

Pipsqueak Device in an RAF fighter aircraft that transmitted a Morse signal on high-frequency radio to enable the position of the fighter to be fixed by Direction Finding.

Plastic armour Armour consisting of granite chips embedded in a 70mm thick layer of mastic (a bituminous cement-like asphalt) used on vessels. In some coast artillery sites it was poured onto 18mm steel plates to provide overhead cover for gun houses. Officially known as plastic protective plating.

PPI Plan Position Indicator, a device showing radar plots on a circular map base, centred on the radar station, showing both the fighter and enemy aircraft allowing the operator to guide a fighter towards its target.

PRN Primary Record Number uniquely identifying an entry in a Historic Environment Record.

PRO Public Record Office, official collection of government and court records (from 2003 part of The National Archives).

PS Paddle steamer.

Purple warning A confidential air raid warning passed to establishments giving about 10 minutes warning of an expected air raid so that 'permitted lighting' was immediately switched off.

Pyrotechnic signals Use of flares, rockets or smoke to pass simple pre arranged signals.

Q site A night bombing decoy with lights simulating an aerodrome to attract enemy bombers away from a real aerodrome.

QF Quick Firing. Artillery piece loaded with a combined cartridge and shell enabling a rapid rate of fire.

QF site A night bombing decoy site simulating the fires resulting from smaller scale incendiary bomb attack on an urban area, factory or depot with the aim of attracting enemy bombers away from their target.

QL site A night bombing decoy site with lights simulating an urban area or a specific factory or depot. with the aim of attracting enemy bombers away from their target.

Quadrant tower An observation tower used on air to ground bombing ranges to locate the point of impact of bombs.

Radiolocation A term released for general use when the existence of RDF was disclosed to the public on 18 June 1941 through a House of Commons statement.

RA Royal Artillery (full title, Royal Regiment of Artillery).

Radar Radio Detection and Ranging. The American term for RDF that was also used in Britain from September 1943 to avoid confusion.

RAE Royal Aircraft Establishment, the British aircraft research and testing organisation.

RAF Royal Air Force.

RAF Regiment The RAF organisation, founded in 1942, which took over responsibility from the Army for the ground and air defence of RAF aerodromes.

RCM Radio Counter Measures primarily against German aircraft radio navigation aids.
RDF Radio Detection and Direction Finding. The original British name for radar; the American term was adopted in September 1943 as an allied standardisation measure.
RE Royal Engineers (full title, Corps of Royal Engineers).
Regional Commissioner A senior government appointed person who would take over control of the region if enemy action prevented central government from exercising its functions. The South West was in Region 7 with the Regional Commissioner's HQ in Bristol. The Region covered Wiltshire, Gloucestershire, Somerset, Devon and Cornwall.
Retd retired, used after the previous rank of a retired officer (eg Colonel retd)
RN Royal Navy.
RNAS Royal Naval Air Station.
RNO Resident Naval Officer, a shore-based appointment with responsibilities for control of shipping and operational control of the Coastguard and Coast Artillery in a designated area.
ROC Royal Observer Corps (originally the Observer Corps).
ROF Royal Ordnance Factory.
Romney shelter or hut A large prefabricated building designed like a Nissen hut.
RSS Radio Security Service, the RSS was established before the Second World War to monitor illicit transmissions from spies or enemy agents within Britain. It was run by the GPO on behalf of MI5 and also used part-time volunteer radio amateurs.
RT Radio Telephone or radio telephony voice communications.
Ruffian British code name for the *Luftwaffe X-Gerät* beam navigation system for bombers.
Ryder flares Pyrotechnic lights used by Coast Artillery to illuminate targets.
SAAD School of Anti-aircraft Defence.
Satellite fighter station A simplified fighter aerodrome commanded and administered from a parent aerodrome.
Schnellboote or S-boote Heavy, fast German motor-torpedo boats.
SD Special Duties, a branch of the GHQ Home Forces Auxiliary Units trained to collect and transmit information about German forces from within a coastal area in Britain occupied after an invasion.
Sea Raid Zone an area up to about 5 miles deep in which military installations and important civilian factories of infrastructure might be attacked by enemy forces landing on the coast.
Secret Service Historic term used to describe MI5.
Self-propelled anti-tank gun Anti-tank gun capable of moving under its own power but normally not capable of firing on the move.
SF site Special Fire or Starfish, a very large fire decoy site designed to replicate the fires caused by *Luftwaffe* pathfinder aircraft when attacking a major town or city with the aim of attracting mass bomber raids away from their target.
Shadow aircraft factory Factories set up by the Ministry of Aircraft Production to provide resilience against air attack through duplication and dispersion of the factories of major aircraft manufacturers.
Shaped charge An explosive charge which concentrates the explosive force into a narrow jet that can burn a hole through armour.
SHER Somerset Historic Environment Record covering the current administrative county of Somerset except those parts within Exmoor National Park.
Slapping The rapid movement of a vertical searchlight beam downwards to indicate to a night fighter the direction in which an enemy raider had been identified.
SLC Searchlight Control (radar), the original was also known as Elsie.

Abbreviations and Glossary

Somerset An administrative county which then included the City of Bath but which since 1974 has been divided into what are now the administrative counties of Somerset, North Somerset and Bath and North East Somerset.

Somerset Light Infantry (Prince Albert's) or SLI The county infantry regiment, with its Regimental Depot in Taunton. The Regiment comprised a number of battalions.

Somerset Sub Area The Army administrative HQ for Somerset.

Sound locator A device to establish the elevation and bearing of an aircraft by using directional microphones to receive the noise of the aircraft engine(s).

South Western District The administrative area covering the counties of Somerset, Devon and Cornwall which replaced the 8 Corps area in January 1943.

Southern Command An administrative HQ responsible for the South and South West of England. In the event of operations, Command HQs became Army HQs and commanded the corps HQs in their area.

Spigot mortar Weapon developed primarily for the Home Guard firing anti-tank and anti-personnel bombs. Also called the Blacker Bombard and first issued in late 1941.

Spoiler transmitter A transmitter used to prevent enemy aircraft from using a civilian broadcast transmitter as a navigation aid.

SRO Somerset Record Office, now part of the Somerset Heritage Centre.

Stand to Army alert measure ordered when conditions were particularly suitable for an invasion to bring Home Forces to a complete state of readiness to resist an invasion and to call out the Home Guard. Also abbreviation for 'Stand to arms' a procedure carried out by all units in the field before dawn and again before dusk to be fully prepared for any enemy attack.

SS Steamship, a merchant vessel driven by either reciprocating or turbine steam engines.

Stop line A linear defence line, primarily to stop tanks, using natural futures like rivers or canals or artificial anti-tank obstacle(eg excavated ditches or concrete cubes) with road or railway blocks on routes crossing over the obstacle and pillboxes sited to provide defensive fire.

Stuka (*Sturtzkapfflugzeug*) A *Luftwaffe* dive-bomber, the Junkers Ju 87.

Swept lanes Designated lanes for shipping which are regularly patrolled by minesweepers to keep them clear of mines.

TNA The National Archives, formerly the Public Record Office.

U-boat (*Unterseeboot*) German submarine.

Ultra The British codename for intelligence gained from interception and decryption of high-level enemy radio traffic. Its very existence was secret to ensure that the enemy believed their codes were secure.

UP Unrotated projectile, a rocket developed for anti-aircraft use.

V1 The German flying bomb (*Vergeltungswaffe 1*).

VCP Vehicle check point, a roadblock manned by the Army or Home guard to check civilian traffic.

VE Victory in Europe (day, 8 May 1945).

VHF Very High Frequency (radio transmission).

VIII Corps (or 8 Corps) The Army formation responsible, between July 1940 and January 1943, for the area of Somerset, Devon and Cornwall.

VJ Victory in Japan (day, 15 August 1945).

VP Vulnerable Point, important civilian infrastructure (eg power stations, bridges, BBC transmitters) which required a military guard.

Waist of the South West Colloquial Army term for the area between Bridgwater Bay on the Somerset coast and Lyme Bay on the south coast.

War-diary Daily historic record kept by Army units and formations.

Western Area The Army administrative area in 1941 that included Somerset.
Western Approaches Command Royal Naval Command responsible for the protection of shipping in the Atlantic, originally based at Plymouth and later moved to Liverpool.
Wheezers and Dodgers Nickname for Royal Navy's Department of Miscellaneous Weapons Development (DMWD.
Wireless Intelligence and Development Unit The name given to the RAF flying unit used to monitor and evaluate *Luftwaffe* bombing navigation aids.
WO War Office, the executive Department of State responsible for the Army.
Works order An order issued by the Royal Engineers for a civilian contractor to undertake construction, maintenance or repair work.
WRNS Women's Royal Naval Service, commonly known as the Wrens.
WT Wireless telegraphy (communications using Morse code).
X-Gerät The second generation of *Luftwaffe* beam navigation systems for bombers.
Y-Gerät The third generation of *Luftwaffe* beam navigation systems for bombers.
Y-Service In this book, the RAF intercept and monitoring organisation which primarily monitored *Luftwaffe* ground-air and air-to-air communications.
ZAA Anti-aircraft batteries or units equipped with unrotating (rocket) projectiles (UP).

Chapter 1

Introduction

SOMERSET may seem at first sight to be of little maritime strategic significance. It has few harbours: all of them small and none accessible at all states of the tide. Only Watchet, Dunball, Highbridge and Portishead provided facilities for coasting cargo steamers and these facilities were of very modest capacity in terms of the cargo they could handle and distribute by rail. Piers at Minehead, Clevedon, and Weston-super-Mare provided landing points for the Bristol Channel passenger steamers but had no strategic significance. The county does however form the southern flank of the Bristol Channel, an important waterway giving access to the Port of Bristol, to the coaling ports of Newport, Cardiff, Penarth and Barry (all owned by the Great Western Railway) and to a network of waterways leading to the heart of the Midlands. In an age when the whole transport system, particularly the railways and the shipping industry, was geared to carrying the main flows of heavy minerals the shortest possible distance by rail to the nearest port and then by water to the customer, the strategic importance of the Bristol Channel was much wider than its significance to international trade through the Port of Bristol. Somerset was also in close reach of the English Channel and straddled the main communication routes from London and the Midlands to the marine facilities of Devon and Cornwall, notably the naval bases at Plymouth.

These geographical considerations have to be set in the context of the three main maritime strategic issues that affected the homeland throughout the war. The first was the defence, maintenance and development of international and coastal seaways and the ports and infrastructure that ensured their effectiveness. Britain was utterly dependent on the success of this strategy for keeping open its links and supplies of people and materiel with both the Empire and Britain's allies from day one of the war right through and beyond VJ day. That meant defending its ports and keeping open the seaways to them, such as the Bristol Channel. The second was defending Great Britain from invasion. In the past, invasions had come by the sea, in practice far more commonly and successfully than popularly imagined. Now added to this was the new and then indefinable threat from the air. The third and ultimate element on which victory depended was the successful support of offensive activity directed against the enemy on a worldwide scale. Roskill (1954) summarises this as the ability to 'transport armies overseas, to place them on shore in the chosen theatres, to support and supply them as may be necessary and to shift their bases forward as their land campaigns advance'. In all these Somerset had a modest but important part to play.

The threat from the air, mentioned above, was only one of the ways in which the traditional distinction between naval and military areas of operation became more blurred during the war; there had always been activities such as Coast Artillery which, literally, spanned land and sea. The ability of aircraft to cross land and water with equal ease, however, meant that everywhere in Britain was 'in the front line'

Somerset and the Defence of the Bristol Channel

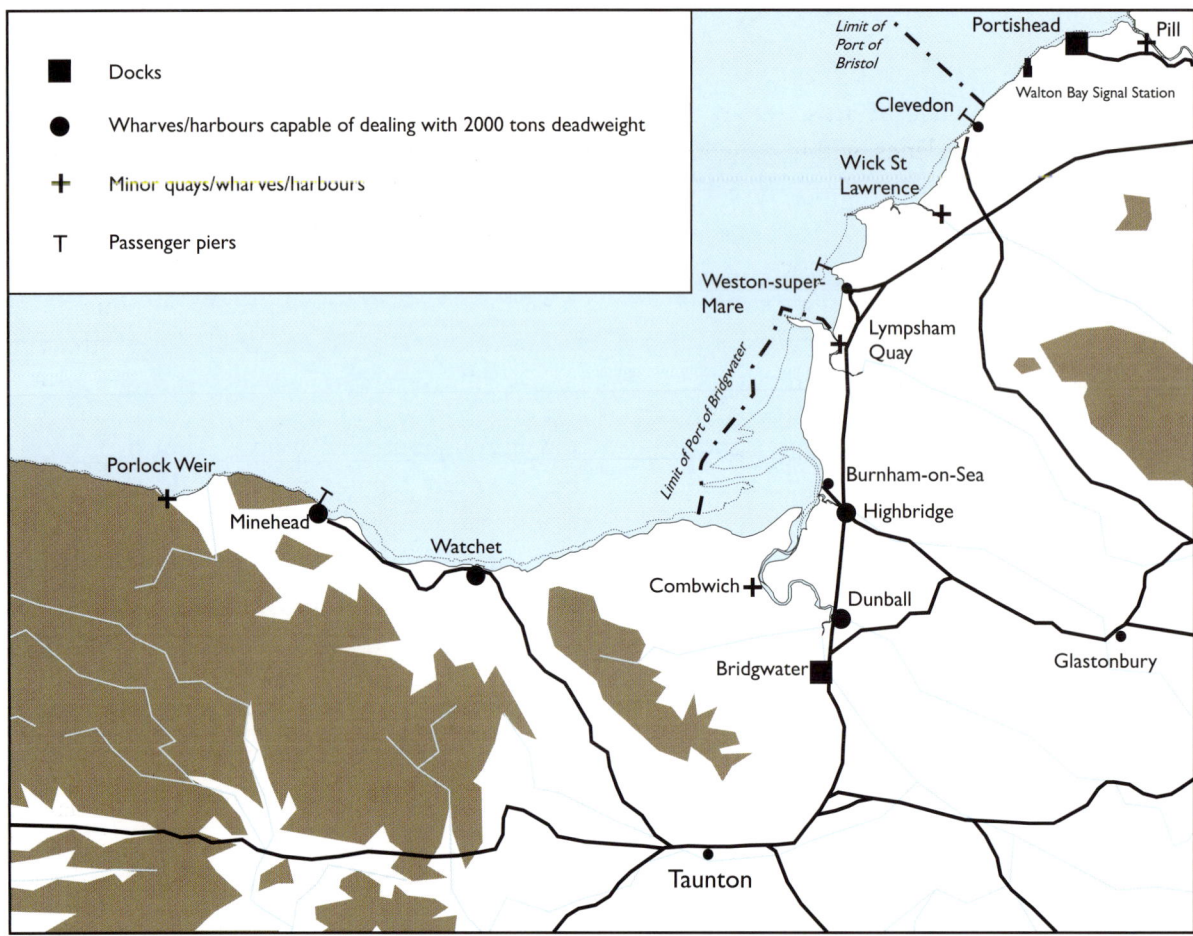

Figure 1.1: Somerset's ports, harbours and passenger piers with their rail links in 1939.

and more relevantly to the present theme, on the way to a maritime target. Thus Somerset's air defences were part of a strategy to defend the industrial heartlands and also the ports of the western coast through which vital supplies flowed. Radar played a critical role here but was also employed to detect shipping. The coast was also important to land-based forces, as an area to defend but also as an area to train for raids, and ultimately, a platform for invasion. It was also useful as the background to live-firing exercises as exclusion areas were easier to establish than on inhabited land.

It is helpful to consider each of these issues as they changed in each of the three phases identified by the *Official Histories* of the Second World War. The first phase runs from the outbreak of war in September 1939 through to the final evacuations from mainland France in late June 1940. Although this phase is often called Defensive (by Roskill 1954, for example), it was characterised by the immediate implementation of an elaborate system of ocean and coastal convoys and the transportation and supply of expeditionary forces to France, to the Mediterranean and latterly to Norway. As it was so distant from Germany, Somerset was regarded as a safe area to which people and organisations such as the Department of Naval Construction could be moved away from London (Lavery 2006, 74). This phase ends with the evacuation of these forces from Norway and France and the fall of these countries to German occupation, which also meant that Great Britain's ability to blockade Germany by sea was outflanked.

The second phase runs from late June 1940 to the invasion of mainland Europe in June 1944. Britain was faced by German arms operating from stations along the length of the coastline from the Pyrenees to the North Cape. It brought shipping, ports and manufacturing centres within close range of attack from the air, it brought the sea lanes within range of attack from under the sea and it brought an imminent danger of invasion. In this phase these threats were met and to some extent contained, yet throughout it Britain retained the ability to prosecute its strategic aims in the Mediterranean theatre. From December 1941, war with Japan brought further reverses which by June 1944 were contained but it also brought the firm armed alliance with the United States and the ability to realise the plan to use Britain as the major launch pad for an invasion of mainland Europe, both from Britain itself and from north Africa. The third phase from July 1944 is one in which offensive action predominates with the defeat of Germany in the west and the release of increasing resources to defeat Japan in Burma and support naval operations in the Far East. The threat of invasion may have receded but the struggle to secure the sea lanes, the grim Battle of the Atlantic, continued until VE day.

A note on sources

The primary source of inspiration for this study has been the extensive but fragmentary scatter of archaeological field monuments across the historic county of Somerset. These have been interpreted with the aid of surviving documentation and together give an insight into the county's maritime history.

The main sources for plans, intentions and activities are in **The National Archives** in the War Office and General Headquarters (GHQ) Home Forces papers. These papers include the war-diaries that Army Field Service Regulations required formation HQs and units to maintain. The object of the war-diary was to 'furnish a historical record of operations and to provide data upon which to base future improvements in army training, equipment, organisation and administration.' The document was classified 'Secret' and was to be updated daily in duplicate. Many unit and formation war-diaries are available in The National Archives but others have not survived. The war-diaries of HQ staff branches may contain extensive policy papers and operational orders which are extremely useful to the researcher while other war-diaries contain the bare minimum of information. These files include those from the War Office and GHQ Home Forces down to brigade or area HQs. In almost all cases any attached maps or plans appear to have been removed. Likewise some files have been 'weeded' and enclosures which were deemed less important at a later date have been destroyed. Fort Record Books exist for some Bristol Channel forts but those for Brean Down and Steep Holm cannot be located. In the case of the RAF, Operation Record Books have a similar purpose to Army war-diaries. The Air Historical Branch summarised many HQ files into concise histories of aspects of RAF operations but local detail, for example exact grid references of sites, is not included. The **Somerset Record Office** has some useful files on Home Guard and roadblocks but there is very little available about coastal defences. The **National Monuments Record** of English Heritage has an extensive collection of RAF wartime and immediate post-war vertical air photos together with excellent low level oblique photos of some of the Somerset invasion beaches. These often show defences such as trenches or pillboxes although many may not be obvious due to effective camouflage or good siting in shadows. Unfortunately there are no pre-war air photos to compare them with.

There are few **personal recollections** from those who served in Somerset and manned the defences and the more senior commanders and their staff-officers who made the plans, and might explain the rational behind them, are most unlikely to be still living. Moreover, the serving personnel came from across the UK which would make attempts to contact them extremely difficult and time consuming. On

1 February 1940, it was estimated that over 5700 troops were serving in Somerset, many in training establishments. In some cases, individuals, particularly those involved with the so-called 'British Resistance Organisation' or RAF Radio Counter Measures, still feel bound by the Official Secrets Act and are reluctant to share their knowledge. Communal memory also appears to be fragile, for example, all recollection of HMS *Iliad* at Watchet has been overlaid by memories of post-war operation of the local ranges.

Reference to **published works** include the *Official History of the Second World War* in particular Roskill (*The War at Sea*) and Collier (*Defence of the United Kingdom*) and a number of Council for British Archaeology reports by Dobinson, together with other local works including Hawkins (*Somerset at War*), Wilson (*Somerset Home Guard*) and Brown (*Somerset v Hitler*). Other references are listed in the bibliography. Particular mention should be made to the use of contemporary military training pamphlets and books published during the war, which give invaluable background information, particularly on organisations, equipment and tactics, for the interpretation of other documentary sources.

Little use has been made of **Internet** sources as there is a growing number of amateur and enthusiast websites on the Second World War, particularly covering pillboxes, which often propagate theories which do not stand up to closer examination. Sadly such theories and suppositions soon become embedded in folk memory and official literature. An example may be taken from the BBC *Peoples War* website where a report includes a mention of the Coast Artillery battery sited in 1940 at Minehead Harbour. The memory of an individual is quoted as 'they tested the guns and found that they shook the harbour wall so much it wasn't possible to use them.' This story was embellished by English Heritage in their *Severn Estuary Rapid Coastal Zone Assessment Study* (readily accessible on the web), which noted that 'the guns were only ever test-fired once nearly destroying the harbour wall and as a result were removed' (Crowther and Dickson 2008, 212). Examination of the war-diary of 20 Coast Artillery Group in the National Archives shows that the Minehead battery fired a practice shoot of ten rounds full charge on 27 March 1941 while the war-diary of 558 Coast Regiment RA records that on 17 September 1941 the Minehead battery fired a 30 round practice shoot. The battery remained fully operational until 1942 when the Royal Navy had more pressing needs for its guns elsewhere.

Finally acknowledgement should be made of the Somerset County Council **Historic Environment Record** (SHER), with which the authors are all closely involved. This records the field work of many including individual studies and the Defence of Britain project. It serves as the most up-to-date and reliable readily available source of the extent of surviving identified installations and structures in Somerset associated with the Second World War. Similar HERs cover Exmoor and the northern parts of Somerset (once in Avon) and sites mentioned in the text are given the reference numbers (where known) in the HER where further information may be found.

The Somerset HER is available online from www.somerset.gov.uk/heritage.

Both the Somerset and the Exmoor HERs can also be accessed via the Heritage Gateway (www.heritagegateway.org.uk), which allows cross-searching of local and national records.

Chapter 2

Naval activities

As soon as war was declared on Sunday 3 September 1939, the Admiralty's plans for the protection of trade were implemented. In fact, a number of measures anticipated the event including on 26 August assumption of control of all British merchant shipping (Barnett 1991, 55). Somerset had no major ports (Figure 1.1 on page 2); the largest dock, an area separated by locks from the effects of the huge tidal range in the Bristol Channel, was at Portishead. This was a small part of the Port of Bristol complex and specialised in coal and imported timber. The only other dock was part of the Port of Bridgwater which also included tidal wharves along the Parrett at Bridgwater, Combwich and Dunball and, further north, the railway wharf at Highbridge. There was a scatter of minor wharves and quays used increasingly less often by local sailing craft at places like Lympsham Quay and Wick St Lawrence. Watchet was the largest of the other harbours (Porlock Weir, Minehead) and was capable of berthing small coasters. Piers for the Bristol Channel ferry services were located at Minehead, Clevedon, and Birnbeck at Weston-super-Mare.

The Admiralty's main concerns in the Bristol Channel were initially transportation of supplies to Cherbourg, Brest, Nantes and St Nazaire for the British Expeditionary Force in France (both the British and the French commands were anxious that these bases should be as far as possible from threat of enemy air attack) from Avonmouth, Barry, Swansea and Newport (Roskill 1954, 63; Winser 2009, 7), and the protection of the south Wales coal and metal trades and the important import trade of Bristol. In 1938 out of the nearly three million tons of cargo imported through the Bristol dock complex, about 940,000 tons was grain and 900,000 tons oil (Brown 1945, 59).

To support this the RN Cardiff sub-command was established ashore with its principal base at the Fish Dock, Swansea, to cover the Upper Bristol Channel. It formed part of Western Approaches Command then based at Plymouth (Roskill 1954, 37; Figure 2.1 on the next page). Its main role was to ensure that Bristol Channel shipping was integrated, where appropriate, into the system of convoys, both ocean going to and from the Americas, Africa and the Mediterranean, and from July 1940 the vital coastal coal convoys to south-east England. Speedy unloading and reloading of vessels was essential to keep the whole system operating efficiently. The pilot cutters of each of the main ports maintained their station off Breaksea lightship (see Figure 2.3 on page 8) for inward bound vessels (Rich 1996, 132).

Flag Officer in Command Cardiff (FOIC) proceeded with the planned establishment of a Naval Port Service to work with the Haven Masters, pilotage, towage and other services at the major ports such as Bristol and Cardiff. To process inward bound ships, a Naval Control Service was established at Barry with an examination area off Lavernock Point covered by an artillery battery on the Welsh side and a further anchorage in Walton Bay under the gaze of the Port of Bristol Authority's Signal Station (Figure 2.2 on page 7).

Somerset and the Defence of the Bristol Channel

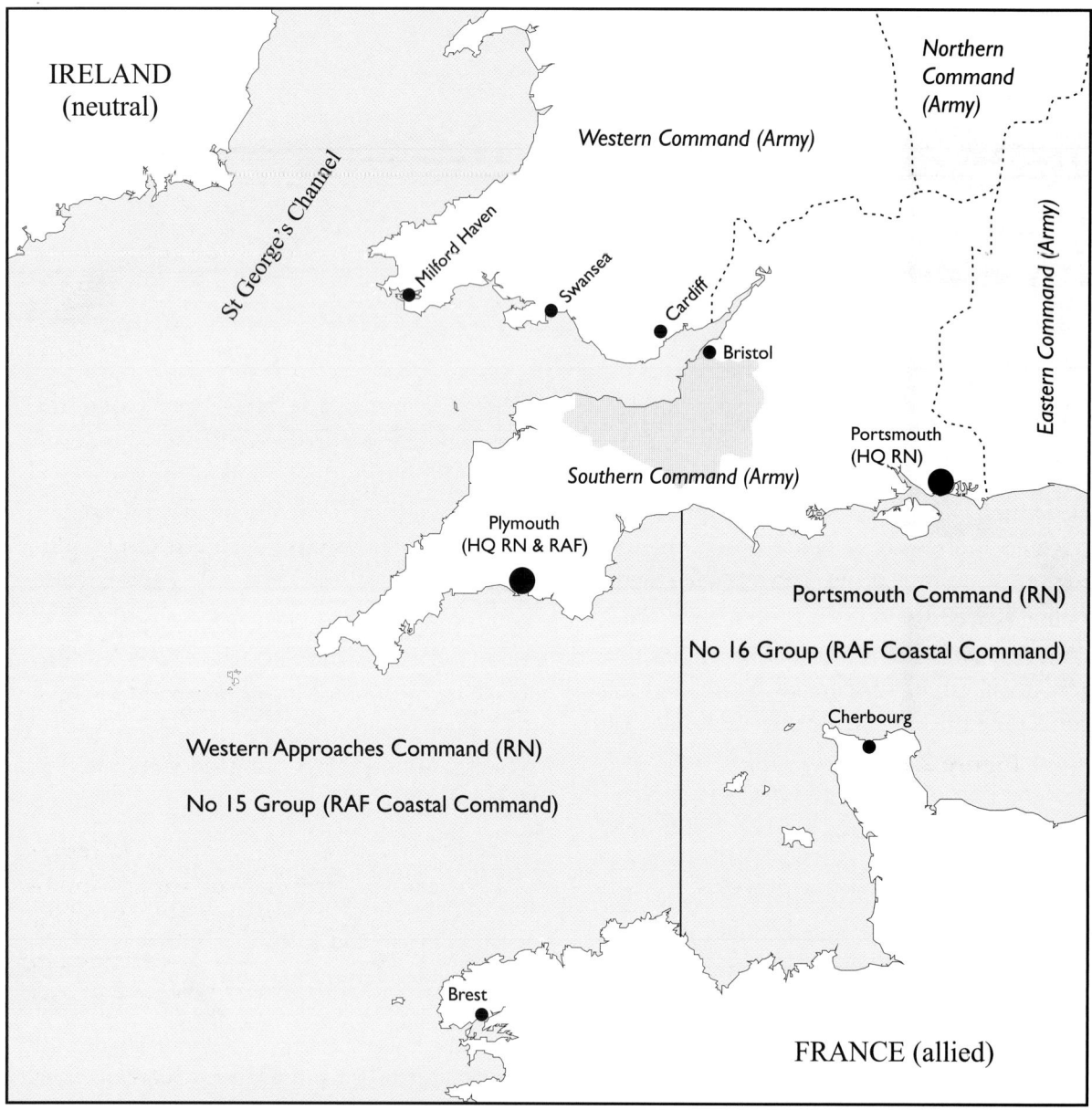

Figure 2.1: *Command areas of the Royal Navy, Army and RAF Coastal Command in 1939/40 (after Collier 1957, maps 4 and 5, pages 49 and 85).*

Admiralty instructions for merchant shipping and fishing boats issued in October 1940 did not allow any merchant vessel to approach within three miles (5km) of the coast or ports in the UK between sunset and sunrise except as part of an organised British convoy. Vessels on passage were permitted to use the main coastal swept channel when this encroached on the three-mile limit. Vessels inside the limit, that could not make their destination before sunset, had to anchor or proceed outside the limit. In fog or low visibility merchant vessels were not allowed to approach UK ports or coasts unless permission had been received from patrols or examination vessels. Fishing boats were also subject to search before arrival in port. If visibility deteriorated, vessels were to anchor or proceed to seaward. Vessels failing to comply with these instructions were liable to be fired on by coastal guns. The Navy also had authority to issue local restrictions for fishing boats or to order their complete

Naval Activities

Figure 2.2: The Port of Bristol Authority's signal station at Walton (David Dawson, 2008).

immobilisation. British or allied warships were permitted to enter defended ports after exchanging recognition signals. Elsewhere they had to follow the rules and if they needed to approach within three miles of the coast, the nearest naval authority had to be warned.

Minesweeping and minefields

Minelaying by enemy aircraft and submarines was a problem from the first and, although in the early phase from 1939 to 1940, emphasis lay on anti-submarine forces the balance shifted toward minesweeping as anti-submarine defences in St George's Channel improved and as the threat of aerial minelaying increased. A main swept channel was kept clear along the length of the area with branches into, for example, the mouth of the Parrett. All this had to be achieved with a growing force of requisitioned vessels, mainly trawlers and drifters from the east coast, many of which originally came with their own skippers and crew. By June 1940 the sub-command consisted of 45 vessels which included three Anti-submarine Groups and one Minesweeper Group (Figure 2.3 on the following page). By January 1941 there was just one Anti-submarine Group but a force of four Minesweeper Groups.

The immediate noticeable effects on local trade were the increasing numbers of vessels large and small requisitioned for war service. For example, ten out of P & A Campbell's fleet of eleven paddle steamers were taken for conversion and commission into the Royal Navy as minesweepers, for service initially in the North Sea (Farr 1967, 265). Even small coastal sailing craft were required for the balloon service (Mote 1986, 8; Slade 1959, 98).

For those vessels still engaged in trade, hazardous incidents increased as enemy submarines penetrated the Bristol Channel: on 21 January 1940, a mine laid off Swansea by *U-28* so badly damaged the 9577-ton Blue Funnel freighter, SS *Protesilaus*, inward bound for Barry, that she had to be beached and

Somerset and the Defence of the Bristol Channel

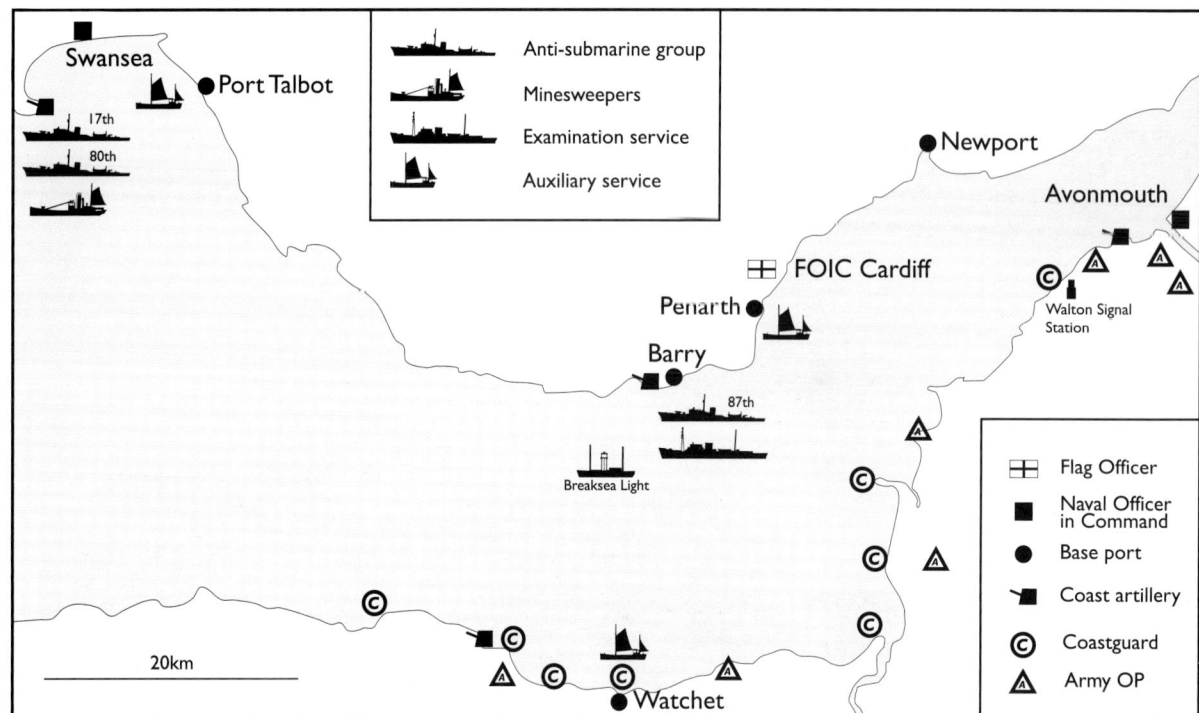

Figure 2.3: *Royal Naval and Coast Artillery dispositions in the Bristol Channel in 1940 with coastguard stations and Army observation posts (not shown in north Devon and south Wales).*

the Bristol Steam Navigation Company Ltd's 710-ton coaster, SS *Cato*, was sunk with the loss of 13 of her crew of 15 on 3 March off Bull Point whilst inward bound from Dublin to Bristol in a minefield laid by *U-29*. On the 28 May 1940, the Minehead lifeboat was called to assist in the rescue of the crew and passengers of Elders & Fyffes' liner, SS *Carare* of 6878 tons (Figure 2.4), which had struck a magnetic mine, probably laid from the air, and sank off Foreland Point with the loss of ten lives (Parsons 1982, 49). In August the same year, the Bristol tug, *John King* (now preserved in Bristol, Figure 2.5 on the facing page), was strafed whilst delivering pumping equipment to Swansea (Parsons 1988, 68). In the face of such threats from the air, P & A Campbell withdrew and laid up *Ravenswood* from their sole surviving Bristol Channel ferry service between Weston-super-Mare and Cardiff on 4 July 1940 (Farr 1967, 248).

For coastal traders under sail, the minefields laid by the Royal Navy were a further hazard (Slade 1959, 96). Individual mines commonly

Figure 2.4: *Elders & Fyffes' liner, SS* Carare, *mined and sinking off Foreland Point on 28 May 1940. Seven crew and three passengers were killed (Ilfracombe and North Devon Sub-aqua Club).*

came adrift in the extreme weather and tidal conditions of the Bristol Channel and the minefields were awkwardly placed for those relying on sail and desperately short of skilled crew.

Laying the extensive minefield across St George's Channel from Hartland Point to the Irish coast (Figure 2.9 on page 14) was undertaken early in 1940 with the main purpose of preventing U-boats penetrating the Irish Sea

8

Figure 2.5: *CJ King & Son's tug,* John King, *which was strafed on route to Swansea in August 1940, now preserved in the collections of Bristol City Museum and Art Gallery (David Dawson, 2007).*

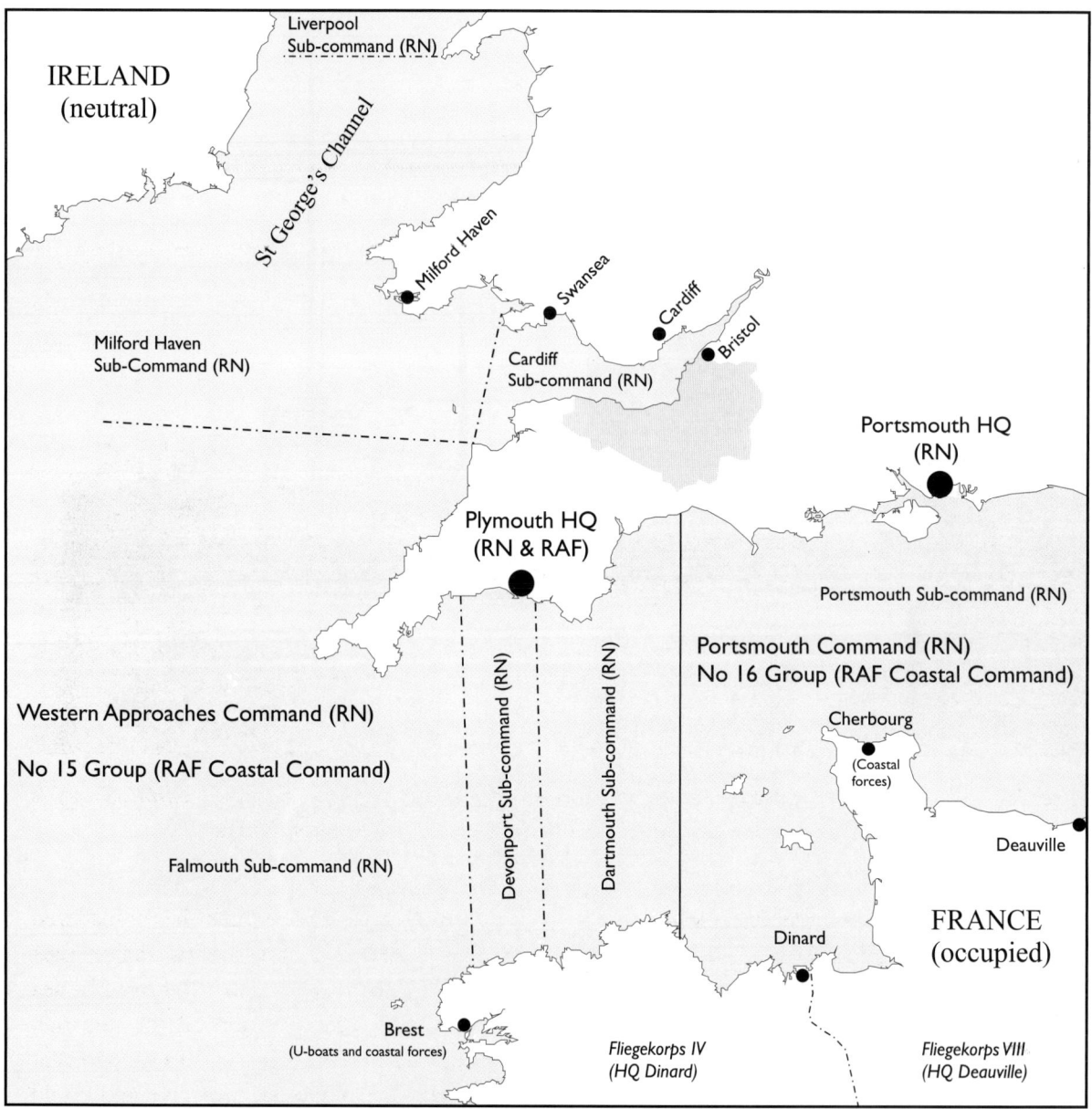

Figure 2.6: *Royal Navy and RAF Coastal Command boundaries and German maritime and air force dispositions in 1941 after the fall of France (after Collier 1957, maps 9 and 11, pages 142 and 159).*

and Bristol Channel. After Andrew Murdock's extraordinary feat in sailing the 120-ton ketch, *Garlandstone* (now berthed at the Morwellham Quay Museum, Figure 2.7 on the facing page), single-handed over the minefields from the small Irish port of Courtmacsherry to Lydney, more traders took the risk of ignoring the minefield's presence (Slade 1959, 100). This was possible because of the light draught of the vessels and the phenomenon of 'dip': a mine is moored to be invisible from the surface at neap (low) tide but the tide running against this mine will pull it even deeper below the surface. In August 1940, in an assessment of the likely effectiveness of these measures against surface shipping, the Admiralty acknowledged that with 'dip' and the lack of density of the field, 'If the enemy use ships of over 14 feet [4.25m] draught it is estimated that 20% would be sunk or damaged. If ships of a lighter draught were used the percentage of losses would be considerably smaller. In low visibility or at night

Figure 2.7: *The ketch,* Garlandstone, *which Andrew Murdock sailed single-handed from Courtmacsherry to Lydney through minefields, now preserved at Morwellham Quay, Devon (David Dawson, 2006).*

a large force of enemy transports might pass through the mine field and proceed towards the Bristol Channel without being reported' (TNA WO 166/57: Letter GHQ Home Forces to Southern Command 29 August 1940).

Auxiliary patrols

The local recipients of the above memorandum might be forgiven for wondering how the Navy with a minefield which was ineffective against surface vessels and a cockleshell flotilla under Vice-Admiral Tomkinson proposed to intervene in an invasion attempt on the Somerset coast. In fact Sir Charles Forbes, C-in-C Home Fleet, was locked in a row with Churchill and the Chiefs of Imperial Staff over the correct disposition of his warships and their ability to intervene should an invasion be launched. Forbes always maintained (and Churchill later asserted privately it was always his view too) that if invasion came, which he considered extremely unlikely given that a major part would have to come by and be reinforced by sea without any effectual support of the German navy, he had 200–300 vessels at sea on patrol at any one time to detect such a move and could intervene within 24 hours with his major units (Roskill 1977, 119; Grove 2005, 188).

The bulk of the 1000 vessels on watch were vessels of under 100 feet (30m) overall organised into the Auxiliary Patrol. Most were deployed on the east coast between Invergordon and Portland but there were at least three groups in the Bristol Channel based on Port Talbot, Penarth and Watchet (Collier 1957, 135). Of the particular group based at Watchet, relatively little is known. On 19 June 1940 Temporary Lieutenant LR Lord RNVR was appointed to command a group of four vessels based at the port and commissioned as HMS *Iliad* (*Navy List*, December 1940). The patrol boats maintained a coastal night patrol from the mouth of the Parrett to the Foreland. Lamp or pyrotechnic signals would have been used to warn of any invaders discovered at sea (TNA WO 166/1317: *Somerset Sub Area Coast Defence Scheme*, para 11a, appendix H, 15 August 1940). The patrol is not mentioned in 1941 or later Army documents.

After the fall of France

The fall of France changed the situation markedly – the removal of almost the entire striking force of U-boats to new bases on the Atlantic coast of France, and of *Luftwaffe* units to Brittany and Normandy. The English, St George's and Bristol Channels were now within easy range of minelaying and bomber aircraft and the losses of ships and their crews increased. There were also more targets: from July 1940, it was decided that, because of the lack of capacity in the railway network from south Wales, it was essential that coal be shipped by sea to keep the power stations and gasworks of south-east England supplied (Roskill 1954, 323). Convoys of colliers from south Wales would have to be fought through the English Channel, no matter how appalling the losses might be. Traffic in the Bristol Channel was increased by these convoys and also ships travelling to those ports of north Devon and Somerset which were linked to the railway system. Highbridge, for example, handled 64,650 tons (3113 in 1941; 25,747 in 1942; 24,001 in 1943; 11,789 in 1944) reaching a peak of 1500 tons per day (Handley 2001, 67). The convoys were however well-protected compared to small local vessels, such as the steam dredger *Durdham*, sunk a mile and half (2km) off Lavernock Point on 27 July 1940. For these ships, contact with a mine often meant total loss and the death of most of the crew.

In July 1940, with convoys depleted of their meagre escorts (withdrawn for defence of the homeland), Britain suffered its greatest shipping losses yet (over 200,000 tons, Roskill 1960, 92–93). Between July and October, 217 merchantmen were sunk (Costello and Hughes 1977, 94). In August 1940 came the first bombing raids on Bristol and Cardiff (Collier 1957, 197). The only bright spot was that among the many fishing and other minor vessels that had escaped from France and Belgium, some were allocated to FOIC Cardiff.

This major change in the strategic position put Somerset in the position of providing the last line of defence of the Bristol Channel and its ports against aerial attack and finally crystallised what was to be its major role. The change was reflected in organisational changes (Figure 2.6 on page 10). In early 1941 a re-invigorated Western Approaches Command was set up at Liverpool where it was better placed to fight the Battle of the Atlantic (Costello and Hughes 1977, 112). Although its Cardiff sub-command retained control of the Bristol Channel and its ports, the Somerset coastline together with north Devon was reallocated to Appledore, a sub-command of Plymouth. The main overseas convoy route now avoided St George's Channel and went north about Ireland (Roskill 1960, 89–91) but despite this the importance of the Bristol Channel ports should not be underestimated. By June 1945, the Port of Bristol Authority had handled:

Vessels docked	53,723
Net registered tonnage of ships	22,990,800
Foreign imports tons	24,998,383
Coastwise imports tons	7,391,640
Foreign exports tons	1,138,220
Coastwise exports tons	5,256,474
Hospital ships docked	89
Troops and other personnel	247,232
Mail bags	577,320

(Parsons 1988, 70)

Between July 1940 and June 1944, naval defensive measures in the Bristol Channel steadily improved. By January 1942, Cardiff Command's allocation included six minesweeping trawler groups, one group of

Naval Activities

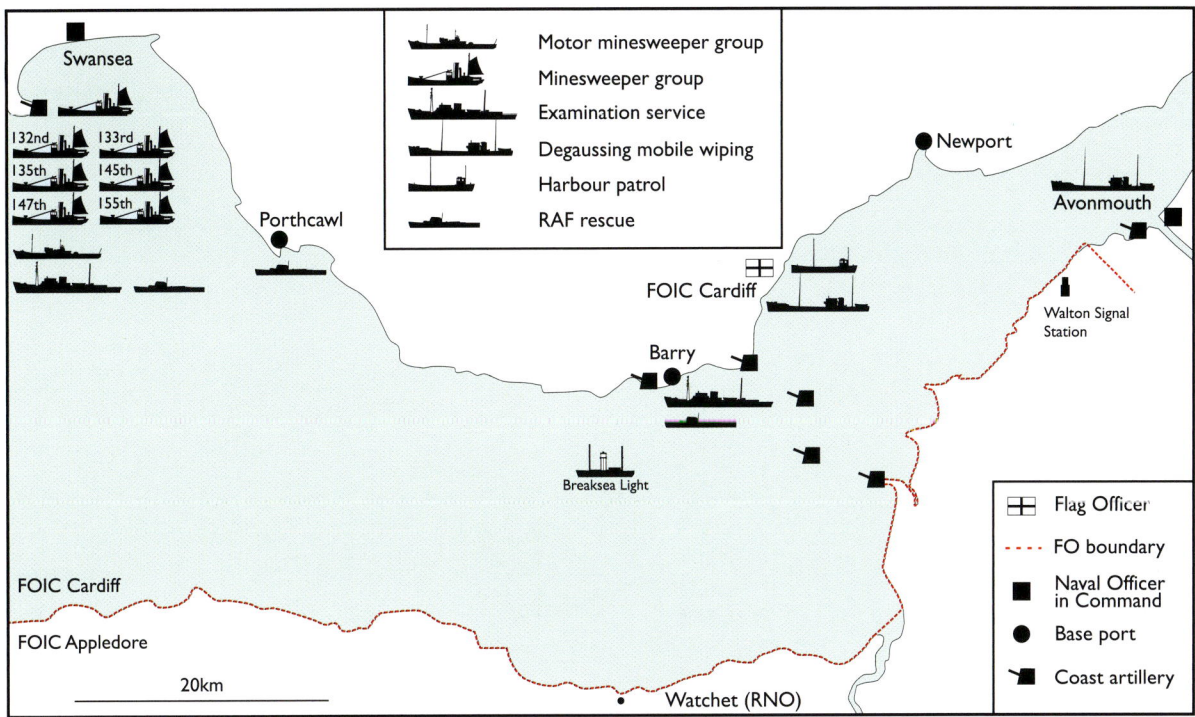

Figure 2.8: *Royal Navy and Coast Artillery dispositions in 1942.*

modern purpose-built motor minesweepers, three degaussing mobile wiping units for providing protection for merchant vessels against magnetic mines, based at Swansea, Cardiff and Avonmouth, and a number of mine detection ships and other ungrouped minesweepers. In addition were the vessels of the Examination Service, the more recently acquired RAF rescue groups based at Porthcawl, Swansea and Barry and a number of miscellaneous craft (Figure 2.8). Further defensive minefields were laid, such as Fields 560, 130X, and 86Y between Foreland Point at Countisbury and Nash Point which were notified on 29th October 1941 (Figure 2.9 on the next page).

The Somerset coast

From 13 January 1941 on the Somerset coastline up to but not including Portishead, the system of coast-watchers, the regular coastguard (Figure 2.3 on page 8), control of emergency Coast Artillery and other naval concerns (which included taking the salute at Williton and Watchet Warship Week on 7 March 1942) was brought under the command of Admiral (retired) JM Casement CB, in the newly created post of Resident Naval Officer (RNO) Watchet (*Navy List*, June 1941). Casement was typical of the many officers on the retired list upon whom the Navy depended heavily to underpin the enormous increase in its responsibilities and personnel. He had commanded the light cruiser, HMS *Blanche*, at Jutland in 1916, and on being recalled for service, had gone to sea again in 1940 as vice-commodore of convoy HGF 25 and commodore of convoy HX 86.

Casement's arrival in the Minehead district on 1 February 1941 is recorded by the Coast Artillery group responsible for this part of the coast (TNA WO 166/1757). As RNO he would have assumed responsibility for control of Auxiliary Patrol vessels, fishing boats and shipping entering and leaving port, informing the authorities when British or allied warships approached within three miles (5km) of the coast, operational control of Coast Artillery, coordination and filtering of reports from coastguards, auxiliary coastguards and coast-

Somerset and the Defence of the Bristol Channel

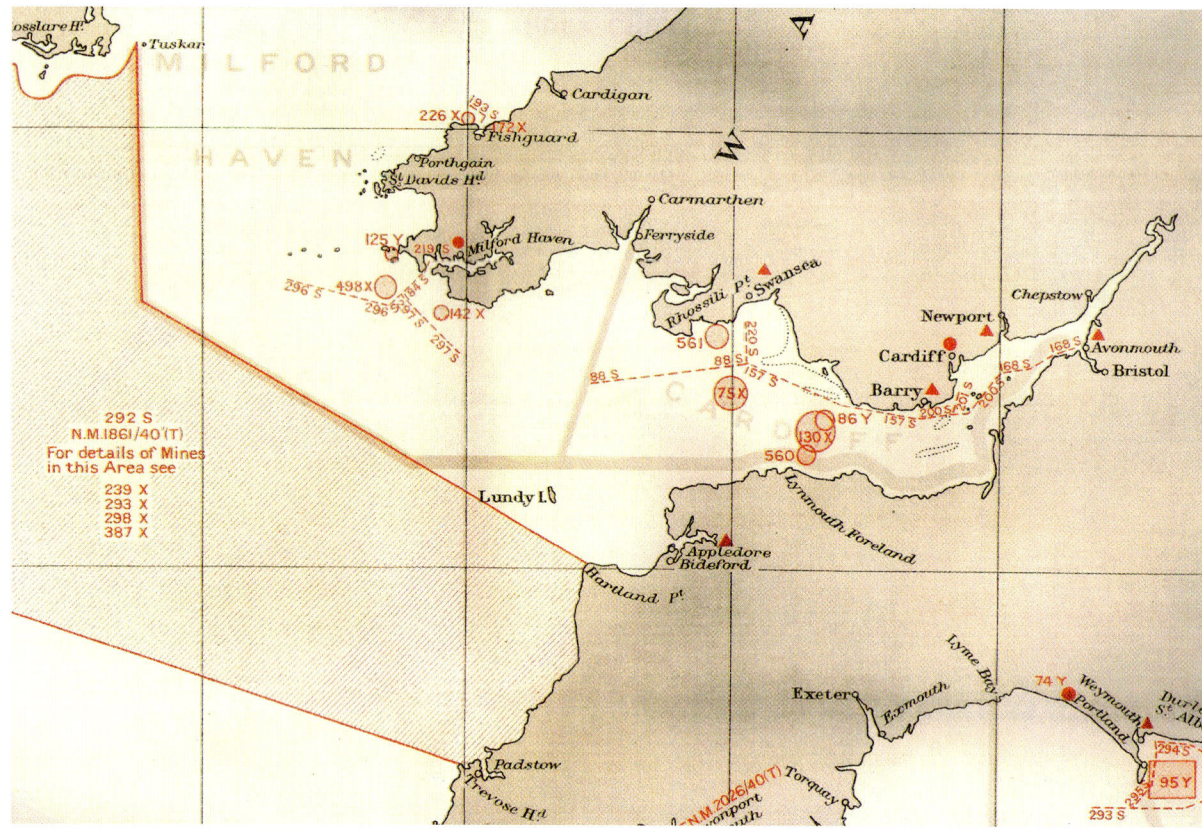

Figure 2.9: *An extract of the chart accompanying the* Notice to Mariners *dated 29 October 1941 of the laying of minefields 560, 130X and 86Y (UK Hydrographic Office).*

watchers and finally port denial measures (TNA WO 166/1275). Before his appointment there had been problems for the local Coast Artillery communicating with the naval officer in command at Swansea (TNA WO 166/1757, January 1941). Probably to ensure more immediate contact with the local defensive artillery at Minehead and Blue Anchor, who required his permission to open fire on any target out at sea, he established himself and a staff which included four from the Women's Royal Naval Service (WRNS) at the Langbury Hotel at Blue Anchor (Binding 2007, 75; Figure 2.10 on the next page).

By the end of 1941, it appears that the threat of invasion was believed to have receded. HMS *Iliad* at Watchet had a change of commanding officer on 23 July 1941 when IHL King relieved Lord but by June 1942 the command had disappeared completely (*Navy List*, January/February 1942, June 1942).

Casement moved to Weston-super-Mare in December 1943, an indication that his responsibilities there had assumed greater importance.

Early in 1941, Birnbeck pier had been identified as a suitable site to test a forward firing depth charge known as Hedgehog, which was to improve substantially the offensive capabilities of convoy escorts (Brown 2007, 115–19). As an embryonic experimental outstation of the Department of Miscellaneous Weapons Development, it was regarded with some suspicion by the rest of the naval experimental establishment but under Casement's command the situation was regularised (the pier had been commissioned as HMS *Birnbeck* on 2 February 1942; Warlow 2000, 25), and when Casement himself moved his command to Weston-super-Mare, he ensured its rather maverick staff got on with designing and getting acceptance of a variety of new weapons and equipment (see Chapter 6).

Naval Activities

Figure 2.10: *The Langbury Hotel, Blue Anchor, HQ of RNO Watchet (David Dawson, 2010).*

The invasion of Europe

By 1944 the war was moving into its third phase: taking the land war back to mainland Europe. The Bristol Channel ports had a crucial part to play in operations Bolero and Neptune, the build-up of troops and supplies and the naval deployment to deliver and support the invasion of France (Operation Overlord, Figure 2.11 on the following page). Volume Four of the *Orders for Operation Neptune* (ON4) designated the Bristol Channel as the western base for the phase one build-up (the phase before any permanent port installations could be captured and restored to working condition) to ensure the armies ashore were supplied with all that they needed to fight (Barnett 1991, 783–84). Between 4 and 26 May 1944, 132 coasters were loaded with ammunition, vehicle fuel in jerry cans and other supplies for delivery direct to Omaha and Utah beaches in support of the landings that went in on 6 June (Bykofsky and Larson 1990, 259–60). A modest seven coasters at a time were allocated to Portishead for loading ammunition and stores (Winser 2009, 47).

The history of the US Transportation Corps states that the Bristol Channel ports were 'all important in the shipment of Overlord cargo' and goes on to acknowledge that between May 1944, when loading began, and the end of September, they loaded 868 vessels with 1,037,332 long tons of US cargo in addition to routine discharges and loadings which 'fluctuated between 104,000 and 246,000 long tons per month' (Bykofsky and Larson 1990, 267).

Amongst this fleet of vessels running to and from Normandy, and typical of many of the smaller vessels requisitioned because, if necessary, they could be beached to unload, were two of the Osborn & Wallis Portishead Power Station coal boats, the 456-ton sisters, *Downleaze* and *Rockleaze* (Winter 2005, 55-60). *Downleaze* had been taken up on 15 April 1944 for running cased petrol to the American beachheads from the English Channel ports of Poole, Southampton and Weymouth and *Rockleaze* on 9 April to run ammunition, first from Swansea to Omaha beach and then from Southampton and Newhaven to the British beachheads (Winser 2009, 78, 112). Both suffered damage from collisions during

15

Somerset and the Defence of the Bristol Channel

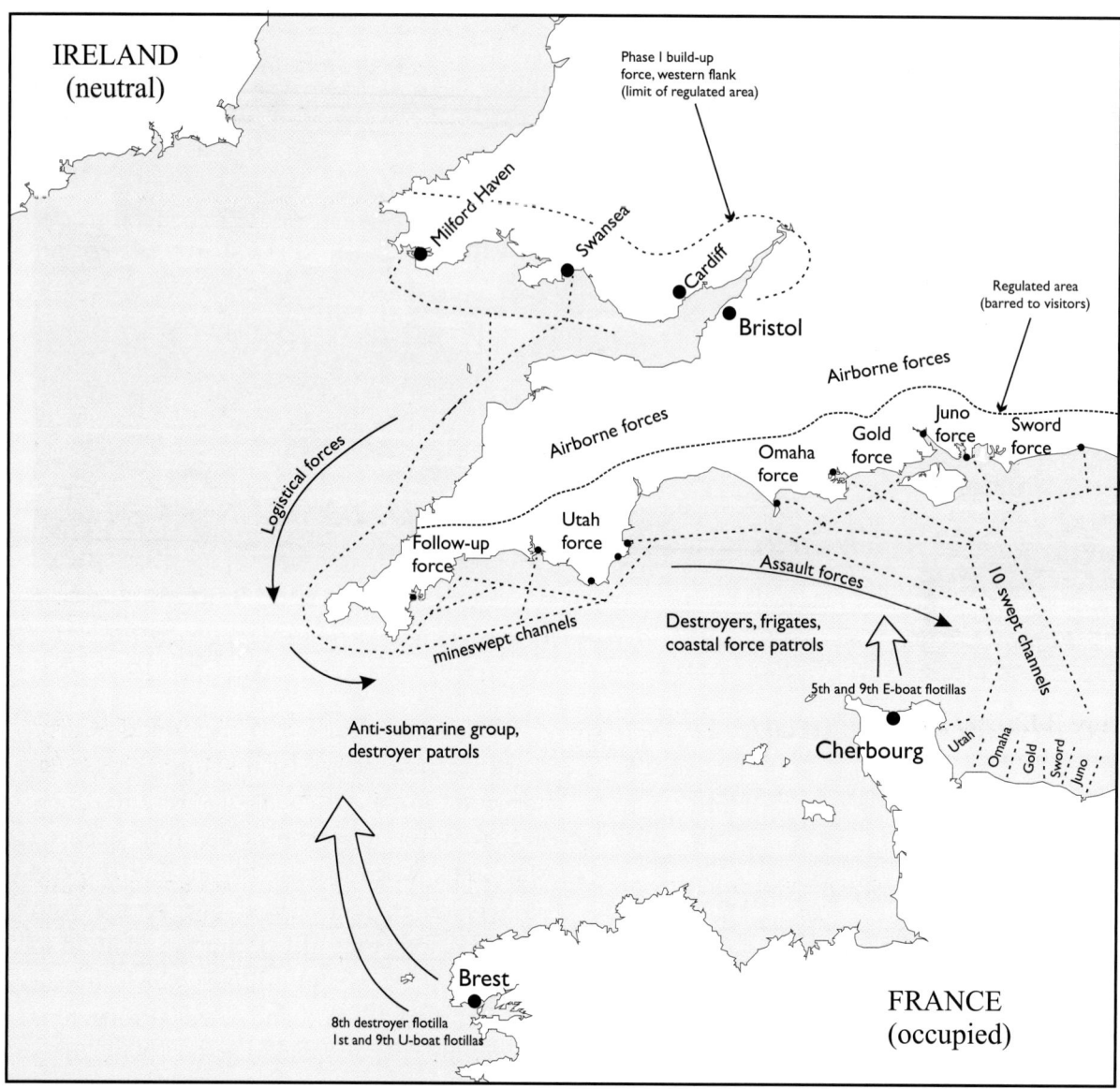

Figure 2.11: The invasion of Normandy in June 1944 and the South West ports (after Roskill 1960, 367).

this service. A review of the supply system in early July resulted in a reduction of the number of vessels involved and a concentration of effort in fewer ports. In the Bristol Channel, Portishead was one of those deleted in favour of ports in south Wales (Swansea, Port Talbot, Penarth) and the English Channel (Winser 2009, 58).

With the successful invasion of France, the gradual elimination of the Atlantic coast bases of the U-boats and north French bases of the depleted German airforce, the perceived and actual threat of invasion and aerial minelaying in the Bristol Channel diminished. However, technical innovations in U-boat design which potentially could see the introduction into service of true submarines was perceived to be a potent threat against which no immediate counter remedy was to be found (Barnett 1991, 852–53). So from early October to November 1944, minelaying between Ireland and north Devon intensified (Hinsley *et al.* 1988, 470–71).

The new deep-laid minefield extended in a broad swathe from Hartland Point and

Figure 2.12: Post-war aerial photograph of RNAS Henstridge on the Somerset/Dorset border, showing the five-runway layout with outlying accommodation and technical areas. The dummy carrier deck can clearly be seen on the most northerly runway (Somerset Studies Library, RAF CPE/UK/1974 4170, 11/4/1947).

Boscastle across to the boundary of Irish territorial waters off Brattin Head and Carnsore Point in an attempt to limit incursions into the Irish Sea. At least one U-boat, *U-1169*, was caught and destroyed in the St George's Channel field as late as 5 April 1945 (Roskill 1961, map 41, 287–288, 298). The order to the U-boats to surrender on 4 May which took several days to effect may have marked the end of hostilities at sea in the European war but the demands on merchant shipping to supply allied armies remaining in the field in Europe and continuing fighting in the Far East did not start to relax until after the surrender of Japan and the consequent gradual demobilisation. The last FOIC Cardiff, Vice-Admiral AD Read (retd), lowered his flag in July 1945, and with him went the organisation of NOICs at the Bristol Channel ports such as Avonmouth and Barry (*Navy List*). The base at Swansea, HMS *Lucifer*, finally closed a year later on 12 July 1946 (Warlow 2000, 87). Somerset's ports and harbours had come through unscathed but the same was not true of the vessels and their crews who were once familiar to them.

Other naval activity

It is appropriate to acknowledge other uses made of Somerset by the Royal Navy in its wider prosecution of the war. The Department of Miscellaneous Weapons Development found an ideal location for its experiments in its outstation based at Birnbeck Pier, Weston-super-Mare, and commissioned it as HMS *Birnbeck* (see page 85). Bath seemed to be an ideal place to locate departments evacuated from London in face of the threat from the air and in 1939 the Naval Constructor's Department was removed to requisitioned hotel accommodation in the city centre until bombing made it clear that it was no safer place than London to where the department returned in 1942 (Lavery

2006, 74). By then it is also likely that pressure to house the increasing numbers of staff, taken on to cope with modifying existing vessels and designing and managing the increase of new types of vessel required for the war, made a return to new more suitable accommodation near the capital an urgent necessity. Before the war, the Hydrographic Department had planned to move its entire staff to the West Country but the speed of events forced it to move its compilation staff to Bath in 1940, while the new site, initially only for printing and supply, was being built at Creechbarrow, Taunton. Plans to move the Bath staff to Taunton came to nothing and they were moved out of the city to a hutted camp at Ensleigh on Lansdown Hill. The staff at Bath returned to London after the war before the entire Department was finally centralised, some twenty years later, at Taunton where it remains (Adrian Webb pers. comm.).

The Fleet Air Arm, though primarily a ship-borne force, needed airfields to train air and ground crews and receive disembarked flights (ships normally flew off their aircraft before returning to harbour). In 1939 it was hurriedly decided that one of its first new air stations (there were eventually to be three in Somerset) was to be established in the county. The reason for the hurried decision was that despite accepting the recommendation made in 1937 of the prolonged inquiry by Sir Thomas Inskip that the Fleet Air Arm be restored to Admiralty command, it was not until 24 May 1939 that the Admiralty took over full administrative control. Even then the RAF only released five airfields to the new service (Roskill 1978, 14; Grove 2005, 176). Lee-on-Solent (near to Gosport and Portsmouth) was chosen as the HQ of the new manning division. All five of the ex-RAF airfields were either too exposed to enemy bombing or too far from operational fleet bases so the Navy launched its biggest civil engineering project of the war to provide 31 new Royal Naval Air Stations (in common with all shore establishments these were commissioned as ships) and 15 'tenders' or dependent outstations (Lavery 2006, 207).

On 18 June 1940 HMS *Heron*, RNAS Yeovilton, was the first to be commissioned and it served as a base for naval fighter aircraft (in 2010 it is still a major Royal Naval facility, home to both the Lynx and Commando Helicopter Forces, to the Fighter Control School and the School of Aircraft Control). It is sited on a tract of relatively flat land alongside the then course of the A303. An outstation was commissioned as its 'tender' at Charlton Horethorne in January 1943 utilising a former RAF fighter satellite for Exeter (Berryman 2006, 26–27). A second station, HMS *Dipper*, was commissioned at Henstridge in April 1943 (Warlow 2000, 47, 72). Given the need to train for shipboard take-off and landing, runways were always built with distinctive characteristics but Henstridge (Figure 2.12 on the previous page) is unusual in having five, two of which are parallel (Smith 1989, 158). The northernmost runway was equipped with a dummy carrier deck including arrestor wires.

Chapter 3

Anti-invasion defences

THIS CHAPTER discusses the perceived invasion threats along the Somerset coastline during the Second World War and the measures taken to counter them. It covers the period from the summer of 1940, when the invasion threat was greatest, to the autumn of 1944, when the threat had vanished. It is based on an analysis of the available sources of information, which are primarily in the National Archives but in some key areas documentary evidence is patchy or appears to be non existent. In other areas there is a plethora of detail, which can only be summarised. Unfortunately no maps showing detailed layouts of defences or areas of responsibility have yet been discovered; neither has any Home Guard documentation referring to the defence of the Somerset coast. This chapter attempts to give a broad overview of the main features of the plans, which were prepared to defend the Somerset coastline, its ports and facilities in the hinterland. It is not intended to be a history of anti-invasion defences along the Somerset coast and, as key information sometimes only appears in later documents, it does not attempt to follow a strict chronological sequence.

The perceived German threat

After the deployment of German forces into France following the French capitulation in June 1940, the threat of seaborne invasion of the United Kingdom was considered to be greatest along the coast between the Wash and the Isle of Wight. On 5 August 1940 Churchill identified the western coastal sector from north Cornwall to the Mull of Kintyre (which included the Somerset coast) as the least vulnerable to seaborne invasion (Churchill 1949, 259). It was recognised that, along the coast to the west of Portsmouth, sea conditions would rule out the use of the river barges that were being then assembled in the Channel ports. Landings in the South West were likely to be from either modified merchant vessels or specially constructed flat-bottomed landing-craft. By 1941, the perceived threat was increased to include 'fast armoured motor craft and amphibian tanks'.

Anti-invasion strategy

Before considering the anti-invasion measures taken in Somerset, it is first necessary to briefly review the national anti-invasion strategy. This was first to mount air attacks on any invasion fleet before it left the continental ports. On the sea voyage (which would be hampered by minefields), ships of the Royal Navy, together with RAF aircraft, would attack the invasion fleets. When the invader reached the coast, beach defences with anti-tank obstacles and barbed wire, covered by fire from pillboxes, trenches and gun emplacements formed a 'coastal crust' to impede his landing. The troops manning these defences were expected to 'fight to the last man' to destroy the enemy on the beaches and to delay any move inland so that mobile forces could be moved into position to destroy the invader (Churchill 1949, 257–59). Key routes towards the threatened beaches were

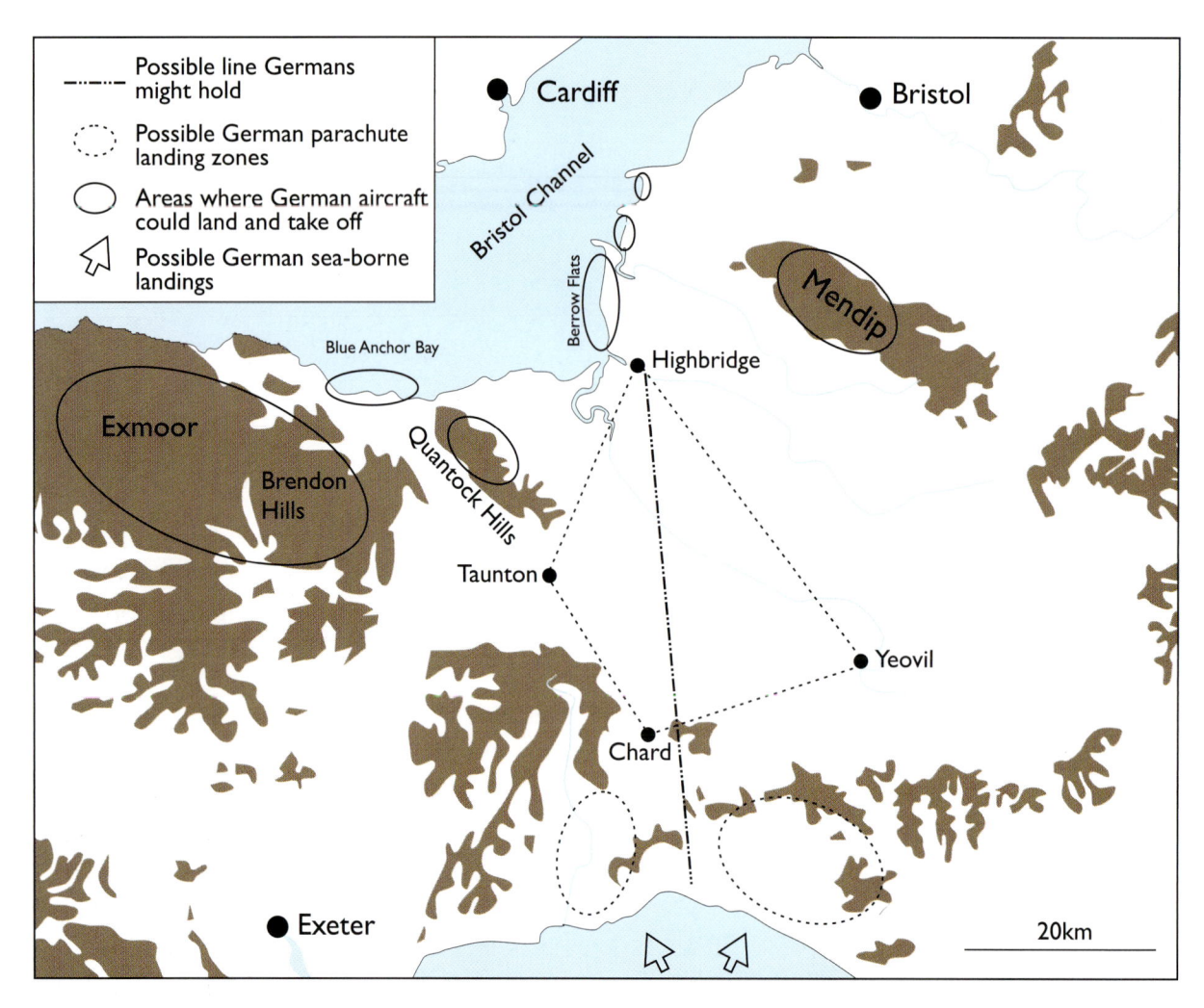

Figure 3.1: The perceived German threat to the Waist of the South West, following a successful capture of Plymouth.

kept open to allow the rapid deployment of reinforcements. At the same time, denial measures were prepared to prevent the enemy from using docks and harbours or from capturing transport and fuel stocks.

The threat to the South West

On 19 July 1940 Southern Command issued *Operation Instruction 16* to the newly formed 8 Corps which was taking over responsibility for the defence of Devon, Cornwall and Somerset. This identified that the most likely threat to the South West was an enemy diversionary attack to capture Plymouth, which might be a prelude to a main invasion elsewhere or, more likely, follow such an attack with the aim of drawing off reserves. Plymouth would have given the Germans a major port to land follow-up forces and sustain operations. The city incorporated Devonport, an important target in its own right as a major Royal Navy dockyard, one of its three manning divisions and home of the Royal Navy's HQ Western Approaches which controlled all shipping sailing to and from the Atlantic (Lavery 2006, 31, 107, 177). This HQ also included the HQ of 15 Group RAF Coastal Command (Collier 1957, 57–58).

A major German force landing in the South West would seriously threaten shipping in the Western Approaches and the Bristol Channel (TNA WO 166/57: *Operation Instruction 16* to 8 Corps, 19 July 1940). It would offer an advanced base from which to attack Ireland with a view to gaining Irish ports and airfields to attack shipping further out into the Atlantic and in the Western Approaches. German bases in Ireland would have posed a serious threat to key western ports in the UK especially those in the Bristol Channel (Butler 1957, 276). After the capture of Plymouth, the Germans were expected to mount a second attack to cut off the whole of the south-west peninsula by taking and holding a defensive line from Bridgwater through Ilminster to Lyme Regis (Figure 3.1 on the facing page). This would allow them to build up their forces in the South West and launch an attack to capture the Port of Bristol. Southern Command warned 8 Corps that enemy occupation of the south side of the Bristol Channel would deny Britain use of the waterway and its ports with serious implications for the country (TNA WO 166/57: Southern Command *Operational Instruction 16 to 8 Corps*, 19 July 1940). As Churchill later noted, one tenth of British imports were coming through the Bristol Channel ports in August 1940 (Churchill 1949, 580). A number of courses open to the Germans for this operation across what the British called the 'Waist of the South West' were postulated, including seaborne assaults in Dorset or east Devon but the most likely option was believed to be a large scale airborne attack near the Dorset coast combined with airborne landings in Somerset. These landings might be on Somerset beaches, on the low ground in the area bounded by Highbridge, Yeovil, Chard and Taunton or on open spaces on Exmoor and the Brendon Hills (TNA WO 166/1317: *Somerset Sub Area Coast Defence Scheme*, 15 August 1940).

In contrast to the situation in west Wales, where significant defences (including beach anti-tank obstacles and stop lines) were constructed, the threat from Ireland itself is hardly mentioned in any documents about anti-invasion defences in Somerset. The only reference found is in the *Severn Sub Area Defence Scheme 2* dated 14 December 1940 where the first threat listed was 'landing in force after bases have been established in Ireland' (TNA WO 166/1314). Nevertheless the authors have found that when discussing the war with older members of the population in Somerset, a threat from Ireland (often called by its Irish name, Eire) is frequently mentioned. There is evidence to suggest that recurrence of this theme was because of a general belief during the war, particularly in the South West, that this was a distinct possibility. From 10 May 1940 the Home Intelligence Department of the Ministry of Information (MOI) compiled daily reports on the morale of the nation using the Mass Observation social survey organisation together with a network of contacts and covert sources. During June and July 1940 the south-west region of MOI reported (Addison and Crang 2010, 62, 131, 149, 201) that: 'the invasion of Eire is also rumoured in a large number of places' (1 June); 'some anxiety on the coast about the possibility of invasion from Eire' (19 June); 'dangers from Eire are often discussed' (24 June); 'many references in the morale reports to fears of invasion and some speculation that Hitler would seize control of Ireland and turn it into a springboard for an assault on Britain' (week 8–13 July). These rumours still appear to be firmly embedded in local folklore in and around Somerset.

British plans

Inland defences (stop lines)

Inland from the beaches, a series of 'stop lines', based primarily on features like waterways or escarpments, were built to impede enemy movement forward, particularly by tanks, and to buy time for any available reserves to counter attack. A key feature of stop lines was the creation of a continuous anti-tank obstacle to attempt to prevent the rush of armour that had been recently experienced in France and Belgium but many stop lines also included sufficient defences along their length to prevent infantry from crossing the obstacle or from attacking to build a bridgehead. The most important stop line was the GHQ Line (GHQ

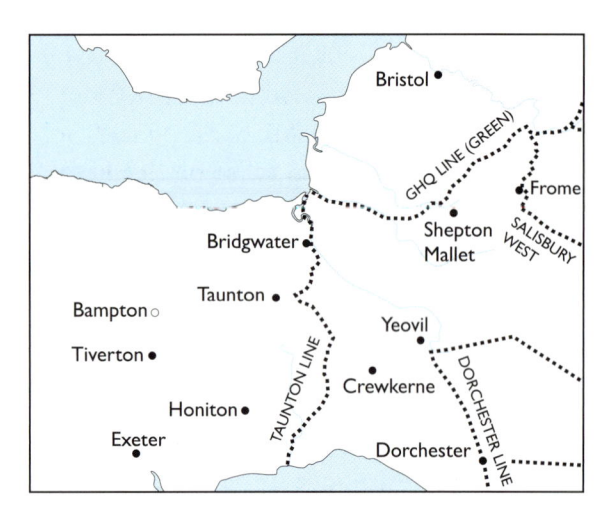

Figure 3.2: Somerset's stop lines with anti-tank islands in the Waist of the South West. The island at Bampton was abandoned in favour of Tiverton and the islands formed along the Taunton Stop Line are not shown.

was an abbreviation for General Headquarters Home Forces). This was intended as the final line to keep the invader from reaching London or the industrial heartland of the country in the Midlands (Collier 1957, 129). The GHQ Line ran from Burnham-on-Sea eastwards along the river Brue and across Somerset to join the river Avon (Figure 3.2). This section was called the 'GHQ Line Green'. One part of the line then ran north via Chippenham into the Cotswolds to join the Severn estuary as the 'Bristol Outer Defence Line' but in August 1940 work was suspended on the northern part. The main GHQ Line ran eastwards along the Kennet and Avon canal (GHQ Line Blue) to Reading then south of London and finally northwards towards Yorkshire.

To stop enemy infantry or armour from advancing out of the South West, the Taunton Stop Line was built across the 35-mile (56km) land gap between Burnham-on-Sea and Seaton (TNA WO 166/1317: *Somerset Sub Area Coast Defence Scheme*, para 16, 15 August 1940). This line followed the river Parrett to Bridgwater, where it joined the Bridgwater and Taunton canal and ran to Creech St Michael, where it used the bed of the old Chard canal to Ilton and then ran along the Great Western Railway line to Chard Junction. From there the stop line followed the river Axe to Seaton; a total distance of about 51 miles (82km) (Figure 3.2). The basic line with westward-facing anti-tank and anti-infantry obstacles covered by pillboxes and some gun emplacements was completed during the autumn of 1940 but the in-depth defences were never finished and the line was abandoned in 1941 (TNA WO 199/1803).

After General Ironside handed over as Commander-in-Chief of Home Forces to General Brooke on 20 July 1940, the policy of building stop lines was curtailed and was finally abandoned in April 1941 with a new emphasis on mobile operations and the creation of anti-tank islands and centres of resistance. (TNA WO 166/1251: Southern Command letter SC.Z/7347/G (Ops), April 1941).

Anti-tank islands

Towns that were at important nodal points on the road system were defended as 'anti-tank islands' with roadblocks on all routes into the built-up areas to deny enemy tanks and transport columns use of the roads through them. In most of these towns, two rings of roadblocks were constructed with the inner ring utilising buildings and other obstacles to form an enclosed 'tank proof' area. In the summer of 1940 anti-tank island defences were prepared at 37 towns in the Army Southern Command including Exeter, Bampton (later Tiverton), Taunton, Honiton, Yeovil, Frome, Shepton Mallet, Bristol, Crewkerne and Dorchester (TNA WO 166/57: OpI 24–Annex B, 15 August 1940). Somerset County Council files show that work started in July (SRO S/5/3).

In 1941 the 12 major crossing points on the Taunton Stop Line were given extensive all-round defences to make them into anti-tank islands. These included Bridgwater (east of the river Parrett), Durston Station, Creech St Michael, Ilminster, Chard (east of the railway) and Axminster. In contrast, none were constructed on the GHQ Line in Somerset. By 1942 some 80 towns in Southern

Command had been prepared as anti-tank islands (TNA WO 199/544: Southern Cmd letter S.C.Z/11098/G (O), 3 March 1942).

The threat from the sea

A seaborne invasion of Somerset was considered to be unlikely. The August 1940 *Coast Defence Scheme* issued by HQ Somerset Area (TNA WO 166/1317) stated that 'Landing of troops on the beaches from the sea is not to be greatly feared; the approach from the enemy shore is long, the Bristol Channel is difficult for small boats to navigate and except for an hour or two before and after high tide a mud bank is disclosed by the tide which it would be very difficult if not impossible for armed and heavily equipped men or AFV [Armoured Fighting Vehicles] to cross.' The writers of the defence scheme believed that an invader would need to land on a rising spring tide, within two hours of high water, so that the disembarked forces did not have to cross vast expanses of mud or sand under fire from the shore and so that landing craft would not become stranded until next high tide. This greatly restricted the times when landings would be possible and, as the enemy was expected to land at dawn, the number of suitable dates was even more limited.

In the Bristol Channel, high water at Burnham-on-Sea is some eight hours later than at Dover or the beaches along the Kent and Sussex coasts. On the East Anglian beaches (to the south of Southwold) high water is about one hour before high water at Dover. It would be impossible to coordinate dawn landings in these two areas, which were considered to be the most likely options for the main thrusts of any German invasion. Despite this, it was estimated that between five and six hours notice of a seaborne attack might be anticipated in Somerset except in poor visibility, but that airborne attacks could take place with little or no warning (TNA WO 166/1317: *Somerset Sub Area Defence Scheme*, part II, para 16, 4 December 1940).

Assessments of the Somerset coast concluded that the harbours at Portishead, Bridgwater, Watchet and Minehead would be of value to the enemy and must be defended while Combwich and Dunball might possibly be. None of the harbours were considered sufficient to provide the Germans with a permanent base. Porlock Weir and Highbridge were not mentioned (TNA WO 166/1317: *Somerset Sub Area Defence Scheme*, 4 December 1940). All these harbours would have been of limited use to the invader. Access was totally dependent on tidal conditions and navigation of the Parrett estuary requires expert knowledge of the river and its constantly changing conditions.

The Coastguard Service, which had been moved from the Board of Trade to the Admiralty in May 1940, made an assessment of UK landing beaches in August 1940 and confirmed that the Somerset beaches were not well suited for seaborne landings. The Somerset coast was therefore placed in Priority Four (the lowest priority) for beach defences within the South West. This overall assessment remained unchanged from 1940 until the threat of invasion had passed in 1944 (for example, TNA WO 166/298: Appreciation of Defence Problems, 18/2/1941). Nevertheless, operation orders continued to set defence commanders along the Somerset coast the primary task of repelling a seaborne invasion but often in conjunction with airborne landings.

Blitzkrieg tactics

The use of airborne forces in the invasion of Norway and Denmark and later of the Netherlands and Belgium, confirmed that surprise was the key element of the German 'blitzkrieg' strategy and Germans were to be expected to appear in strength, with little or no warning, at the most unlikely places. Any invasion was expected to be preceded by intense fighter and bomber attacks on ground objectives like beach defences. Large scale drops by paratroopers dressed in British uniforms and equipped with

British weapons captured at Dunkirk would attack military posts from the flank or rear. The Germans were expected to take high risks, to use unorthodox tactics and exploit new weapons, and to be prepared to suffer high losses in order to achieve their objectives. The use of persistent gas to contaminate areas on the flanks of their attack and choking gas in the area being attacked was predicted. Once any selected landing grounds had been secured, troop carrying aircraft and gliders would land and their air-portable transport might include British vehicles captured in Flanders. Any attack was expected shortly before sunrise to allow a night approach to maximise the chance of surprise and to give the attacker the benefits of long hours for the first and most important day of the operation (TNA WO 166/1317:*Somerset Sub Area Coast Defence Scheme*, para 2, August 1940).

Aircraft landing on beaches

Luftwaffe aircraft landing on some of the beaches of Somerset as part of an invasion force was considered to be a high threat. The sandy beaches considered most suitable for both airborne or seaborne landings were (from north to west) Sand Bay, Weston Bay, Berrow Flats, Blue Anchor Bay and Porlock Bay, although the latter had shingle. The beach at Steart was identified in early plans but was rapidly excluded presumably because the mud flats would make landings by sea or air extremely difficult if not impossible. The threat of aircraft landing on the sand strips near to the high water mark of most of these beaches was taken very seriously.

By August 1940, Sand Bay, Berrow and Weston beaches had all been partially obstructed against aircraft landing. Cairns of Mendip stone were used at Weston-super-Mare and Middle Hope Cove, which survived until after the war. Burnham-on-Sea, Berrow and Sand Bay beaches were obstructed with rows of poles set in large squares and in 1941 Blue Anchor Bay beaches were similarly obstructed (see page 32). Examination of the defences built to obstruct aircraft from landing on these beaches clearly indicates that the threat was from Junkers 52 (Ju 52) transport aircraft, each of which could carry up to 16 fully armed men (Figure 3.3 on the next page).

Unlike a seaborne landing which it was assumed would be restricted to a relatively short period before high water, aircraft could land on the sands at the head of the beach from perhaps an hour after high water on the ebb tide until the next flood tide reached the sand again some eight or ten hours later. For example, high water at Watchet is typically seven and a half hours later than high tide along the south coast between Portsmouth and Dover but low water is about six and a quarter hours before high tide at which time the upper sand on the Somerset beaches would be available for aircraft. This could have allowed German seaborne landings on the south or East Anglian coastlines to be coordinated with simultaneous air-landing of troops on Somerset beaches. It should be pointed out that this conclusion was not recorded in any wartime documents.

The use of gliders to capture the key Belgium fortress of Eben Emael on 12 May 1940 greatly increased the awareness of the potential glider threat. However, along the Somerset coast glider landings were considered to be unlikely as it was believed that gliders would be released from their Ju 52 tug aircraft before crossing the south coast of England as towing over hostile territory was assessed as being too risky and with typical glide ranges of perhaps 20 miles (30km, depending on the release altitude and wind speed and direction), it was thought unlikely that they could have reached Somerset beaches. As gliders were able to land in a very short distance and the Germans were prepared to accept major damage to them on landing, there were no practical ways of obstructing potential landing grounds against gliders as these would have to to ensure that the gliders were so badly damaged that their passengers would be seriously injured.

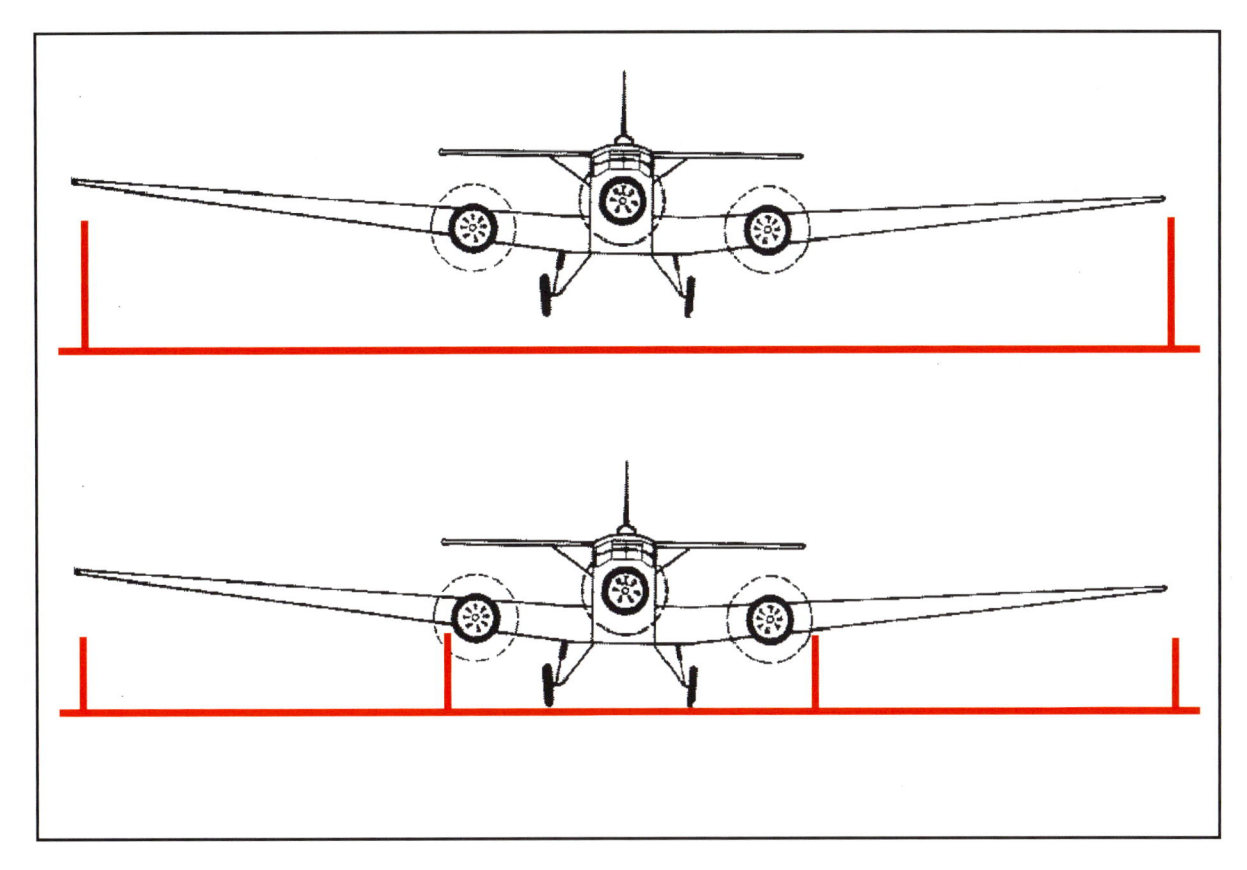

Figure 3.3: *Dimensions of obstruction posts to damage Ju 52 on landing and prevent take off. Upper 12-foot (3.65m) poles at 30-yard (27.5m) spacing, lower 6-foot (1.8m) poles at 10-yard (9m) spacing. Both set in lines to form 150-yard (137m) squares. The wingspan of a Ju 52 is 29.25m.*

The Ju 52 however, was capable of landing on a wide road or beach and taking off again to return to base to shuttle in another load of soldiers. Ju 52s needed to land and take off into the wind and the use of open spaces like beaches rather than fields would allow them to take off immediately after unloading without having to taxi back to the other end of a field and turn in order to take off again into the wind. Landing ground obstructions on moors, open spaces and beaches were designed to damage any Ju 52 sufficiently badly to ensure that it could not take off and return with more troops or supplies.

The operation orders issued for Somerset Coast Defence in 1940 stated that it was not clear whether the enemy aircraft would land on the beaches or on the moors. (The use of the term 'landing' can be confusing but in this context implied the landing of aircraft like the Ju 52 rather than any seaborne landings.) It was considered that if the beaches were heavily defended, the enemy would be more likely to land on the moors. The vast expanses of Exmoor and the Brendon Hills with open moorland, large fields and, in many places, straight wide roads running roughly east–west into the prevailing wind, offered numerous potential landing grounds, which were impossible to obstruct or defend. With relatively few isolated villages, the Germans might achieve surprise and land a significant force unseen and unopposed.

The Mendip Hills and, to a lesser extent, the Quantocks were also considered to be potential landing grounds. The Defence Scheme document states that throughout Somerset, 'numerous other landing grounds' were also obstructed, but no comprehensive lists have yet been discovered. Sites have been identified on immediately post-war aerial photographs at Maes Knoll, Dundry, Fry's Hill,

Figure 3.4: *Aircraft landing obstructions on the open moorland of Black Down near Shipham. These obstructions were constructed of double lines of heaps of stone or turf. It is likely that they survived wartime clearance for agriculture because the site was used for several bombing decoys (Somerset Studies Library, RAF 3G/TUD/UK/15/25/PART I 5279, 14/1/1946).*

Axbridge (SHER 11520) and Black Down (SHER 24114, Figure 3.4); at the last, the earth and stone mounds erected as obstacles still survive.

It is of interest that the MOI surveys of public opinion include a report on 27 May 1940 from Bristol: 'some anxiety over the hills and the moors in the west as parachute landing sites', while on 23 July 1940 Bristol reported: 'concern in Somerset about number of flat fields containing no obstacles' (Addison and Crang 2010, 42, 261).

It was also believed that seaplanes might land on the reservoirs at Cheddar, Blagdon (Mendip), Ashford, Cannington (site so far unidentified) or Durleigh and it was stated that the local authorities responsible had taken steps to obstruct them. Blagdon and Cheddar reservoirs were obstructed by Bristol Waterworks Company with moored rafts (Brown 1999, 32). The lower reaches of the Parrett, Brue, Axe and Yeo were also considered to be suitable for seaplane landings at high tide but no specific defence measure against seaplanes are cited (TNA WO 166/1317: *Somerset Sub Area Defence Scheme*, 11e, 11f).

On 13 July 1940, Army Southern Command issued guidance about how the Germans were expected to attack and capture airfields. Assuming that Somerset beaches were thought to be potential temporary airfields, similar tactics might be used (Smith 1989, 100). It would have been suicidal to attempt to land paratroops or aircraft on defended beaches before the defences had been suppressed. An attack might therefore start at dawn with a sweep by enemy fighters over the beach at medium height to assure local air superiority. The fighters might then be followed almost immediately by very low-flying bombers at about 25-50 feet (8–15m) dropping sticks of light bombs on the defences. Heavy fighters would then attack the defences with their front cannons and machine guns.

At the same time companies of parachute troops would be dropped (as companies) at several points about 1000 to 1500 yards (900–1400m) inland. These parachute troops would form up again in their companies in about 12-15 minutes and storm the beach defences from the rear. Beach obstructions would then be cleared to allow significant numbers of Ju 52 and large troop transports to land on the beach at the rate of about six a minute. On landing, these troop transports would disgorge troops armed with heavy and light machine guns, 2-inch and 3-inch mortars and possibly 3-inch mountain guns. The aircraft might also carry motor cycle and side-car combinations. Light anti-aircraft guns (20mm automatics with an effective range of about 4500 feet (1.4km) and capable of use as anti-tank and anti-pillbox weapons) might also be landed to defend the beach and a fighter 'umbrella' would be maintained over the area until the beachhead defences were ready (Smith 1989, 100).

Clearly not all these stages might be part of an attack on a beach intended as a landing ground but, as will be seen from the following paragraphs, the Somerset coastal defence plans were primarily based on this airborne threat. The paramount need would be for the Germans to achieve local air superiority and British air defence systems are therefore discussed in some detail later.

Defence of the coastal area

The Somerset coastline is about 65 miles (100km) long and the hinterland included in the coastal defence plans varied in depth from between five to ten miles (8–16km) from the sea. The 1940 concept for the defence of the Somerset coastal areas was to maintain an aerial and seaward watch over the area, to station troops near to all beaches to repel any landings, to have mobile reserves ready to reinforce troops defending beaches or to contain enemy landings on the moors and to prepare, and if necessary 'immobilise', the sea ports (TNA WO 166/1317: *Somerset Coast Defence Scheme*, 4, 15 August 1940). Beach defences were to be organised in defended localities prepared for all-round defence and defence schemes were designed to meet both landings from the beaches and also attacks by air-landed troops near to the coast. Pillboxes, intended primarily to house machine guns or concrete infantry section posts for riflemen, were built along the threatened beaches and fire trenches dug for infantry sections.

The Coastguard Service manned stations along the Somerset coast. These were supplemented by permanent Army observation posts and, during the night, by coast-watchers (Figure 2.3 on page 8). Observer Corps posts and Army searchlight sites near to the coast watched both air and sea. Across the area the Home Guard manned observation posts of their own from dusk to dawn, while Somerset Police and Customs & Excise gathered intelligence. All troops holding defensive positions on beaches and aerodromes 'stood to' daily at one hour before sunrise and only 'stood down when visibility justifies such action.' During the hours of darkness, beaches (including cliffs where landings were possible) were to be patrolled and one third of the garrison was ready for immediate action. At other times half of the troops on beaches or aerodromes were to be instantly available (TNA WO 166/1243: *Somerset Sub Area Defence Scheme*, para 40, 30 December 1940).

In addition to RAF Coastal Command sorties flown west of Lands End towards the Bay of Biscay and in the English Channel, 8 Corps ordered the RAF Army Co-operation Squadron based at Weston Zoyland to fly dawn patrols around the south-west coastline with a view to identifying any invasion fleet at sea or in the process of landing (TNA WO 166/298: 8 Corps *Operation Instruction 1*, 9 August 1940).

Units manning coast defences were also expected to be able to communicate by visual lamp signalling to any naval vessels in the area. Procedures were issued with brevity codes for requesting naval gun-fire from warships onto land targets. Basic signals were also laid down for intercommunication between ground forces and RAF aircraft.

On 23 June 1941, HQ Western Area, which was by then responsible for both Somerset and Bristol, issued the *Western Area Defence Scheme*. This listed defence commitments in priority order with aerodromes first, Bristol and Avonmouth docks second and 'the small harbours at Minehead and Watchet' in third place out of ten commitments. Lower priority commitments included manning anti-tank islands, vulnerable points and the north Somerset coast (TNA WO 166/1251: *Western Area Defence Scheme*, S4, para 11, 23 June 1941). Anti-parachute reaction forces were held ready to attack landings on the Quantock Hills, in central and south Somerset and in the valley to the north-east of Clevedon (TNA WO 166/1317: *Somerset Sub Area Defence Scheme*, part V, plan).

As will be discussed below, many of the troops assigned for beach defence came from training units in Taunton and orders were given that no roadblocks were to be erected along the A358 between Taunton and Williton, the A39 between Porlock and Othery (except in Bridgwater), the A38 between Taunton and Bristol (except again in Bridgwater) and the A370 between Highbridge, Weston-super-Mare and Bristol. This was to minimise any delays in deploying troops to counter an invasion in the coastal area (TNA WO 166/1317: *Somerset Sub Area Coast Defence Scheme*, appendix I, 15 August 1940). For the same reason, arrangements were made for the police to close certain roads to all civilian traffic within one to three hours of the request being received.

Centres of resistance

The coast defence plans required the Somerset ports and major coastal towns (Portishead, Weston-super-Mare, Burnham-on-Sea, Bridgwater, Watchet and Minehead) to be placed in a state of all-round defence as 'centres of resistance'. This was a pre-war concept laid down in *Field Service Regulations* and was not based on the blitzkrieg experiences of 1940. Later in the war, many centres of resistance were not provided with all-round anti-tank defence. By December 1940, Highbridge and Brent Knoll hill were also included and infantry slit trenches survive at the latter (SHER 15995, Figure 3.5 on the facing page). At Portishead the defence plans included the town, harbour and power station and eight roadblocks were built in December 1940 on main routes into the town (TNA WO 166/1317: *Somerset Sub Area Defence Scheme*, para 33; SRO C/S/5/3). The importance of Bridgwater lay not only in its docks but also because it was the only crossing point on the Parrett between its mouth and Burrow Bridge, and was also at the intersection of the A38 and A39 main roads which joined to cross the river. The town between the Parrett and the Great Western Railway to the east was fortified as an anti-tank island on the Taunton Stop Line in 1941. Loop-holed walls near the docks on the west side of the river suggest earlier harbour defences (SHER 12381).

The beach defences of Watchet were authorised on 18 January 1941 (TNA WO 199/1812) and several anti-tank roadblocks were erected on routes into the town (Wilson 2004, 165; SRO C/S/5/3). At Clevedon approval for beach defences was given in April 1941 (TNA WO 199/1812). There is no evidence to suggest that these 'centres of resistance' were ever provided with effective all-round defences, which is in stark contrast to the anti-tank islands constructed in 1941 on the Taunton Stop Line. These stop line anti-tank islands all had a perimeter of continuous anti-tank obstacles and barbed wire fences covered at all points by substantial pillboxes.

Figure 3.5: Surviving slit trenches on Brent Knoll. The angle-iron pickets would have supported sides (revetment) formed from expanded metal; some small areas of this survive (Somerset County Council HER, 2003).

The threat of tanks

The threat of tanks landing on the Somerset coastline was considered to be minimal and along the coast and throughout the immediate hinterland, there was an absence of any anti-tank cubes, scaffolding, ditches, mine fields, bridge demolitions or other anti-tank obstacles other than those on the stop lines, or in anti-tank islands and centres of resistance (SRO C/S/5/3). Nevertheless, a major assumption in the defence plans was that the Germans had the capability to transport special light tanks in aircraft capable of landing and taking off on roads or open spaces. Contemporary documents mention the *Luftwaffe* constructing special planes to carry two five-ton 'tankettes' (TNA WO 166/298: 8 Corps *INTSUM 7*, para 5b, 22 September 1940). Senior RAF officers also identified a tank threat from the air. General Pile noted that in May 1940, Dowding (the Air Officer Commanding-in-Chief of Fighter Command) and Portal (the Chief of Air Staff) were 'of the opinion that the Germans might land small tanks by air' (Pile 1949, 103).

An analysis of the works orders for the construction of anti-tank roadblocks in the coastal defence zone (SRO C/ S/5/3) and the absence of blocks on routes leading off the beaches suggests that the tank carrying aircraft that the Germans were believed to possess were only expected to be capable of landing on the hard surfaces of roads and not on beaches. This lack of anti-tank obstacles on exit routes from the Somerset beaches is in stark contrast to the Dorset or east Devon beaches where dual rows of anti-tank cubes or beach scaffolding together with barbed wire were erected. Unlike the Dorset, Cornish and both the south and north Devon coasts, there were no pre-arranged RAF targets planned against tank exit routes off the Somerset beaches (TNA WO 166/298: *8 Corps Defence Scheme*:

Beach Targets, March 1941). The HQ Western Area *Defence Scheme* instruction issued on 23 June 1941 advised that: 'This coast is already well provided with artificial defences and wire obstacles but has not yet been prepared for anti-tank defences. Schemes will be prepared for the blocking of exits from harbours or favourable landing beaches against tanks so that they can be put into effect if the priority of this coast rises and labour and materials become available' (TNA WO 166/1251).

There is no documentary evidence or surviving infrastructure to suggest that any anti-tank obstacles were ever constructed on or near Somerset beaches. Anti-tank roadblocks were built on the approaches to the harbours of Watchet and Portishead to prevent access to the ports rather than to contain any tanks landed in them. However, as will be discussed later, anti-tank roadblocks were definitely constructed on some routes north off Exmoor and the Brendon Hills against air-transportable tanks landed on the moors. Throughout Somerset there was also the threat of tanks which had landed to the west or south attempting to move across the county.

Port denial measures

Denial measures for the ports of Avonmouth and Portishead were prepared by the local Flag or Naval Officer in Charge (FOIC/NOIC), and were intended to prevent the off-loading of military vehicles, tanks and stores for a period of between seven to ten days. No denial measures are recorded for Minehead or Watchet (TNA WO 166/298: *8 Corps Defence Scheme*, amendment 2, 8 Feb 1941). However at Watchet, the West Quay and the slipways to both the West Beach and main harbour appear to have been prepared for demolition with large charge-chambers constructed in the roadway (Vernon Stone pers. comm.). The Admiralty intended to remove a section of Birnbeck Pier at Weston-super-Mare to prevent its use by an invader but it was found that the pier was built of continuous-girder construction and removal of any section would cause the whole structure to collapse (Pawle 2009, 141). The piers at both Minehead and Clevedon were not included in these denial measures but Minehead pier was removed in 1941 (Figure 4.1 on page 47) to improve the arc of fire of the emergency Coast Artillery battery sited on the harbour wall (see page 47).

In tidal waters the Admiralty was responsible for the immobilisation of vessels and small craft and the senior Royal Navy officer was responsible for the issue of passes allowing fishing boats to sail from harbours. Private craft on inland waters were always to be immobilised when unattended and, in the event of an invasion, further unspecified denial measures were planned by the Somerset Rivers Catchment Board for implementation by the Bridgwater Port and Harbour Authority (TNA WO 166/10824: *Somerset and Bristol Sub Area Defence Scheme*, appendix L, para 3, 13 April 1943).

Fuel denial measures

Denial measures were vital to ensure that an invader could not capture food, fuel or transport thereby increasing his mobility and reducing his logistics. This was particularly important for parachute or air landed forces, which would have lacked transport for both tactical movement of infantry and for logistic support. Across Britain all vehicles and petrol pumps had to be immobilised every night to deny their possible use to an invader.

Figure 3.6 on the facing page shows the 'Pink Area' where the threat of invasion was considered to be significantly higher and special additional measures were required. This area included the Somerset coast, Exmoor, the Brendon Hills and most of the Quantocks. Within the Pink Area, stocks of fuel were limited to the basic essentials only and measures prepared to enable the Home Guard to immediately cap petrol pump tanks with concrete to prevent the extraction of bulk fuel. Trains of full fuel tank waggons were not

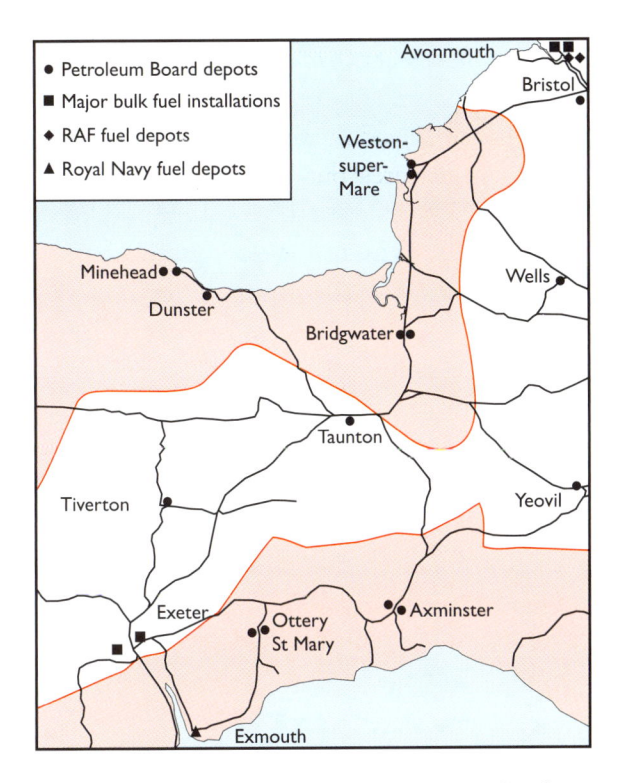

Figure 3.6: The Pink Area, fuel depots and railways (based on plans in TNA WO 166/298). The Pink Area covered locations where there was a higher threat of invasion. Special precautions were implemented to deny the Germans access to the fuel stocks held in the area. The locations of depots are approximate and are not recorded in Dorset.

permitted to remain overnight in the Pink Area and plans were made to destroy the coastal fuel depots at Weston-super-Mare, Bridgwater, Dunster and Minehead.

The 'Fifth Column' threat

Landings were also expected be supported by the 'Fifth Column': a network of agents or Nazi sympathisers, which was (wrongly) believed to have already been set up in Britain. After the successful German attacks in Norway, Denmark, Belgium and The Netherlands, rumours abounded of the decisive role that the Fifth Column had played in the swift defeat of these countries and their governments in exile in London appear not to have denied them. It is not intended to review major concerns of the Government over the Fifth Column threat or measures taken to minimise it but they are well documented in the Official Histories (Hinsley and Simkins 1990, 47–64). There also numerous references in the MOI surveys of the concern in the civilian population about the Fifth Column which was viewed by all as a very real threat (see, for the South West, Addison and Crang 2010, 80, 81, 88, 434). Agents or spies were also expected to be landed by parachute or on isolated beaches (see page 39).

Shortly after the outbreak of war, military guards had been placed on key points like Whiteball railway tunnel on the Somerset–Devon border and the Air Defence of Great Britain (ADGB) Burnett magazine near Keynsham together with measures to defend the only four aerodromes that then existed in Somerset (Whitchurch, Weston-super-Mare, Yeovil and Weston Zoyland). Foreign nationals from enemy countries and 'aliens' were interned in special camps with military guards. These included the holiday camps at Paignton (Internment Camp 23) and Seaton (Camp 24). By mid October 1939, Seaton was holding some 274 Class B internees and Paignton 30 Class A, those internees considered to be the most dangerous (TNA WO 166/1252).

Figure 3.7: Williton Police Station. In May 1940 all placenames and signposts were ordered to be removed to confuse the invader. The bottom left-hand part of the scroll bore the name 'Williton' and was chipped away. Similar action was taken at Dunster Police Station (David Hunt, 2009).

Control of movement

On 31 May 1940 orders were given to remove all signposts and name boards to hinder an invader's road movement (Figure 3.7 on the previous page). The MOI reported from Bristol on 12 July, 'Motorists on Salisbury Plain refused directions by villagers' but on 14 June had recounted a case of 'a stranger to the region travelled 360 miles [575km] in the west country without difficulty, thanks to hotel and other private advertisements on the road, and the clearness of the white lines on the roads leading to towns' (Addison and Crang 2010, 113).

Figure 3.8: The 'EL' emergency licence. The original was 5¼ by 4 inches (133 x 102mm).

In the Coastal Defence Area, ten 'vehicle check points' (VCPs) were set up by the Army to hinder movement of Fifth Columnists or agents landed by sea or air. In total, there were some 50 VCPs across Somerset. In addition, across the county, the Home Guard routinely set up temporary roadblocks and checked night movement along selected roads within their areas of responsibility. If the threat of invasion increased, VCPs would be manned by police supported by armed Home Guard, who would enforce the civilian 'stay put' policy and keep key routes free for the military to move to battle stations or reinforce the coastal areas. 'Immobilisation Parks', also called 'Civilian Car Parks', were set up nearby and after the 'Stand Firm' order had been given, vehicles attempting to leave the area without the necessary 'EL' (emergency licence) would be impounded and either immobilised or immediately requisitioned by the military. If the threat of invasion became imminent, the police were then to centralise and immobilise all civilian vehicles and, if these were likely to be captured, the police were under orders to 'fire' them (TNA WO 166/1317: *Somerset Coast Defence Scheme*, 15 August 1940).

Landings on the coast

Blue Anchor Bay

Extensive defences were constructed across Blue Anchor Bay in the approximately five-mile (8km) wide area between Minehead and Blue Anchor which were commenced in August 1940 and were further strengthened in 1941. A grid of stout 6-foot (1.8m) high wooden posts about 10 yards (9m) apart forming boxes with sides about 170 yards (155m) long was built along the upper reaches of the beaches. These obstructions were specifically designed to damage any Ju 52 troop transport aircraft attempting to land on the beaches to prevent them from returning to base to bring in additional waves of soldiers, supplies or equipment. At least 76 pillboxes have been identified in the Blue Anchor Bay area (details in SHER) and there were possibly more (Figure 3.9 on the facing page). These primarily cover the open beaches and their immediate hinterland with a few providing defences for villages like Carhampton, Dunster and the town of Minehead (Figure 3.10 and Figure 3.11 on page 34). Compared to Berrow Flats or the Taunton Stop Line, over three times more pillboxes per mile have been identified across Blue Anchor Bay.

In January 1941, an Army-manned 4-inch QF naval beach defence gun was installed covering the eastern end of Blue Anchor Bay. This was one of only 12 such guns in the South West and was the sole gun to be deployed in this role in Somerset. These guns were intended to fire at 'hard' targets like landing craft on the beach but would not necessarily

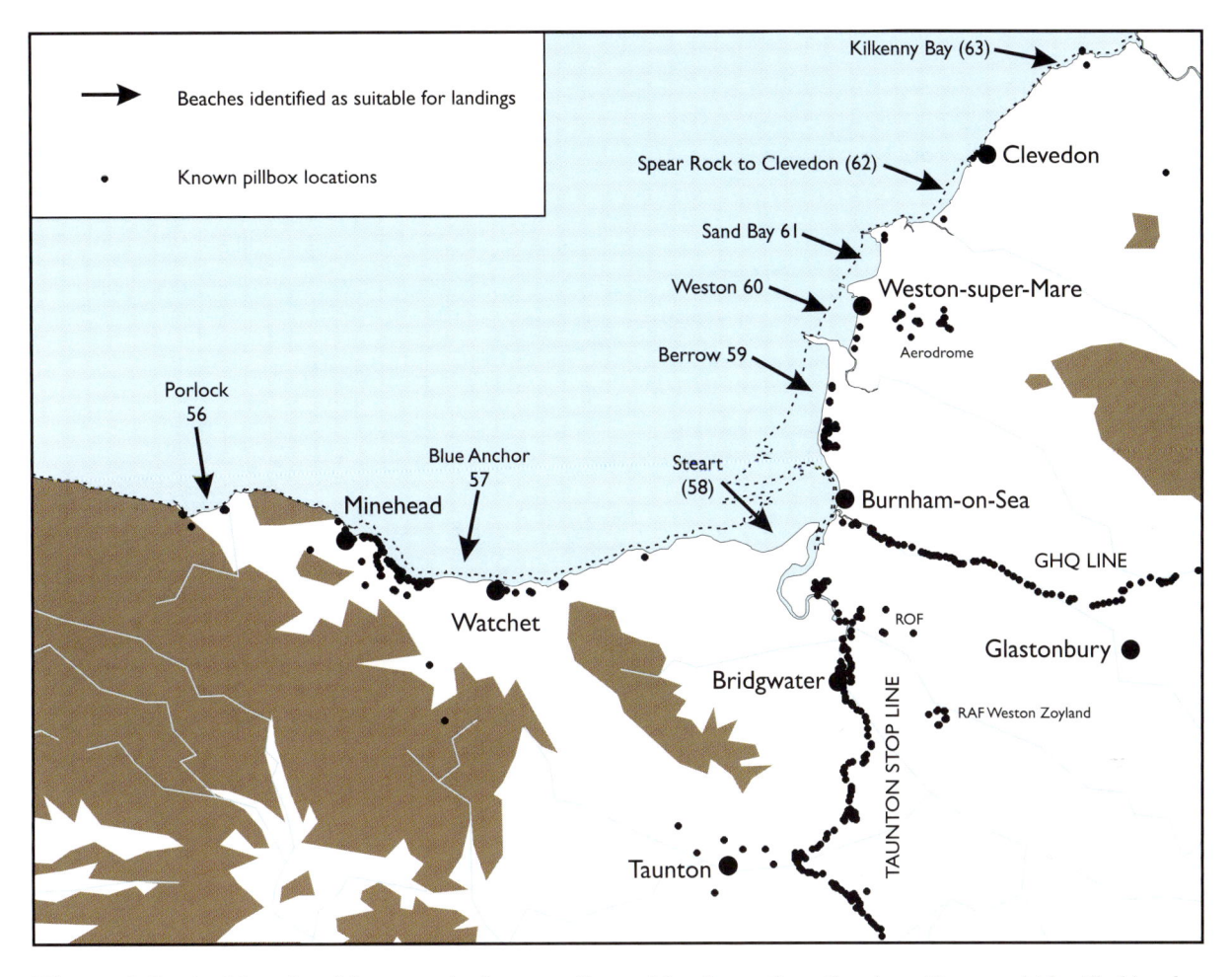

Figure 3.9: *Anti-invasion defences on the Somerset Coast. Numbers refer to Southern Command identified beaches; those in brackets were considered at low risk (listed, for example, in TNA WO 199/1624).*

have been effective against airborne landings, indicating that a seaborne invasion threat was certainly still under consideration. The gun was returned to the Royal Navy in January 1942 (TNA WO 166/2038).

The importance given to Minehead harbour in the summer of 1940 is indicated by the construction of an 'emergency coast defence battery' (see page 47) although the harbour had a significantly lower tonnage landing capacity than Watchet harbour. The current Harbourmaster of both ports estimates that up to two 500-ton vessels could berth simultaneously at Watchet, while at Minehead only one vessel of this tonnage could be berthed (Vernon Stone pers. comm.). Despite this Minehead was protected by a battery while the two 4-inch naval guns planned and reconnoitred for the harbour at Watchet were never implemented (TNA WO 166/2060). In 1941, however, a pair of 6-pounder guns covering the harbour mouth at Watchet were installed, and manned by the Home Guard.

As well as these, the fixed Bofors AA guns at Doniford range were also capable of engaging ships which have to approach the harbour mouth from the north-east. This inward passage to the harbour ran close to the shore past the Doniford AA range firing point. Although anti-tank ammunition was available for Bofors guns, the 2-pound shells of the Bofors are not likely to have been very effective against merchant vessels or landing craft. The guns at Minehead were returned to the Royal Navy in early 1942 and were never replaced although they and the additional two guns for Watchet remained on the list as a low priority replacement (TNA WO 199/1111).

Figure 3.10: *Pillboxes camouflaged with beach pebbles on the coast north of Dunster Beach. SHER 35362, 35363 (Timothy Dawson, 2002).*

Figure 3.11: *Blue Anchor Bay. The only surviving section post of some 23 constructed in the first phase of coast defences in the summer of 1940. The post has 11 loopholes and is sited to cover the beach with rifle or machine-gun fire along the high water line. There is a pit for a light AA machine-gun in the centre of the roof. SHER 35367, Listed Grade II in 2010. The beach defence gun was sited in the woods, just below the horizon (David Dawson, 2010).*

Airborne landings on the moors

The threats of aircraft or parachutes landing on the vast expanses of Exmoor and the Brendon Hills have already been mentioned. In the event of an invasion alert, vehicle mounted infantry were to be deployed to carry out patrols along key routes on Exmoor and the Brendon Hills. These patrols were to be started as soon as the order 'Stand To' had been issued. The order would be given when conditions were particularly favourable for an invasion to bring regular forces to a complete state of readiness to resist an invasion (TNA WO 208/2969, appendix XLI, see Figure 3.15 on page 40). Analysis of both the coastal defence plans for west Somerset and the deployments of troops during the major invasion scare in September 1940 (for example in TNA WO 166/4660), suggest that German troops landing on Exmoor or the Brendon Hills were then considered to be the major threat. By 1941, the objectives of enemy airborne troops landing on Exmoor or Quantocks, or of seaborne troops landing on the Somerset coast west of the river Parrett, were considered to be 'penetration through Bridgwater or Taunton' (TNA WO 166/1251: Conference minutes, 12 July 1941).

The main body of the German air-landed troops was expected to advance southwards towards the A361 or A38 to take the Waist of the South West and would need logistic support. The capability to do this by air was limited, particularly for bulk commodities like ammunition and fuel, so the threat of an attack northwards towards the coast would seem likely to have been a secondary operation with the aim of securing the west Somerset ports and beaches to enable a temporary supply chain to be established. The priority given to their defence has already been mentioned.

Within the western part of the Coastal Defence Area, several anti-tank roadblocks, some with associated pillboxes, were built in December 1940 (TNA WO 166/1317: *Somerset Sub Area Defence Scheme*, amendment of 30

Figure 3.12: *Pillbox at Vale House, Roadwater, with camouflage roof reconstructed in 2008 by Exmoor National Park Authority. It was built in 1940 to cover an anti-tank roadblock closing routes towards the west Somerset coast for German troops landed by air on the Brendon Hills. ExHER MSO12289, Scheduled Monument 35320 (David Dawson, 2009).*

December 1940, para 43(a)(2)). These blocks were sited at defiles on the main routes north from Exmoor to the coast. Blocks are recorded to the north and south of Dunster and at Withycombe, Roadwater, Raleigh's Cross and Sticklepath together with blocks on the A39 at Allerford to the east of Porlock and at Periton on the Porlock–Alcombe road.

The 'works orders' for the construction of these blocks clearly state that the expected direction of enemy attack was from the direction of the moors. Pillboxes still survive at Raleigh's Cross (SHER 35369) and Roadwater (ExHER MSO12289; Figure 3.12). The importance of these anti-tank blocks on the routes north off Exmoor and the Brendon Hills is indicated in the *Somerset Sub Area Defence Scheme* where the Dunster sector commander was ordered to task an ad-hoc battalion of the Somerset Light Infantry, that had been allocated to him, to patrol specified routes across Exmoor and to be prepared to take up defensive positions at these defiles on routes off the moor. The anti-tank blocks were strengthened in May 1941 and again in November 1941 but other blocks on routes leading eastwards from Porlock Bay were not (SRO C/S/5/3). These strengthening measures were similar to those implemented across the South West at this time, to ensure that the blocks would stop the latest and heaviest German tanks (SRO C/S/5/3).

While the open terrain on the moor and hills favoured the invader, once the enemy attempted to advance down the valleys to the coast, the deep narrow and twisting lanes with substantial hedgerows and small fields would make movement along the roads slow and difficult. Unlike the open fields of northern France in the German offensive in May 1940, it would be difficult for armour to break away from the roads to bypass blocks or attack them from flank or rear. Tanks would be at constant risk of close-quarter attacks using rudimentary anti-tank petrol bombs ('Molotov cocktails') or other grenades and would have to advanced 'closed down'. This would severely restrict the vision of the tank commander and driver and hinder navigation in this complex terrain even more.

Infantry movements along the roads would also be slow and it would have been difficult to bring infantry forward to attack roadblocks or blocking positions that were holding up the tanks, particularly as the tanks in a German *Zug* (a troop of four or five tanks) were only equipped with wireless receivers and only the troop leader had a transmitter (Jentz 1998, 272–74). In such close country, the troop leader would be unable to see what was happening to his leading tanks and could not receive reports from them. *Luftwaffe* Stuka ground-attack aircraft might have been available to attack these blocking positions.

These routes to the coast had a very limited capacity compared to those routes southwards off Exmoor and the Brendon Hills along which the main air landed force might move into the Waist of the South West. This difficulty reinforces the suggestion that the advance northwards to the coast was expected to be a secondary operation with German air-portable tanks attacking north towards the coast to capture the harbours and beaches concurrently with the main operation southwards to secure the Waist of the South West. The defences at Watchet included anti-tank roadblocks on routes into the town (Wilson 2004, 165 map) but these blocks do not appear to have been strengthened, later in 1941, to resist more modern tanks when other blocks in Somerset were (SRO C/S/5/3). Roadblocks were also later built on routes off the Quantocks at Spaxton, North Petherton, Nether Stowey and Cannington.

A review of potential invasion beaches carried out in 1943 (TNA WO 199/1624) reported that the beaches of Blue Anchor Bay would be suitable for the landing of infantry, armoured vehicles and trucks. Despite this assessment, the lack of roads from the beaches would have greatly restricted the quantity of supplies and stores that could have been landed. It must be remembered that the support of the airborne troops attacking and potentially holding the Waist of the South West would only be planned to be a temporary measure until the Germans could establish a more effective supply route through Plymouth or other south coast ports. The importance of British denial measures to prevent the enemy from capturing transport or fuel and thereby lightening his logistical requirements has been discussed (above, page 30). Nevertheless, the logistic problems of using the long sea route from France or Plymouth to the Somerset coast and landing over the beaches would have been considerable.

Despite this, the area was still considered a likely invasion site and GHQ Auxiliary Unit patrols trained to operate as 'stay behind parties' were established in the area to attack the follow up forces, landing grounds or logistic traffic from captured ports after the initial thrust had passed (see page 42).

The north Somerset coast

Berrow and Weston-super-Mare beaches, together with their hinterlands, were considered to be more likely options for airborne landings than Exmoor as they would allow troops to form up and to move more easily onto their objectives: particularly Taunton and Ilminster. With low tides, the beaches at Berrow and Weston-super-Mare had large areas of firm sand that the tide might not cover for several days, which would allow the beaches to be used as temporary landing grounds on which the *Luftwaffe* might land up to 3000 men per hour (Figure 3.13 on the following page). At Weston-super-Mare the aerodrome was also near to the beach.

Between September and December 1940, 8 Corps tasked its mobile reserve divisions to be prepared to counter attack both airborne and seaborne landings at Berrow: the only Somerset beach where a seaborne threat was identified (TNA WO 166/298: 8 Corps *Operation Instruction 3* for 3 Division, 10 September 1940 and *Operation Instruction 11* for 50 Division, 1 December 1940). The option of Berrow or Weston-super-Mare then being used to launch a German secondary diversionary attack against Bristol was also mentioned, which might be coordinated with other airborne landings on Mendip. To counter these threats, significant forces including dedicated artillery support with a section of 25-pounder guns and a permanent allocation of five Vickers medium machine guns (MMG) were deployed there, with their crews held at a high state of readiness. Concrete MMG emplacements, together with other pillboxes, still survive and wartime air photos show the emplacements each with an adjacent Nissen hut to accommodate the crews. At least 34 pillboxes were built along nearly seven miles (11km) of the coast between Brean Down and Burnham-on-Sea (details in SHER; Figure 3.9 on page 33). On the issue of the invasion alert order 'Action Stations', mobile Bofors guns (which could have either an anti-aircraft or a limited anti-shipping role) were to be immediately deployed to the Berrow area from the anti-aircraft practice camp at Liddymore near Doniford. The requirement to hold the hill at Brent Knoll with its commanding views over Berrow Flats and the hinterland has been mentioned above. After the fortification of Steep Holm in 1942 (see page 52), the coastal guns from the South Battery were also tasked to fire 'beach barrages' onto Berrow Flats (TNA WO 166/10824: *Somerset and Bristol Sub Area Defence Scheme*, appendix B, 13 April 1943).

The GHQ Line

Both Berrow and Weston-super-Mare were also within the perimeter of the Green Line section of the Bristol Outer Defence Line and were to the rear of the westward-facing defences of the Taunton Stop Line. Southern Command therefore directed that the junction of both stop lines with the coast at Burnham-on-Sea was 'to be made into a strong point capable of prolonged resistance against attack from any direction' (TNA WO 166/298: Southern Command Operation Instruction 24, 15 August 1940). No evidence has yet been found of these all-round defences. Troops at Burnham-on-Sea and Berrow were also ordered to hold the major crossing points of the river Brue on the Green Line at Highbridge, Bason Bridge, River Bridge and Westhay. Significantly, a German guide prepared in 1940 for the invading forces recognised that 'the marshy depressions of the Parrett and the Brue block approaches to Bristol from the south' (Wheeler and Matthews 2007, 56).

Vulnerable installations

Raids on coastal installations

Throughout the period from 1940 to late 1944, the possibility of airborne or seaborne raids on important installations near to the coast was also identified. Such raids might be up to company strength (about 100 men) or small

Figure 3.13: *The vast expanse of Berrow Flats seen from Brean Down as the tide recedes. Note the cars driving onto the firm sand that could have been used to land enemy aircraft (David Dawson, 2010).*

parties landed by parachute or from U- or E-boats. By April 1942, it was 'considered unlikely that the enemy would be able to land in force on the coast of South Somerset Sub Area [the coast to the west of the river Parrett], small diversionary landings by either by sea or air are not improbable' (TNA WO 166/6775). Later in the war, the possibility of destructive raids on key installations within the 'sea raid zone', which extended up to 5 miles (8km) from the coast, was identified. It was expected that raiders would either fight to the last man ('suicide raids') or accept capture after achieving their objectives.

Lists of potential targets for sabotage or 'Vulnerable Points' (VP) include communications installations like the BBC transmitters at Clevedon and Washford (see page 73), the Post Office ship-shore radio transmitters at Portishead and their associated receivers at Burnham-on-Sea (see page 91), the two MI5 Radio Security Service directional finding stations at Stockland Bristol (see page 92), the transatlantic submarine cable station at Weston-super-Mare pier, together with the cable balancing houses in Bridgwater and Perry Bridge, and the GPO telephone repeater station on the Bristol–Plymouth cables at Rooks Bridge. The War Office School of AA Defence (SAAD) at Doniford was another VP. It would have been of particular interest to the Germans as the school specialised in AA radar. Other likely targets included the Avonmouth Docks, and the oil facilities there and at Berwick Wood, aircraft factories at Filton and Weston-super-Mare or the Royal Ordnance Factory at Puriton. The barrage balloon experimental station at Pawlett (see page 89) was also included.

By the summer of 1943, the assessment of the Commander-in-Chief Home Forces was that there was 'no possibility at present of

Figure 3.14: *Pillbox at Uphill covering one of the exits from the beach (David Hunt, 2009).*

an invasion of the United Kingdom' but there was still a threat of sabotage and anti-invasion preparedness must be continued for 'the possibility that a sudden and unexpected change to the war situation might alter existing conditions for the worse' (TNA WO 166/10904: South West District Operational Policy 17, para 6, 1943). On the 22 September 1944 Southern Command advised that there was no longer any need for defence works to be maintained for anti-invasion or anti-raid purposes (TNA WO 199/1779: Home Defence file).

Precautions against enemy agents

Agents or spies were expected to be landed by parachute or on isolated beaches. A report to GHQ Home Forces of April 1941 (TNA WO 199/92: *The Landing of Enemy Agents from Small Craft*, SF.64/2/6/B.2c) relates that 'reliable Secret Service sources' indicated that the German Intelligence Service had become discouraged from attempting to land agents by parachute and proposed to run them in using small boats. Since September 1940 enemy agents had been landed from sea planes and fishing cutters and further attempts might be expected by submarine. Their alarm had been reinforced by the number of small craft found washed up and left abandoned on beaches. The report continues:

> But the value of ... coastal watchers in preventing or detecting landings made under cover of darkness is very limited. There appears to be unanimity of opinion among those who are in a position to judge upon such matters that there are innumerable

State of readiness	Action taken
Normal	Invasion unlikely in the immediate future but raids possible.
Stand to	Conditions particularly favourable for an invasion. Complete state of readiness to resist invasion for all regular troops and for such Home Guard as the Army Commander may decide.
Action Stations	Immediate threat of invasion. Complete state of readiness to resist invasion. Home Guard called out.

Figure 3.15: *Army states of readiness*

places on the coast where an agent would stand a good chance of getting ashore in a dinghy or small boat during the hours of darkness without being detected. It should be borne in mind that the inshore motor-boat patrol maintained by the Admiralty cannot operate in bad weather, and it is in such conditions that an agent would have the best prospect of success and would be most likely to make his attempt. Further, since the coast is not regularly patrolled, the evidence of a landing – eg, in abandoned craft – might not be discovered for several days, and in the interval the agent would probably have disappeared inland into a populated area, where his detection becomes an infinitely more difficult task.

The chances of finding an agent who had disappeared into an urban area through police controls or radio intercept by the Radio Security Service (see page 92) were considered to be small. The Secret Service requested GHQ Home Forces to provide military or Home Guard dawn patrols to search the shore in undefended areas for suspicious persons and signs of landing and to have plans for the capture of any suspected enemy agent. The main undefended areas thought to be at risk in Somerset were Glenthorne, Porlock, Selworthy, Greenaleigh, St Audries, Lilstock, Brean Down and Portishead Point. It was recommended that personnel of the Auxiliary Coastguard Service should be employed. On 21 January 1942 the Secret Service stated that it was also highly desirable for the eastern and southern coast of the UK and the Bristol Channel as far as Burnham-on-Sea on the south shore and Barry on the north to be patrolled daily by the military, Home Guard or Coastguards and those areas not covered were to be patrolled by Auxiliary Coastguards (TNA WO 199/92: Landing of enemy agents, HF/IB/120). The *Somerset and Bristol Sub Area Defence Scheme* (appendix C, 15 April 1943: TNA WO 166/10824) lists Coastguard stations and gives details of dawn patrols from Glenthorne to Porlock Weir, Porlock Weir to 'limekilns' (presumably those near Bossington), Greenaleigh to Selworthy, Warren Point to Blue Anchor, Watchet to Blue Anchor, Kilve to Lilstock, Kilve to St Audries and Stert Point along Stert Flats. These patrols were organised by the District Officer of HM Coastguard, Croyde and consisted of a single man armed with a Sten gun who commenced his search half an hour before dawn. North of Burnham 'coast searchers' at Brean and Brean Down were to search Berrow Flats and Brean Down 'as and when they can, daily if possible.'

Coastal defence troops

The best plans and defences are useless without trained, well-equipped and determined troops to man them. Detailed listings of 'troops to task' for coastal defences for August and December 1940 exist in the relevant editions of the *Somerset Coast Defence Scheme* and analysis of these documents shows that in August 1940 about 11,500 officers and men were available for coastal defence in Somerset. Of these 6800 (about 60%) were Home Guard; a force which had only been in existence since May that year but, based on the national average, some 30% of these men were probably experienced ex-soldiers (Mackenzie 1995, 37). Only half of Home Guardsmen had a weapon, initially with some ten rounds of ammunition, and Molotov Cocktails as anti-tank weapons. Despite the threat of chemical warfare, Home Guardsmen did not receive anti-gas clothing until late into the autumn of 1940 (Mackenzie 1995, 91; TNA WO 166/299).

Three new infantry battalions of the Somerset Light Infantry were formed from 1800 men above the age of 42. These battalions lacked unit training and had minimal communications and logistic support. The 9th Somerset LI were deployed to St Audries near Watchet and 50th Somerset LI to Weston-super-Mare. In addition, two ad hoc infantry 'battalions' were formed from instructors and trainees at the Infantry Training Centre in Sherford Camp, Taunton (over 700 men forming two battalions called K1 and K2) and, from the nearby 222 Searchlight Training Regiment at Norton Manor Camp, two battalions each of over 900 men (called Mod A and Mod B, it appears that 'Mod' may have been an abbreviation for mobile defence). Other troops came from students and staff of the School of Anti-Aircraft Defence (SAAD) at Doniford and the nearby AA practice camp at Liddymore. Despite these numbers, about one quarter did not have a weapon and, had a German invasion occurred in September 1940, a total of only 44 light machine guns (LMG) and 14 anti-tank rifles were available across the whole 65 miles (100km) of the coastal area. The use of so many trainees and students, who had never practised their defence role and would not have known the ground they were defending, would have been a severe disadvantage.

By December 1940, when the winter weather conditions reduced the threat of invasion, about 9200 troops were available but there was still an overall shortage of weapons (about 22%) although adequate ammunition and 370 LMG were now available in the coastal area. About 5600 (60%) of the manpower was Home Guard and two thirds of Home Guard now had a weapon or hand grenades together with 240 LMG. It should be noted that Home Guard numbers depended only on those who volunteered and cannot be taken as a measure of military needs. No data is available after 1940.

The availability of Home Forces troops along the Somerset coast permanently assigned to coastal defence duties, who alone would have borne the brunt of a surprise airborne attack, were 23% of the total forces available in August 1940 and 20% in December 1940. These troops were not in organised field formations with armour, field or anti-tank artillery, or engineer support. They seriously lacked the firepower and support of a normal formation. For example, across Blue Anchor Bay only 360 men were instantly available while at Berrow the number was about 490. If an invasion was expected and the Alert Measure 'Stand To' had been ordered, troops from training establishments would then become available (see Figure 3.15 on the facing page). As previously mentioned, some six hours warning of a seaborne invasion was expected and this should have enabled these troops to move to their defence positions. The Home Guard became available for coastal defence (but only within about three miles (5km) of their homes) when an invasion was imminent and the Alert Measure 'Action Stations' had been ordered.

As the war went on, Home Guard battalion commanders took over responsibility from the Field Army for the defences of their areas against the current threats. The successful airborne attacks in Crete in May 1941 heightened British awareness of the *Luftwaffe* airborne capability and the Home Guard role included dealing with parachute landed troops. Even after Germany invaded Russia in June 1941, it was considered that, once they had conquered Russia, it would only take several months to regroup and prepare for an invasion

(Hinsley 1979, 482). Nevertheless, maintaining the interest and morale of the Home Guard was clearly an important political and social factor, particularly after Home Guard conscription was introduced in early 1942 (Mackenzie 1995, 7–8, 124–25).

GHQ Auxiliary Units

The major threat in Blue Anchor Bay is also indicated by the establishment of six 'operational bases' of the GHQ Auxiliary Units (AU) Operational Branch in the area. The AU was part of what is often called the 'British Resistance Organisation' (BRO) although during the war the AU title deliberately gave no clue to the operational roles of the GHQ AU. The Operational Branch was recruited primarily from specially selected Home Guard members or others with excellent local knowledge, who were prepared to harry the Germans after the initial wave of an invasion. AU patrols were tasked to lie low in specially constructed hides during an invasion and to then surface and attack or sabotage the invaders' supply and command systems. Patrols were equipped with a variety of weapons and explosives and were highly trained in sabotage and assassination and their bases were well stocked with rations to enable them to survive for several weeks. Blue Anchor Bay appears to be the only beach within the Somerset Coast Defences where nearby AU operational bases (OB) were established. Other OBs were sited in the area between the West Somerset coast and the Brendon Hills.

In addition to the Operational Branch, there was a completely separate organisation within the GHQ AU called the Special Duties Branch (SD). This was manned by specially selected and trained civilians who were to act as spies in any coastal areas which the German had occupied. These spies would report through a network of 'dead letter' drops and their reports would be collected by runners delivering to hidden wireless stations (Figure 3.16 on the next page). These civilian-manned 'out-stations' would transmit the reports to military-manned 'in-stations' which would then pass on to the appropriate Army HQ.

Ongoing research suggests that the spy networks were probably established in 1940 or 1941 but that the wireless networks were only rolled-out to east Devon and to west and central Somerset in mid 1942. Secret wireless 'out-station' sites have been identified at Dunball, Brent Knoll, Blue Anchor, Spaxton, Glastonbury, Puckington and Wiveliscombe. These were linked to military underground control stations (in-stations) at Castle Neroche (SHER 28026) on the eastern end of the Blackdown Hills, which was manned by Royal Signals or, in the case of Wiveliscombe, to Volis Hill on the south-eastern slopes of the Quantock Hills, which was manned by women of the ATS. The Blue Anchor station is believed to have had a link to the Blorenge mountain in south Wales or possibly Castle Neroche.

The AU (SD) network only covered the east Devon coast as far as the river Exe and there were no stations in south Devon, Cornwall or north Devon. The relatively high density of AU (SD) stations in Somerset and the distance that some of them were inland from the coast is indicative of the perceived threat to the Waist of the South West even in 1942. A major difficulty in researching the AU and, in particular, the SD is that documentation is almost non-existent and some of the few survivors still consider themselves bound by the Official Secrets Act and refuse to share their knowledge. The AU (SD) was stood down in July 1944 and the infrastructure of the control stations was 'capped off' or destroyed after all equipment had been removed (Tim Wray pers. comm.).

Communications and logistics

Command and control facilities in HQs, particularly communications, were basic. There was no wireless available within any infantry units in 1940 and the first wireless sets for linking battalion HQs to their companies were only then coming into production. Battalion internal communications were by

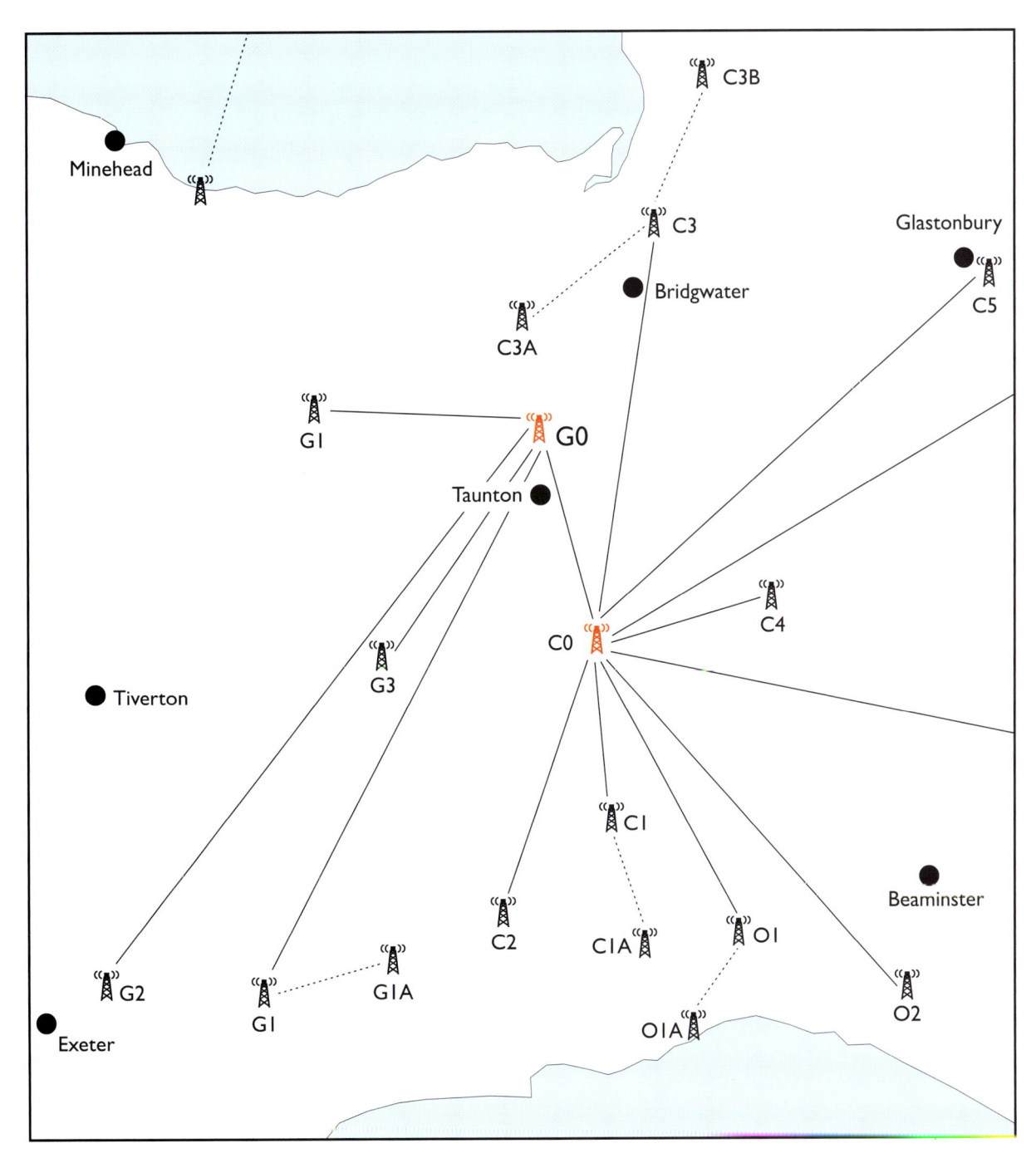

Figure 3.16: *The GHQ Auxiliary Unit Special Duties Branch wireless networks in the Waist of the South West. The two networks, 'Chirnside' with its control station at Castle Neroche (C0) to the south of Taunton and 'Golding' with its control to the north (G0), served HQ South Western District in Taunton. The networks were developed between 1942 and 1944 and were the most westerly of the AU networks along the South Coast.*

runner, motorcycle orderlies, semaphore or daylight signalling lamps with a few field telephones and limited cable (*Signal Training (All Arms)*, Section 147, 1938). The war-diary of 9 Battalion Somerset Light Infantry describes how improvised signalling lamps were used (TNA WO 166/4660, 17 September 1940) but ad-hoc units and the Home Guard had nothing. Both the Observer Corps and searchlight sites had dedicated GPO (General Post Office) communications backed up by wireless at many searchlight sites and these were

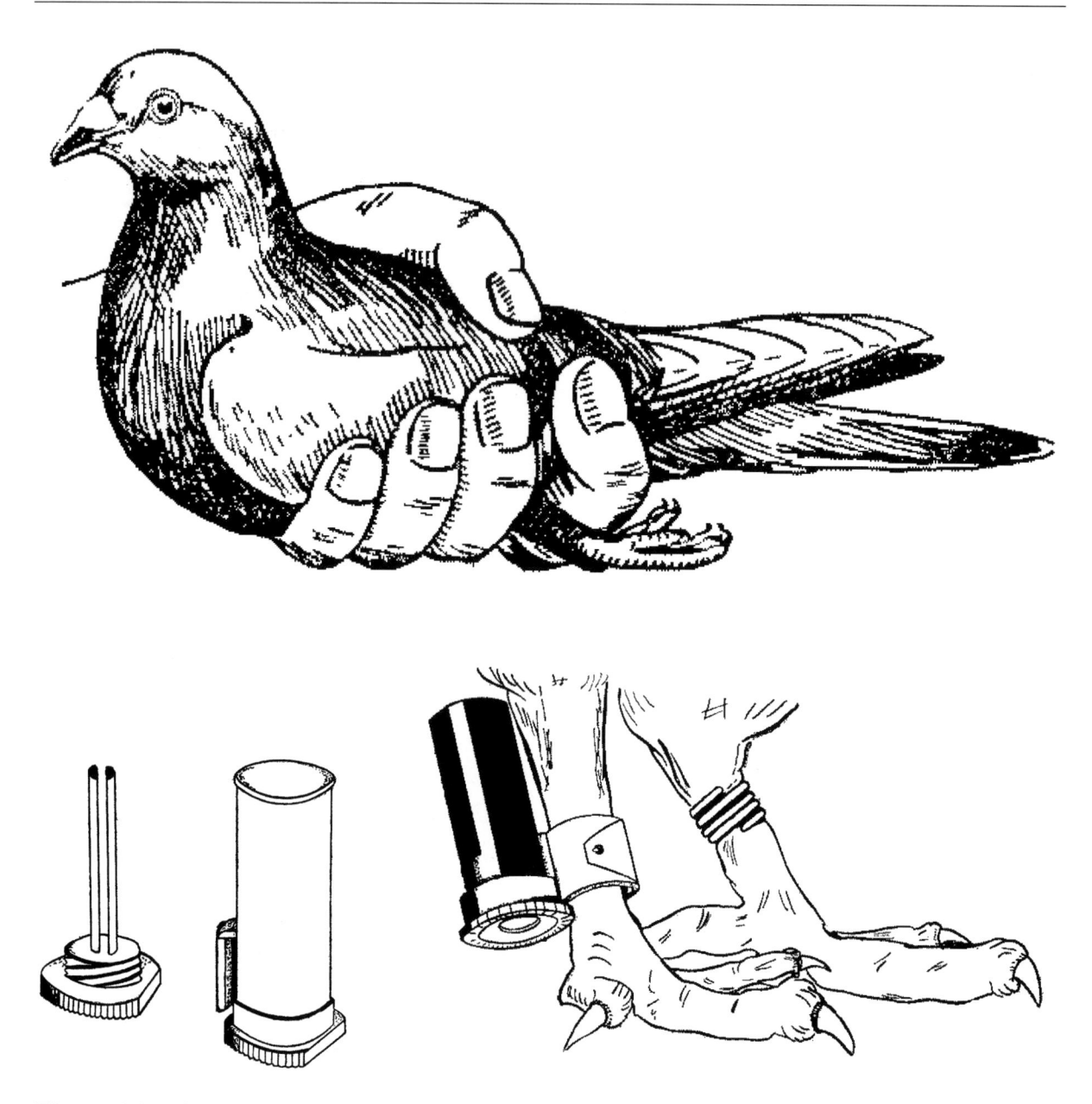

Figure 3.17: *Carrier pigeons: the correct way to hold a pigeon (top), the message carrier (bottom left) and the carrier attached to the pigeon's leg (bottom right) (War Office 1938).*

used whenever possible. Maximum use was made of the GPO telephone network although this was particularly sparse and vulnerable in coastal areas. Dispatch riders, runners and even carrier pigeons were used. A regular pigeon service (Figure 3.17) was run between HQ Somerset Sub Area in Bridgwater and both HQ Southern Area in Sherborne and the Burnham-on-Sea Sector. On the Alert Measure 'Action Stations' the Dunster Sector was included in the system and six birds were sent from both Dunster and Burnham-on-Sea to Bridgwater who dispatched the same number in return. After 48 hours fresh birds were sent out and the original birds released to fly back to their home loft before they became too acclimatised to their temporary surroundings (TNA WO 166/1317: *Somerset Sub Area Defence Scheme*, appendix S, 4 December 1940). According to the Royal Signals Museum, at distances over 50 miles (80km) pigeons were often faster than motorcycles though pigeons would not normally fly in the dark. The rudimentary communications of the Home Guard were improved in March 1942 by the issue of four signalling lamps and 20 semaphore flags to each company but it was August before radio became available when four wireless sets (type WS18) were issued to each battalion (TNA WO 199/392).

An important tri-service system to ensure all formations and land-based units of the Navy, Army and RAF were immediately warned of invasion was the 'Beetle Broadcast' system. HQs and units were issued with civilian wireless receivers which were constantly monitored. A number of long wave transmitter stations were set up across Britain to flash the news to all units. The information came primarily from RAF sources including the Observer Corps. The ringing of church bells had been forbidden except as a warning to the Home Guard that an invasion was taking place. After the invasion alert codeword (Cromwell) had been issued on 8 September 1940 by GHQ Home Forces to bring Southern and Eastern Commands to a higher state of readiness as conditions were particularly favourable for invasion, some Home Guard units became aware of the alert and rang their local church bells assuming an invasion was in progress. Orders were later given that church bells were to be rung only if the local commander had personally seen a minimum of 25 parachutists descending. Rumours of parachutist landings and the ringing of other church bells were not to be acted on (Mackenzie 1995, 60, 63).

Rudimentary supply systems for ammunition included setting up 'ammunition points' at Crowcombe and Winscombe where units could replenish their ammunition. Fuel and rations were based on static supply depots at Bath for the Clevedon area and Norton Fitzwarren. Much of the transport was requisitioned civilian vehicles and in the event of invasion over 80 Western National buses were to be ready to move within one hour. The medical system relied on both civilian facilities and military establishments and instructions were issued on such subjects as casualty reporting, deaths and burials. Detailed orders on varied subjects such as handling of prisoners of war, traffic control, salvage, repair and recovery, dealing with stragglers (soldiers cut off from their unit), crashed aircraft, bomb disposal and gas attacks were also issued.

The end of the threat

In 1944 as the build up for D-Day commenced, the Home Guard was deployed to guard key points essential to the preparations and launch of the invasion. Home Guardsmen were made well aware that with the departure of the invasion forces to Normandy, the defence of Great Britain was in their hands (Mackenzie 1995, 149). On 6 September 1944, Home Guard service once again became voluntary. Finally on 22 September 1944, Southern Command advised that there was no longer any need for defence works to be maintained for anti-invasion or anti-raid purposes (TNA WO 199/1779: Home Defence file). By November 1944, when the Home Guard finally stood down, the strengths of the Somerset battalions with operational areas of responsibility along the coast exceeded 9500 all ranks. It must be pointed out that not all of these were in company areas adjacent to the shore and some battalion areas extended a considerable distance from the coast. For example, the Minehead (originally Dunster) Battalion area ran as far south as Wiveliscombe, which is some 10 miles (16km) south from the sea and only the Dunster and Porlock companies were responsible for coast defences. By this time the Home Guard was well trained, had an impressive array of weapons and was a significant force.

Conclusion

It might be wondered why such elaborate defences were constructed in an area where the seaborne threat was obviously so small but contemporary documentation clearly shows the perceived threat from aircraft landings both on the beaches, in the hills and on the high moors. The 1940 German attacks on Denmark, Norway, Belgium and the Netherlands made the airborne threat significant and the successful airborne invasion of Crete in May 1941 increased the perceived risk. The threat of a German invasion from Ireland was always present in the background but mentioned only once officially in regard to Somerset. It must also be pointed out that with the shortage of materials (particularly cement) and manpower in the construction industry all defence works were carefully controlled yet, despite this, significant defences were constructed, particularly in Blue Anchor Bay in 1941. These were not local initiatives and there is ample documentary evidence that the Commander 8 Corps and his staff reviewed the plans and visited these coastal defences (for example, TNA WO 166/1317: 30 March 1941) while the ongoing works were approved by both his HQ and Southern Command, who allocated the funding and cement.

Without local air superiority, any German airborne or seaborne landings would have been almost impossible and the air defence system that protected the Bristol Channel, Somerset beaches and inland landing grounds will be discussed in Chapter 5. It is not possible to predict how effective the ground defences might have been but it is fair to say that the maximum was done, within the limited resources available, to prepare both the defences and the defenders against the perceived threats from both air and sea. While many may question the German threat to the west country as perceived by the British in 1940, it is worth noting that we now know that Hitler's Directive Number 16: *On preparation for a landing operation against England* issued on 16 July 1940 stated: 'The possible advantages of limited operations before the general crossing (eg the occupation of the Isle of Wight or the county of Cornwall) are to be considered from the point of view of each branch of the armed forces and the results reported to me. I reserve the decision to myself' (Trevor-Roper 1964, 75).

As Churchill wrote in his memoirs for July 1940, 'Nothing moves an Englishmen so much as the threat of invasion, the reality unknown for a thousand years ...' (Churchill 1949, 146).

Chapter 4

Coast Artillery

COAST ARTILLERY had its origins in the Tudor period and reached a peak of sophistication in the late 19th century with the construction of massive forts and batteries, primarily to defend dockyards such as Plymouth and Pembroke Dock. In the Second World War two distinct roles are discernible: close defence of ports to prevent their capture by an invasion force and longer-range weapons defending shipping. Most of these fortifications were referred to as 'emergency batteries', in contrast to the more established batteries around the major dockyards and ports, and were built around naval guns that had remained in store since the First World War. The primary role of emergency batteries was seaward defence to guard the approach channels to ports, landing places and beaches against armed merchant vessels, transports, armoured fighting vehicle (AFV) carriers and similar craft. Secondary roles included assisting the Army in the defence of beaches but direct fire landwards was only permitted against targets that were visible to the battery. There were 28 Emergency Batteries in the South West, mostly at ports, but some, like that at Sidmouth in Devon (TNA WO 166/298), covering only potential landing beaches.

Minehead battery

Port defences are known from Minehead (SHER 35359), which has relatively good survival of documents. On 21 July GHQ Home Forces reported to the War Office that

Figure 4.1: Minehead harbour Coast Artillery battery. Compare with the plan on page 49. The partly destroyed pier can also be seen (RAF S262/8703 36, 27/1/1941. English Heritage (NMR) RAF photography).

the Admiralty had placed about 100 ex-naval 4-inch guns and possibly about 30 ex-naval 6-inch guns at their disposal for coast defence purposes. The lists for the deployment of these guns showed that Minehead was allocated two 4-inch guns as priority 13 out of 28 emergency batteries listed across Britain. The first 14 of these emergency batteries were reported 'in action' on 10 August 1940 but Minehead was not included. All batteries were reported as being 'in action' by 24 August and it is assumed that Minehead was declared 'in action' between these dates (TNA WO 166/11). The battery was visited by the Commander Corps Medium Artillery (CCMA) from 8 Corps on 16 August 1940. The CCMA was a brigadier responsible at that time for all Coast Artillery in the 8 Corps area of Somerset, Devon and Cornwall (WO 166/303). Later, when the Severn Defences were established, the new batteries and Portishead came under HQ Western Command.

The battery was initially manned by 51 Heavy Regiment Royal Artillery (RA) commanded from Portland. They were replaced by 400 Coast Battery RA, part of 20 Coast Artillery Group (later 558 Coast Regiment RA), which was established at the Marine Hotel, Instow (Devon) and controlled batteries at Appledore, Instow and Ilfracombe as well as Minehead (TNA WO 166/1757). The battery comprised officers from the Territorial Army and Officer Emergency Reserve with NCOs drawn from 'various branches of the regiment'. (The term 'regiment' used here is assumed to refer to the Royal Regiment of Artillery in its widest sense and not the Coast Defence Group or 51 Heavy Regiment). The remainder of the manpower was 'Army Class' personnel between the ages of 25 and 30, who had been called up three months previously. The newly-trained 400 Battery took over at 1800 hours on 5 December 1940. The battery was commanded by a captain and had a strength of three officers and 93 other ranks, which enabled the two guns to be constantly manned. This establishment was reduced in January 1941 to two officers and 80 other ranks (TNA WO 166/1862) and there also seems to have been Home Guard involvement (Hawkins 1988, 130, Hurley 1978, 57) but no references have been found in The National Archives.

Their situation at Minehead is described (TNA WO 166/1862: 4 December 1940):

> The battery position consists of two guns and emplacements disguised as small houses, which also contain the two duty watch shelters, and a separate BOP on the quay at Minehead Harbour. Billets are in a loft over a large coal shed at the entrance to the quay and in the Pier Hotel about 40 yds [36m] away.

The Battery Observation Post (BOP) contained a 9-foot (2.7m) Barr and Stroud optical range finder and was connected by internal telephones, tannoys and light indicators to each gun and the searchlights. The guns were 4-inch Mk VII ex-naval BL guns (TNA WO 166/1757) which fired 31lb (14kg) high explosive (HE) or armour piercing (AP) shells to a maximum range of 17,000 yards (15.5km). Emergency batteries, however, were limited from firing 'until the enemy began to lose sea room some three to four [5–6.5km] miles from the shore' (Collier 1957, 131). This policy ensured that the battery remained concealed for as long as possible. Owing to the limited accuracy of the available range finders and the shortage of shells, a general order was given that no ex-naval service guns should open fire at ranges of over 6000 yards (2.7km, TNA WO 166/11). This limitation would also have helped to overcome the lack of experience of the newly trained gun crews. The 4-inch guns were not ideal and it was noted by the Tri-service Coast Defence Committee in February 1941 that a 4-inch gun was insufficient to stop a merchant vessel but batteries with 6-inch guns were considered to be effective (TNA WO 199/1110).

As noted on page 14, the Minehead battery was expected to liaise with the Naval Officer in Command, Swansea but as the 20 Coast Artillery Group war-diary records, 'this liaison appears to have been non-existent for a considerable time.' (TNA WO 166/1757). The problem was resolved on 31 January 1941 when Admiral (retired) Casement was installed as Resident Naval Officer (RNO) Watchet (see page 13). Liaison with the Royal Navy was vital to ensure that coast batteries did not expose friendly warships with their searchlights or mistake them for hostile forces and engage them with fire. The Navy also controlled port entry by merchant shipping and the registration, issue of permits and immobilisation of fishing vessels as well as any local restrictions on their use. Before the RNO Watchet was appointed, the battery commander at Minehead

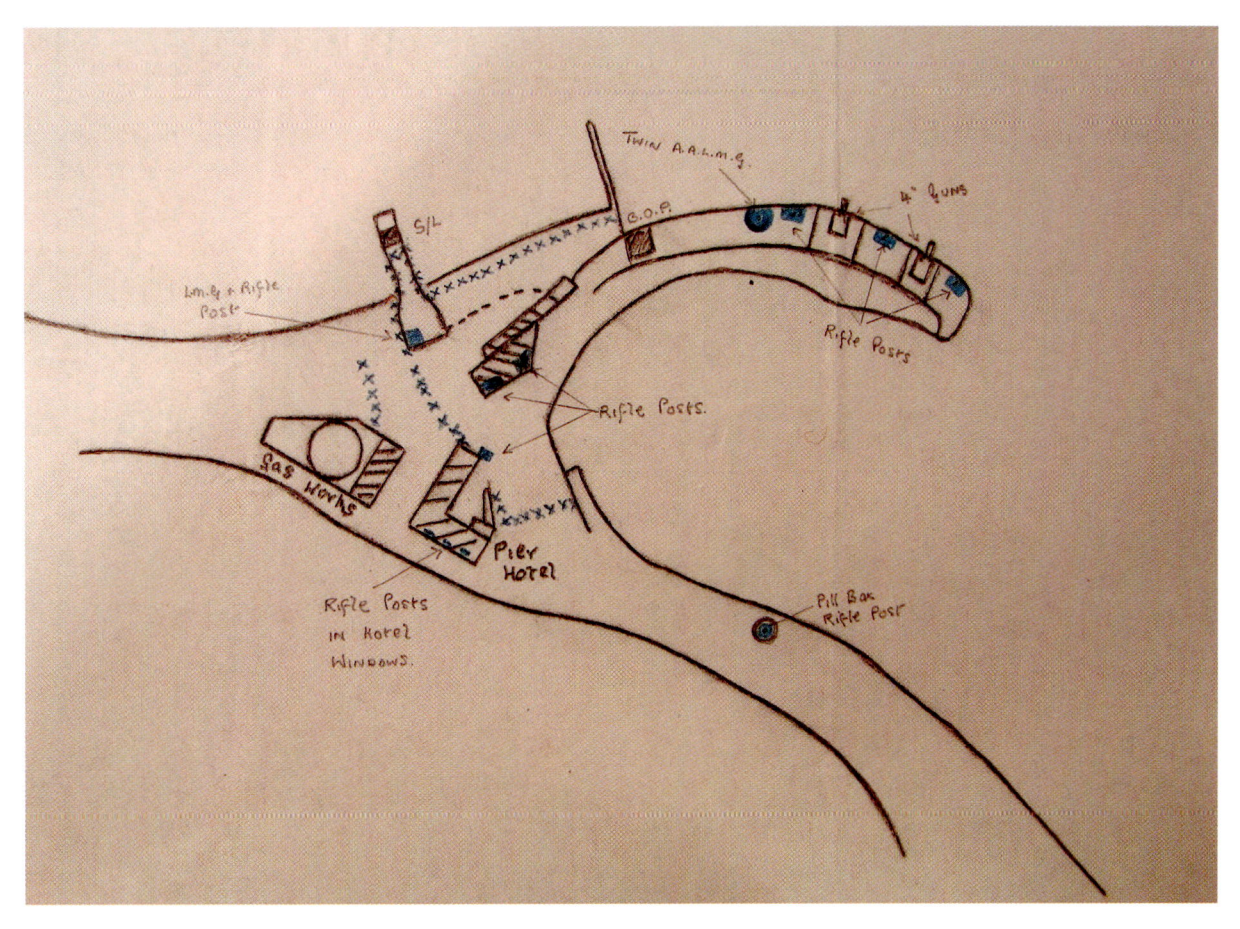

Figure 4.2: *Minehead harbour Coast Artillery battery. Plan prepared to show defences of the battery against ground attack (TNA WO 166/1842).*

was responsible for obtaining a list of fishing boats and ensuring his battery was 'informed whenever a boat leaves the harbour, where it is going, its probable time of return and actual time of return. Fishermen will be warned that if they do not comply with the instructions, which are made largely for their own safety, they may be forbidden to leave harbour.'

The RNO or Coastguards (who were controlled by the Navy) were to be immediately consulted if any vessel did not identify itself correctly or approached harbour during darkness or had been challenged by firing a 'bring-to' round across its bows and failed to stop. The order stated, 'If she does not stop, she will be destroyed' (TNA WO 166/1757: 20 Coast Artillery Group Op Order 1 dated 16 Jan 1941). A direct telephone line was provided between Minehead battery and the HQ RNO Watchet to allow communication. The battery commander also had to consult the RNO about the level of the maritime threat before allowing his battery to reduce the state of operational readiness. Reduced readiness could be permitted if the RNO considered that the state of the weather made it impossible for shipping to approach within range, The RNO was also responsible for liaison with the Army chain of command and for informing them and the Coast Artillery, which was under Army command, of any warships that were approaching within three miles (5km) of the coast and thus avoiding any chance of causing an invasion scare (TNA WO 166/1757).

Construction works to improve the battery continued, and in March 1941 an anti-aircraft searchlight arrived to be used in an anti-shipping role; a shed was requisitioned for its generator. Unfortunately, at this date, 20 Coast Artillery Group ceased to be an independent

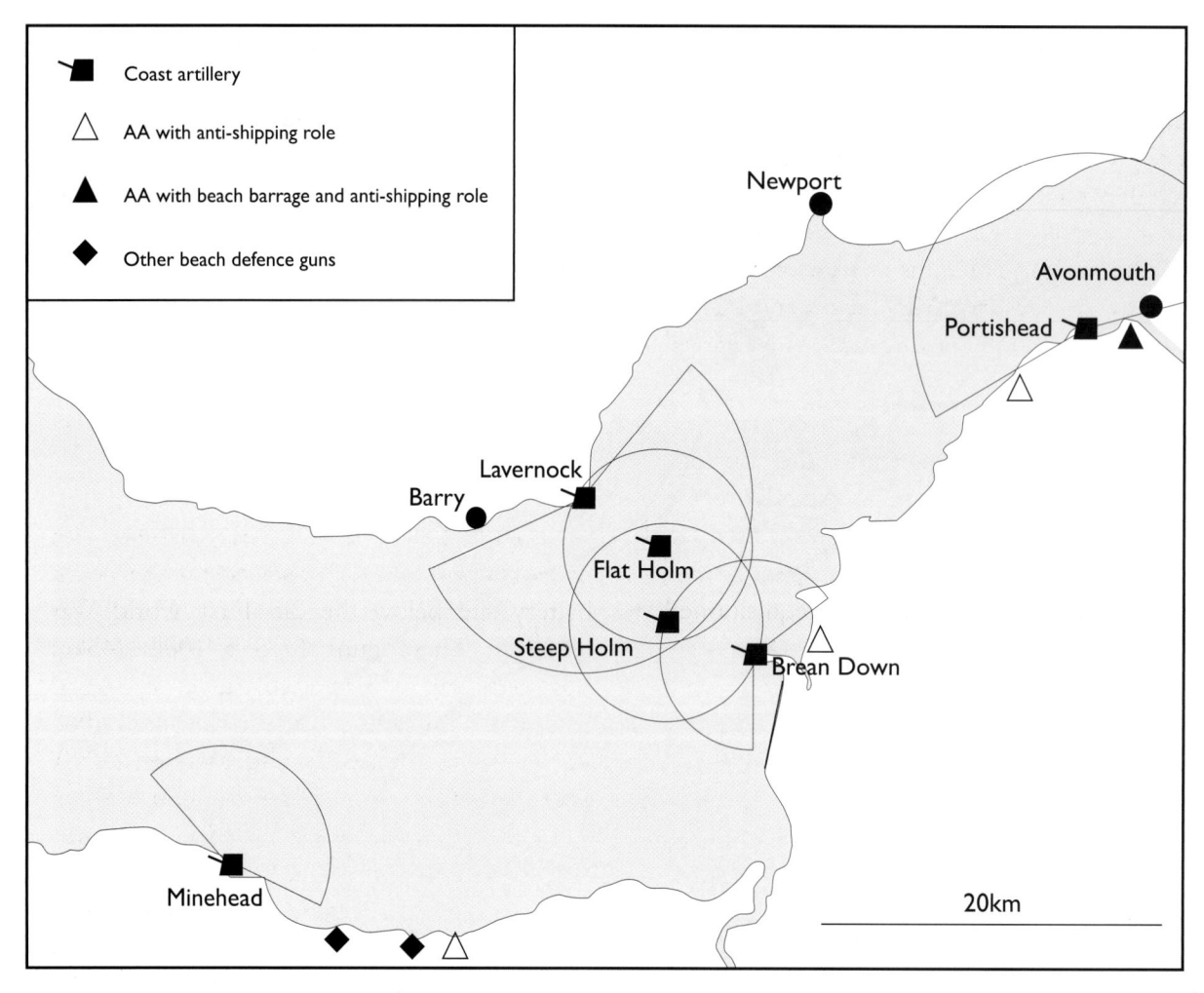

Figure 4.3: *Coast artillery and other artillery defences on the Somerset side of the Bristol Channel, together with the Severn Defences. The area of beach that could be fired on by Steep Holm South is also indicated, see page 56. Note that not all these sites were operational at the same time.*

unit and, on becoming part of 558 Coast Regiment, was no-longer required to keep a war-diary so detailed information ceases.

In September 1941 each battery provided the regiment with a plan for its own defences which gives a good idea of the layout (Figure 4.2 on the previous page). The two guns stood on the harbour wall with Lewis anti-aircraft light machine guns adjacent and also the Battery Observation Post. The searchlight position (SHER 28641) is shown on the remains of the pier, which had been substantially removed in August 1941 to improve the arc of fire of the battery north-westwards along the coast (SHER 35506). Before the searchlight arrived, the battery had four Ryder flares (pyrotechnic lights) to illuminate targets. Minehead did not have an 'examination service' with boats that could intercept and board incoming vessels to check them and relied on the coastguards to identify friendly shipping.

Two practice shoots are recorded in war-diaries. One daytime shoot, on 27 March 1941, comprised five full charge rounds from each gun at a towed target. On 27 September 1941 a night practice shoot was carried out and 30 rounds were fired. The shoot was observed by the Commander Corps Royal Artillery (Brigadier Sir Colin Jardine) from 8 Corps (TNA WO 166/1757).

The battery was short-lived as early in the following year, on 12 February 1942, 'the two

4-inch BL naval guns, mountings and ammunition at Minehead (400) Battery were removed being urgently needed for return to the Navy' but the gunners themselves stayed until April when they moved to the Helford river in Cornwall to establish another new battery (TNA WO 166/7178). The guns at Ilfracombe were removed two days after Minehead's, and Instow was placed in a state of 'care and maintenance' on 11 August.

At Minehead, the only survivals are two ammunition lockers built into the harbour wall and an 'engine house' of standard type (SHER 16579). This would have contained the generators and was presumably built after the war-diary ended to replace the requisitioned shed.

Defence of Watchet harbour

In September 1940 plans were made to emplace two 4-inch static guns for the defence of Watchet Harbour but these never materialised. After the withdrawal of the guns from Minehead, a requirement for the replacement of four 4-inch guns in the Minehead area (including presumably two for Watchet) remained on the Coastal Defence Committee list. However, two 6-pounder short guns from First World War tanks (allocated from 16 guns removed from the Taunton Stop Line in 1941) were deployed to cover the western approaches to the harbour and were later moved to a commanding position on the east side of the harbour mouth.

The Watchet Home Guard manned these guns from 26 July 1941 (TNA WO 199/1638). These guns had a limited practical range of perhaps 600 yards (5.5km) and the 6lb (2.7kg) shell would be significantly less powerful than the 'insufficient' 31lb (14kg) shell of a 4-inch naval gun. Scant remains of the rear of one emplacement survive above the harbour (SHER 35392). The use of the static Bofors AA guns sited at the Doniford AA range to cover the approach to the harbour mouth has been mentioned above.

Avonmouth and Portishead

Both Dobinson (1996) and Hogg (1974) list an Avonmouth battery at South Pier but neither gives sources or locations. Dobinson also mentions that in 1916 the Avonmouth (South Pier) Battery was equipped with two 4.7-inch QF naval guns. No mention of this battery has been found in any National Archives sources of Second World War date but Portishead Battery, which covered the approaches to Avonmouth, is sometimes referred to as Avonmouth (Portishead).

Portishead had an emergency battery with two 6-inch naval guns installed on the beach battery site below the old First World War battery. These guns fired a 100lb (45kg) shell and had a maximum range of 14,000 yards (12.8km), but were restricted to 11,000 yards (10km). There is also mention (TNA WO 199/1638) of a 3-pounder gun and, in 1943, practice firing of both a 2-inch UP (anti-aircraft rocket) and a 75mm gun. Two coast artillery searchlights were provided, which were capable of illuminating ships out to about 4000 yards (3.7km). These searchlights gave the battery the capability of engaging targets using one light while still being able to observe over their arc of fire with the other. There was also a single beach light that could illuminate the shoreline which was sited so that beach defences were not illuminated for the enemy.

The battery had a similar role to that of the Minehead battery but included support of the Examination Service. It was manned by 365 Coast Battery RA formed at 'Avonmouth near Bristol at 1800 hours on 26 June 1940' (TNA WO 199/523). The first entry in the battery war-diary (TNA WO 166/1842) is the same day, when 55 soldiers were posted into the battery referred to as 'The Fort'. The battery was incorporated into the Severn Defences and from 12 July 1942, it was manned by the Home Guard, the task falling to 7th Somerset (Long Ashton) Battalion. Training proceeded with the first Home Guard practice being fired on 6 December 1942.

Somerset and the Defence of the Bristol Channel

Figure 4.4: *Remains of one of the two 6-inch gun emplacements at Brean Down. Compare this with the contemporary painting of an identical emplacement on Steep Holm on the cover of this volume. The ring bolt for mounting the gun lies in the centre with the cut-off remains of the supports for the plastic armour roof around it. Birnbeck Pier can be seen in the distance (Somerset County Council HER, 1995).*

The Severn defences

With the increase in shipping across the Atlantic, the ports of the Bristol Channel became important arrival points for convoyed vessels. By its nature, the convoy system meant that large numbers of ships arrived at port at once and each ship would have to wait its turn to unload. Ports, particularly Cardiff, were improved and working practices changed to unload cargoes as quickly as possible and sort them later, but ships waiting at sea were still vulnerable to attack from the air and by sea. Moreover the port installations at Penarth, Cardiff, Newport and Bristol (Avonmouth and Portishead) were vulnerable targets to attack from the sea. The scale of the perceived threat was defined in the *Coast Defence Reconnaissance Report* of 17 November 1940 as 'a raid by 8-inch cruisers, destroyers and E-boats'

(TNA WO 166/11). What the authors of the assessment seem to have in mind was that the Germans had deployed similarly constituted assault forces with spectacular success to spearhead their invasion of Norway on 9 April 1940. Gunfire from the 8-inch cruisers *Hipper* and *Blücher* (sunk by torpedo during the attack on Oslo Fjord), other cruisers and destroyers had been used to suppress the coast defences to prepare the way and land forces of between 900 and 2000 troops (Roskill 1954, 163–4).

The term E-boats is an entirely British invention which was often initially used for German light naval forces in general. Later it became equated with the heavy fast motor-torpedo boats that the Germans called *Schnellboote* or *S-Boote*. By November 1940 two flotillas of these were already making a reputation for themselves by the ferocity of their attacks from their bases in occupied Belgium and Holland on coastal convoys in the Straits of Dover and off the east coast of England (Roskill 1954, 324, 329). The initial assessment was reinforced by further definition of the perceived threat in a report of 28 March 1941 where 'the scale of the attack might be: (i) Invasion: Landing from merchant vessels supported by cruisers and destroyers, or (ii) Bombardment by cruisers and destroyers' (TNA WO 166/11).

To counter this, the Victorian fortification line across the Bristol Channel was re-armed in late 1941 to block sea-borne attack from the west (Figure 4.3 on page 50). Batteries were established at Lavernock in Wales (Saunders *et al.* 2001), Brean Down in Somerset (van der Bijl 2000; Webster 2001) and on the islands of Steep Holm (Rendell 1981, Legg 1991) and Flat Holm (Barrett 1992). Lavernock had been rebuilt with modern armament in 1900 but new works were required at the other three sites. Flat Holm was armed with 4.5-inch anti-aircraft guns for its dual role while Brean Down and Steep Holm received 6-inch ex-naval guns.

The assessment of November 1940 considered that, 'the defences provided by 6-inch and 4-inch naval equipments will be inadequate, and should be replaced by coast defence equipments when available' and that 'an attack which these defences are intended to break up, is most likely to take place in thick weather, when visibility in the Bristol Channel seldom exceeds 3000 yards [2.7km]. It is therefore considered most important that Coast Defence RDF [radar] sets should be provided as may be considered necessary' (TNA WO 166/11).

The report noted that the main channels ran between Lavernock Point and Flat Holm (5000 yards, 4.5km) and Flat Holm and Steep Holm (4200 yards, 3.8km) and that Flat Holm commanded the whole water area of any attack. The distance between Steep Holm and Brean Down was 5300 yards (4.8km). During low visibility, an attack developing towards either of the main channels and suddenly turning would be better observed from Flat Holm than from elsewhere. The report also stated that there were no naval defences in the area but 'it is believed that a mine-field to cover a large sea area between the islands and mainland is contemplated.' It appears that the minefield was never laid probably because it would have rendered extremely hazardous any access to the ports of the upper Bristol Channel.

The report states that there was an examination battery at Nells Point but 'owing to the width of the channel, hostile craft could pass examination vessels and battery, during reduced visibility, without observation' (TNA WO 166/11). An incident occurred on 13 June 1941 when the Bristol Channel Coast Artillery fired their first shot in semi-anger at 0700 hours from Nells Point. A small 'tanker' seen at about 1700 yards (1.5km) by 130 Coast Battery failed to hoist signals. One 'bring-to' round was fired but the vessel sailed on into the mist. It was later identified as SS *Overton* bound for Burnham-on-Sea (John Penny, pers. comm.).

The Admiralty successfully argued the need for anti-aircraft defences for Flat Holm and suggested dual-purpose guns using 4.5-inch HAA guns mounted in specially designed emplacements. These guns were positioned in two separate batteries each of two guns (Flat Holm North on the west side of the island and Flat Holm South on the south-east side near to the lighthouse), together with a gun-laying radar and fire control predictors. The guns had modified carriages to allow them to depress to engage surface targets and were mounted in uniquely-designed open emplacements allowing fire in both roles but retained the normal steel protective housing as used by such guns in the AA role (see Figure 5.1 on page 58). The guns were incorporated into the Cardiff Gun Defended Area as Site J16 (Dobinson 2001, 292).

Steep Holm received four ex-naval 6-inch guns: two batteries, each of two guns in separate emplacements, were built on the sites of two of the former Victorian batteries. Steep Holm South Battery was sited on the former Garden Battery on the south-east side of the island facing towards Bridgwater Bay and Steep

Figure 4.5: *Coast Artillery searchlight on Steep Holm. The searchlight was sited in a low position to maximise the area of sea swept by the narrow beam (David Hunt, 2001).*

Holm North Battery on the Summit Battery on the west end of the island facing towards Lavernock Point. Each battery was equipped with two Coast Artillery searchlights powered by generators in protected buildings at each battery site. These searchlight were positioned as low as possible on ledges in the cliffs to enable them to sweep the sea more effectively in the search for suspected enemy craft (Figure 4.5). A single Battery Observation Post (BOP) was built directly on the site of the former Rudder Point Battery at the western end of the island. Six static Bofors AA guns were also deployed on single-gun sites across the island (Legg 1991, map in preface, 102).

The normal range of spring tides in this part of the Bristol Channel is 12m which makes landing on both islands difficult at certain states of the tide, particularly at Steep Holm as on a falling tide a race develops over the shingle bank to the east of the island adjoining the only landing beach (TNA WO 166/11). Work started on the fortifications of Steep Holm on 6 July 1942 (Penny pers. comm.). The steep cliffs and only two small beaches whose access was limited by the weather and state of the tide made it difficult to land men and materials. It was first necessary for the Army to construct two piers and a zigzag tramway with winches up a cliff path to the summit of the island to allow stores and material to be landed, winched up to the top of the island and then pulled by mules on further tramways to the building sites. The four 6-inch guns were delivered by tank landing craft on 30 September and 1 October 1941. All supplies were shipped from Barry in south Wales and after a typhoid outbreak on the island all fresh water had to be brought by sea (van der Bijl 2000, 100). To weather and tide, the frequent mining of the Bristol Channel added to the difficulties of landing stores.

There are detailed records for the construction of the jetties on the islands and for the plans to treat Brean Down as an offshore island of Wales where the Commander, Fixed Defences, Severn was based (TNA WO 166/3937). The military records for Steep Holm and Brean Down appear to have been lost but the Flat Holm (TNA WO 192/155) and Lavernock fort record books survive (TNA WO 192/316, WO 192/317). The Second World War remains at Lavernock are fragmentary but there are extensive remains at Brean Down and, particularly, Steep Holm and Flat Holm where the transport difficulties made clearance less attractive. At both sites are concrete emplacements for the guns, together with crew rooms, observation posts, searchlight emplacements, engine houses and large numbers of hut bases for the accommodation buildings: nearly 30 remain at Brean Down (Figure 4.4 on page 52; Webster 2001).

A particular feature of the Steep Holm and Brean Down batteries was the use of plastic armour consisting of granite chips embedded in a 2¾inch-thick (70mm) layer of mastic (a bituminous cement like asphalt) poured onto ¾-inch (18mm) steel plates to provide overhead cover for the gun house (Figure 4.6 on the facing page). The plates of armour, which were supported on a grid of 5- by 6-inch (128 x 155mm) steel H-girders, had been originally developed by the Royal Navy's Department of Miscellaneous Weapons Development to provide lightweight bullet-proof protection for merchant ships bridges and gun positions against machine gun fire from aircraft – a welcome innovation for the ships of the

Figure 4.6: *Sections of surviving plastic armour roof at Steep Holm South Battery. Most of the armour has been removed to prevent the collapse of the steel frame. Brean Down can be seen in the background (Chris Webster, 1995).*

coastal convoys routed to and from the Bristol Channel to London and the south-east of England through the English Channel (Pawle 2009, 52–57). A key feature of the plate, which was officially designated 'Plastic Protective Plating', was that it was non-magnetic and did not affect magnetic navigation compasses.

By 7 April 1942 the Bristol Channel artillery had become operational (John Penny pers. comm.) as 'Fixed Defences Severn' under the Army's Western Command, which covered Wales and the West Midlands; the south-west peninsula was part of Southern Command which can make finding records for these sites complicated. Shortly afterwards in May 1942 a Coast Defence/Chain Home Low (CD/CHL) radar in the surface watching role was established on North Hill, Minehead some 20 miles (32km) to the west (see page 68), which would have considerably enhanced the early warning of craft entering the Bristol Channel.

Legg records that Major David Benger, who was a staff officer in Fixed Defences Severn voiced concern about their possible effectiveness when engaging fast-moving E-boats (then thought to have a maximum speed of 34.5 knots and known to be highly manoeuvrable, TNA WO 208/2969): 'Given fast moving targets like E-boats, the only thing possible was locating them by searchlight and then engaging them over open sights at close range' (Legg 1991, 100). This would have presented a particular challenge to the 4.5-inch dual role guns on Flat Holm which as anti-aircraft guns were not equipped with direct fire sights. The original assessment of November 1940 had envisaged installation of 12- and 6-pounder guns at Newport and Cardiff to cope with this particular threat (TNA WO 166/11).

Proposals to establish a long-range battery at Nells Point and Nash Point on the Welsh coast or at Hurlstone Point on the west

55

Somerset coast were rejected by the Coast Defence Committee on 2 May 1942 as the only advantage gained would be the extension of the 6-inch gun cover further to seaward by day in conditions of good visibility (TNA WO 199/1111, 4 May 1942).

The run-down of the Severn Defences began in March 1943 when Steep Holm South Battery ceased operations and was put on a care-and-maintenance basis. Under the 'Flood Tide' plan implemented by Western Command on 20 October 1943, the batteries at Lavernock, Brean Down and Steep Holm North ceased to have an operational role and were reduced to care-and-maintenance status. On 1 April 1944 orders were issued for disbanding the Headquarters Fixed Severn Defences and by July all batteries had been put on care-and-maintenance. 184 Battery continued to have a presence at Portishead where an officer and eight men were placed under the Home Guard (Mixed) Battery (van der Bijl 2000, 115–17). Seaward-firing practices continued during 1944 at Portishead and are known to have taken place during June, August, October and November. The Home Guard stood down on 1 November 1944 and shortly after, on 18 December, both batteries on Flat Holm became non-operational (John Penny pers. comm.).

AA guns in other roles

At some coastal anti-aircraft gun sites, guns were able to engage surface vessels and these sites were given a secondary anti-shipping role. These included four static 3.7-inch guns at each of four sites at Bristol (Lodge Farm, Pilning, St George's Wharf and Rockingham), two static 3-inch guns (Figure 4.7) at Uphill and four static 40mm Bofors guns at the 'Watchet AA Practice Camp' (presumably Doniford). The Uphill, St George's Wharf and Rockingham sites were also identified as 'capable of firing

Figure 4.7: *A 3-inch anti-aircraft gun on the Doniford ranges before the war. The same type was used at Uphill in both anti-aircraft and anti-shipping roles (courtesy Vernon Stone from a postcard by HH Hole).*

beach barrages' (TNA WO 166/298: *8 Corps Defence Scheme* Annex T: Coast Artillery).

It was also noted that, under 'certain conditions', the two 6-inch guns at Steep Holm South Battery were capable of firing 'beach barrages' onto most of Berrow Flats.

Conclusion

Although the Coast Artillery along the Somerset coast and in the Severn Defences never fired a seawards shot in anger, they were deployed and reorganised to counter changing perceived threats, none of which ever materialised. Nevertheless they would have formed a deterrent to enemy naval action as important components of the defences of the ports of the upper Bristol Channel and their approaches. As will be discussed in Chapter 5, the dual role guns on Flat Holm also played their part in the anti-aircraft defences of these same ports.

Chapter 5

Air defence of the Bristol Channel

BY THE TIME of the negotiations for the Munich Agreement in September 1938, the German Ministry of Propaganda had managed to sell to the world the idea that the German airforce was capable of subduing any other country by mass bombing. Vastly over-inflated figures of the size and power of the *Luftwaffe* were supplied to the press of one country and, as intended, these were picked up by other media organisations and reported as sensational news. The occupations of Austria and the Sudetenland had provided demonstrations of the actual effectiveness of the *Luftwaffe* and it began to be feared throughout Europe. When in March 1939 German troops invaded Czechoslovakia, they were accompanied by 500 aircraft from which airborne troops were landed in and around Prague. As the possibility of war with Britain became a probability, exercises were carried out to simulate attacks on British harbours and forward aerodromes were built in western Germany (PRO 2001, 18–19). Over the following year Britain invested considerable sums on both air defence and Civil Defence (Air Raid Precautions – ARP) but when war was declared the expected massive air strike against London did not materialise.

At the outbreak of war, Somerset was considered to be in the safe area outside the 400-mile (640km) radius of bombers operating from airfields in Germany. Because of this minimal risk of German air attack, part of the British Expeditionary Force was deployed from the Bristol Channel to Brest and Nantes. Children were evacuated to Somerset from London. The invasions of Poland, Norway, Denmark, Holland, Belgium and France demonstrated convincingly the threat of German air power as a bomber force against land and naval targets, in close support of ground forces and its ability to land airborne troops. After the fall of France in June 1940, the move of two *Luftwaffe* Air Fleets into the north of occupied France (Figure 2.6 on page 10) brought Somerset and the Bristol Channel to within 200 miles (320km) of the new aerodromes in the Brest and Cherbourg peninsulas. This allowed enemy fighters to escort their bombers over most of the Bristol Channel (Collier 1957, 160).

In the period from 7 September 1940 to 16 May 1941, Bristol suffered seven significant bombing raids, Avonmouth five, Cardiff three and Swansea three (Collier 1957, 503–4). Mines laid by aircraft had a major effect on shipping, for example closing Barry Dock between 7 and 10 October 1941 (Jory 1995, 48). The German bases in France also allowed increased air reconnaissance for attacks against ports and shipping. In March 1941, the *Luftwaffe* moved a special unit (III KG 27) into the Brest peninsula with aircraft equipped for guiding submarines onto shipping in the Bristol and St George's Channels (Hinsley 1979, 330). Devon and Somerset were now on main routes for bombers flying to attack cities and industrial targets in the Midlands and the western ports in addition to the Bristol Channel.

The 1940 UK air defence network consisted of the Chain Home (CH) radars along the coast looking out to sea primarily over the

Figure 5.1: *A 4.5-inch AA gun on the ranges at Doniford. These guns were also used in a dual anti-aircraft and anti-shipping role on Flat Holm (courtesy Vernon Stone from a postcard by HH Hole).*

North Sea and the eastern end of the English Channel but with very limited coverage inland. There were wide gaps in the radar coverage along the coasts of the south-west peninsula, particularly to the south of Somerset in east Devon and west Dorset, and no coverage along the Bristol Channel coast (Collier 1957, 149). While the CH radars provided tracks that enabled controllers to direct fighters towards the enemy over the English Channel, once the enemy crossed the south coast, the only source of tracking and identification information came from Observer Corps posts and additionally from searchlights by night.

Daytime interception worked reasonably well but by night it proved extremely difficult for searchlights to locate the enemy and the night fighters then to find the illuminated aircraft. The later use of aircraft interception (AI) radars fitted in fighters is discussed below (on page 63). The air defence warning installations in Somerset and along the Somerset coast were vital in tracking the raiders before they reached their targets in the shipping lanes of the Bristol Channel and the ports and industrial installations along the south Wales coastline, where it was obviously not possible to deploy forward defence installations.

Anti-aircraft guns

The importance of the Bristol Channel ports may be gauged from the allocation of anti-aircraft guns to defend them. In June 1940, before the threat from France had been fully assessed, only Bristol, Newport and Cardiff were gun-defended areas (GDA) with a total of 36 heavy AA guns (HAA). This was about 3% of the national total at the time. By August 1940, the defences had been strengthened to 90 guns, including a new gun-defended area at Swansea, which then represented about 7% of the national total (Collier 1957, 449). On 6 March 1941, Churchill directed: 'We must be prepared to meet concentrated air attacks on the ports on which we specially rely (Mersey,

Clyde and Bristol Channel). They must therefore be provided with a maximum defence.' (Churchill 1949, 109). The number of guns was further increased in 1941 to 190 which was about 11% of the national total. By 1944, with the preparations operation Overlord, the totals had further increased to 247 guns. Later in February 1941 HAA guns were deployed near the Somerset coast to protect Weston-super-Mare aerodrome and the nearby aircraft factory (Dobinson 2001, 519).

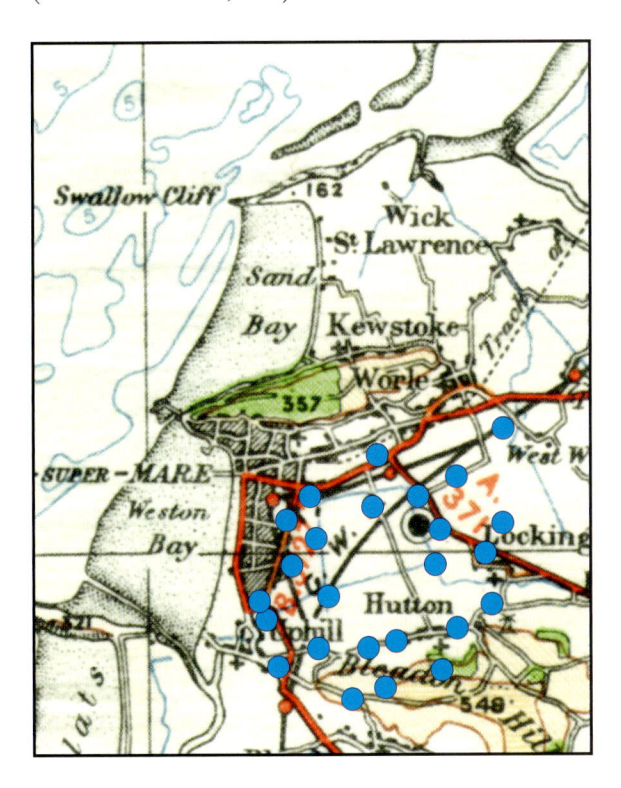

Figure 5.2: Barrage balloon sites (superimposed blue dots) around the aerodrome (black circled dot) at Weston-super-Mare and the Bristol Aircraft shadow factory at Hutton. The 24 balloons were deployed in an inner and outer ring around the targets. Base map: Ordnance Survey 1:253,440 sheet 11. Fourth Edition, 1945, full revision 1930.

RAF balloon barrages were also deployed to the main ports. On 27 August 1939 the first barrage of 32 balloons was deployed to protect Avonmouth and Portishead docks and remained in place until 12 July 1944 when the balloons were redeployed to the south-east of England against the threat of flying bombs. At Bristol, balloons were first deployed on 7 September 1939 while on 2 April 1940, 40 balloons were deployed to protect the city docks. Deployment of barrages, of 24 balloons each, to the Bristol Aeroplane Company factories at Filton and Weston-super-Mare were made on 1 June 1940 and 3 May 1941 respectively (John Penny pers. comm.). By 31 July 1940, Bristol had 72 balloons and Cardiff 39 of which seven were waterborne. By the end of August 1940, additional balloons had been deployed (Collier 1957, 480): to Swansea (35 balloons), Port Talbot, (16), Newport (40) and Barry (16).

RAF fighter organisation

In July 1940, RAF Fighter Command established a new fighter group at Box (Rudloe, Wiltshire) near Bath to cover the South West. The new group (10 Group) took control of the three sectors based at Pembrey in south Wales, Filton near Bristol and St Eval in Cornwall (Figure 5.3 on the following page). In August the Middle Wallop sector was also transferred to 10 Group. The four Sector Operations Rooms each received information about the position of enemy aircraft from 10 Group that was based on Chain Home radar plots and reports from the Observer Corps. On orders from 10 Group HQ they were then responsible for 'scrambling' their fighters into the air and directing them by RT (radio telephone) towards the enemy. Sectors had geographically separated direction finding (DF) 'fixer' stations. Two or three of these took simultaneous bearings on the VHF wireless transmissions of their fighters and thereby 'fixed' their positions.

A new fighter sector station was established at Exeter Airport in June 1940 which took over the role from St Eval. The new Exeter sector covered the English Channel coast and northwards towards the Bristol Channel. Raiders making for the latter waterway should have first been intercepted over the English Channel or the south Devon or Dorset coastline. In the autumn of 1940, the Filton sector control

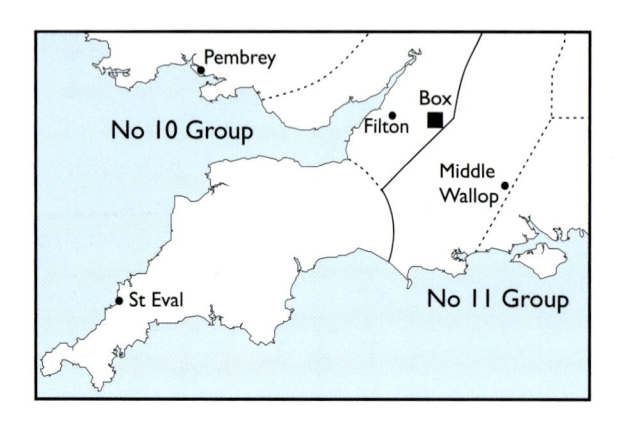

Figure 5.3: RAF Fighter Command organisation on 9 July 1940 (after Collier 1957, map 12, 161).

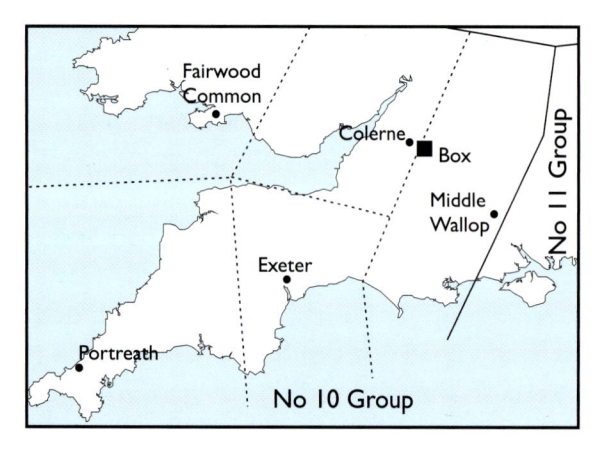

Figure 5.4: RAF Fighter Command organisation in Spring 1941 (after Collier 1957, map 24, 267).

was moved to Colerne in Wiltshire and the sector boundaries changed so that it covered the Bristol Channel north of the north Devon and west Somerset coastline and was renamed the Colerne sector (Figure 5.4). This provided the second line of defence to the north of the Exeter sector while the raiders were over Somerset (Collier 1957, 149). A satellite day fighter station to Exeter was opened at Churchstanton (later renamed Culmhead) on the Blackdown Hills in Somerset on 1 August 1941. Among other duties, fighter aircraft flying from the aerodrome were involved as convoy escorts in the English Channel (Berryman 2006, 55).

Observer Corps

The Observer Corps was the primary source of information about the position, type and strength of enemy aircraft that had crossed the coast. The Corps was run by the RAF using both paid civilians, who contracted to work 24 or 48 hours per week, and volunteers to run small observation posts approximately six to ten miles (10–16km) apart. These were connected by direct telephone lines to their associated group centres at Bristol (23 Group), Yeovil (22 Group) and Exeter (21 Group). Each group typically controlled 35 to 45 posts. Observer group centres with posts near the coast had direct lines to the appropriate Chain Home radar station allowing posts to be warned of incoming raiders. The posts along the Somerset coastline were all operational from 1938 (Wood 1976, 307–9). Each post needed about 20 people to run it continuously with two on duty. Observer group HQs typically needed 150 to 180 staff and from July 1941 women were enrolled.

In addition to their primary role of identifying and tracking aircraft, both hostile and friendly, the Observer Corps posts assumed a number of other important roles. These included reporting landings of parachutists or troop carrying aircraft, enemy submarines or surface craft, aircraft laying mines in coastal waters, aircraft in distress, lost aircraft and crashes. Posts near the coast were often linked to nearby Coastguard stations by landline and in Somerset, the Porlock (ExHER MSO12292) and Highbridge (SHER 12830) posts were both connected. If communications broke down, posts fired red rockets with red stars to indicate enemy action on land and green rockets with stars to warn of approaching enemy surface craft. Posts also assisted lost aircraft and in late 1942 some posts, including those at Porlock and Holford, were equipped with 'Darkie' wireless to communicate with lost aircraft at night. Searchlight sites could then be called to direct the aircraft to the nearest aerodrome using their light beam. Other posts were equipped with 'Granite' flares, which could be lit to warn friendly aircraft in conditions of poor visibility of the proximity of high ground. The posts at Porlock (ExHER MSO12292) and

Dunster (SHER 35805) were both equipped with 'Granite' to warn approaching aircraft flying south from the Bristol Channel of the cliffs along the coast and the high ground of Exmoor beyond them. The Holford post also had 'Granite' to warn of the proximity of the Quantock Hills (Wood 1976, 308).

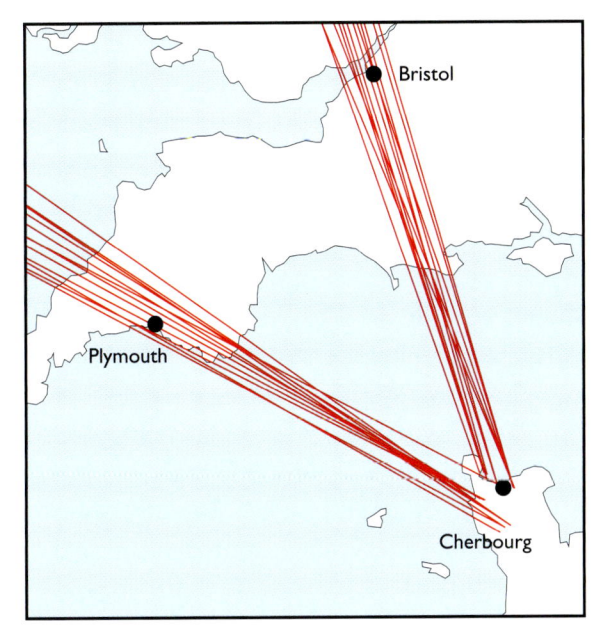

Figure 5.5: The threat of V1 missiles to the South West. The lines of flight were projected from aerial photographs showing the orientation of the launch ramps on the Cherbourg peninsula. The missiles could be timed to fall onto targets along the line (after Babington Smith 1957).

The information provided from the Observer Corps was also critical for the air-raid warning system. In particular, special 'purple warnings' enabled 'permitted lighting' to be used in certain principal ports, which enabled stevedores to work a three-shift system throughout the hours of darkness, as the lighting could be extinguished when there was warning of an imminent threat of air attack. The Somerset Observer Corps posts were a vital part of the warning system for the Bristol Channel ports and particularly those in south Wales (Wood 1976, 126).

In April 1944 RAF air photographs identified the threat of V1 flying bombs being launched from sites under construction in the Cherbourg peninsula (Figure 5.5), which were clearly aligned towards Bristol and Plymouth (Babington Smith 1957, 199). The Observer Corps Bristol and Yeovil groups were ordered to be ready to track V1 attacks. In the period up to D-Day, Bristol was to be defended by 96 heavy AA guns and 216 light AA guns and a key aspect of the plans was the assumption that the Observer Corps would be able to identify and track the missiles, giving ample warning for fighters to attack and thus avoid the need for standing air patrols (Collier 1957, 364). The attacks never materialised as the initial successes of the Allied invasion over-ran the launch sites.

The Corps was granted the title 'Royal Observer Corps' (ROC) by the King in April 1941, in recognition of their outstanding work; it was believed to be unprecedented for the title 'Royal' to be awarded in wartime.

Searchlights

By night, the observer posts were often unable to track raiders or fighters effectively and the main method of locating hostile aircraft was the network of Army searchlights. These were initially deployed at approximately 6000 yards (5.5km) spacing and sites were equipped with a primitive sound locator to guide the searchlight towards the hostile aircraft. The primary role of the lights was to locate and illuminate enemy aircraft so that the fighters could find and attack them. The lights also forced the enemy to take evasive action by weaving or flying higher, which might impair the ability to accurately bomb. Searchlight sites were all equipped with a Lewis anti-aircraft light machine gun, which turned out to be an effective weapon against aircraft flying down the searchlight beam to attack the light and was also important for defence against potential parachutists (Price 1977, 52, 54). Before gun-laying (GL) radars became available, searchlights were also essential for illuminating targets for the heavy AA guns defending the major ports and without them the guns were powerless to engage targets by night. An increased density of searchlights was therefore deployed around gun-defended areas for this purpose but it was found that this actually assisted the enemy to identify their target (Cooper 2004, 52). Searchlights were connected by telephone and wireless through their battery HQs to an Army cell in the RAF Sector Operations Room (Collier 1957, 483).

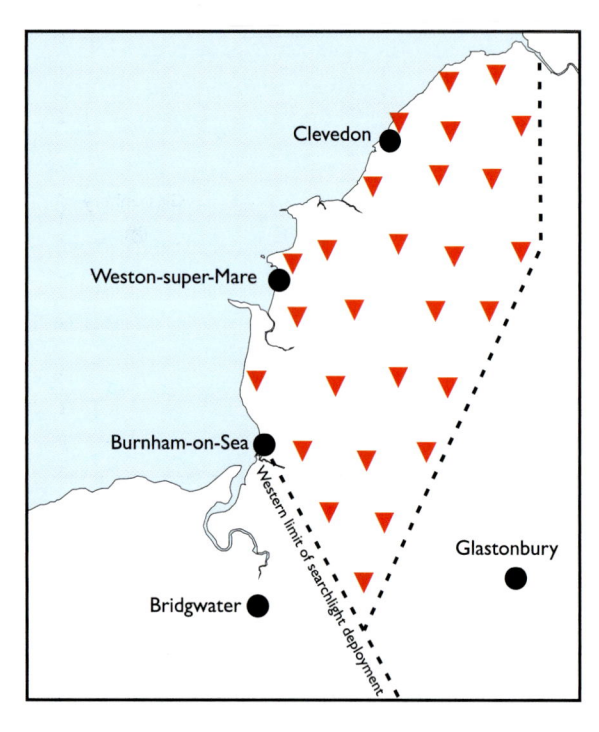

Figure 5.6: Searchlights deployed in the Coastal Defence Zone in mid 1940. Inland searchlights in the Glastonbury area are not shown.

The initial searchlight deployment in Somerset only covered the coastline north of Burnham-on-Sea and southwards to Yeovil and Portland (Figure 5.6) but, during the summer of 1940, the coverage was extended westwards. Cover had also been deployed along the Welsh coast as far west as Swansea (TNA WO 166/3292, map). In November 1940 with the arrival of more powerful searchlights and with increasing manpower shortages, it was decided to 'cluster' the lights in groups of three with clusters spaced uniformly at 10,400-yard (9.5km) separation across both gun-defended and fighter-defended zones to avoid giving the enemy any indication of gun sites or targets (Figure 5.7 on the facing page). Each cluster had one of the new 150cm searchlights which could illuminate targets up to 20,000 feet (18.3km) and two of the old 90cm lights. This was intended to improve the chance of picking up and 'coning' enemy aircraft in three beams. Practical experience showed that although a single searchlight might illuminate a raider, the night fighter might not be able to see the raider and an intersection of two beams was essential to ensure the fighter could identify the position and height of the enemy aircraft (TNA WO 166/2076, letter of 8 November 1940).

In the autumn of 1941, it was decided to once again redeploy the searchlights, this time into 'fighter boxes' each 14 miles deep and 44 miles (22 x 70km) wide with radar controlled searchlights deployed at 6000 yard (5.5km) intervals to form a 'killer zone' (Figure 5.8 on page 64). On the enemy approach side of the box, lights at 10,400 yard (9.5km) separation gave early warning of the approach of the enemy. A searchlight shining vertically near the centre of the box provided a marker beacon for the waiting night fighter to orbit around until directed by the orbit beam 'slapping' down towards the enemy which was by then illuminated by other lights in the box (Dobinson 2001, 344–45). Even so, it still proved difficult for night fighters to find the intruders. Searchlight control radars (SLC), which were also known as 'Elsie', were deployed as they became available. These had a range of about eight miles (13km) (Price 1977, 112). Gun-laying (GL) radars were also deployed to some searchlight sites to assist in locating enemy aircraft and to give warning of raiders up to 30 miles (48km) away.

Figure 5.9 on page 65 shows a typical 1942 searchlight battery deployed with 24 searchlight sites and 15 radars in the approximate area between Lynton, Porlock, Tiverton and South Molton, as part of the Exeter Sector 'Fighter Box' deployment, with the battery HQ at Exford. The four searchlights to the north are part of the indicator belt to give warning of

Air Defence

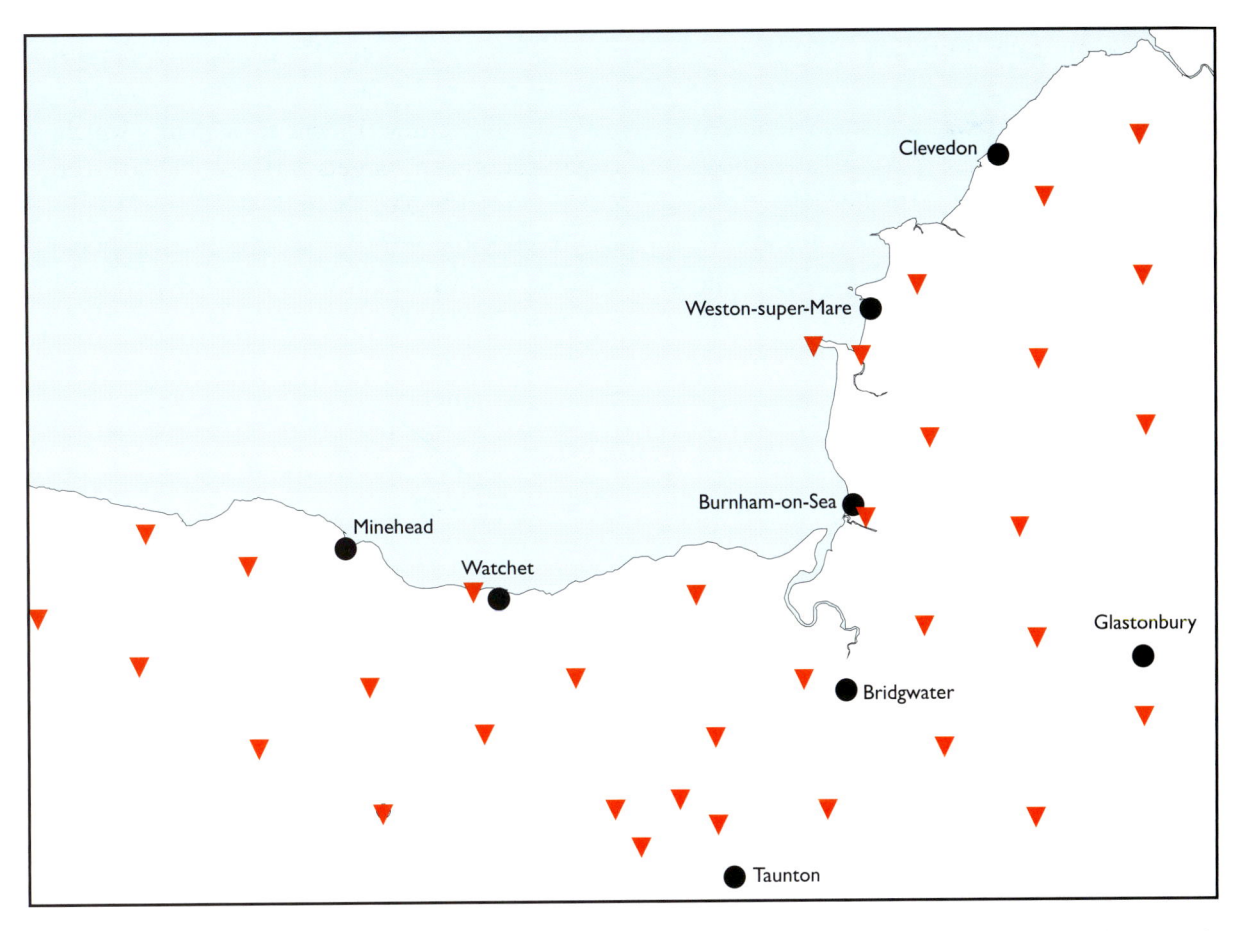

Figure 5.7: *Searchlight clusters in 1941 within the boundaries of Somerset. Each cluster consisted of three searchlights.*

enemy aircraft returning to their bases in north-west France. There was also the main indicator belt to the south, which is not shown on this map.

Air defence radar

Until September 1943, the British used the term RDF which was a compression of the initials RD for Radio Detection and DF for Direction Finding. A further term, radiolocation, was released for general use when the existence of RDF was disclosed to the public on 18 June 1941 in a House of Commons statement. The American term radar (radio detection and ranging) was later adopted to avoid differences in terminology between the Allies (Air Historical Branch 1950a, iii, note 1, 8).

The use of radar is a complicated subject, both because of the secrecy that surrounded its invention shortly before the war and because of the many types developed for use by the Royal Navy, the Army and the RAF in both air defence and coast defence roles. Army and some RAF radars were mobile and were moved to meet changing *Luftwaffe* tactics or to improve coverage.

The South West, including Somerset, was not part of the original Chain Home system, whose primary role was distant warning of hostile aircraft, concentrated on the south and east coasts looking seawards only. These radars had an average effective range of about 80 miles (130km) depending on the height of the aircraft. On 19 January 1939 it was decided that Chain Home should be extended westwards with a station at Prawl Point in south Devon to give warnings of attacks from the south of the Bristol and south Wales industrial areas and that a second station should be built

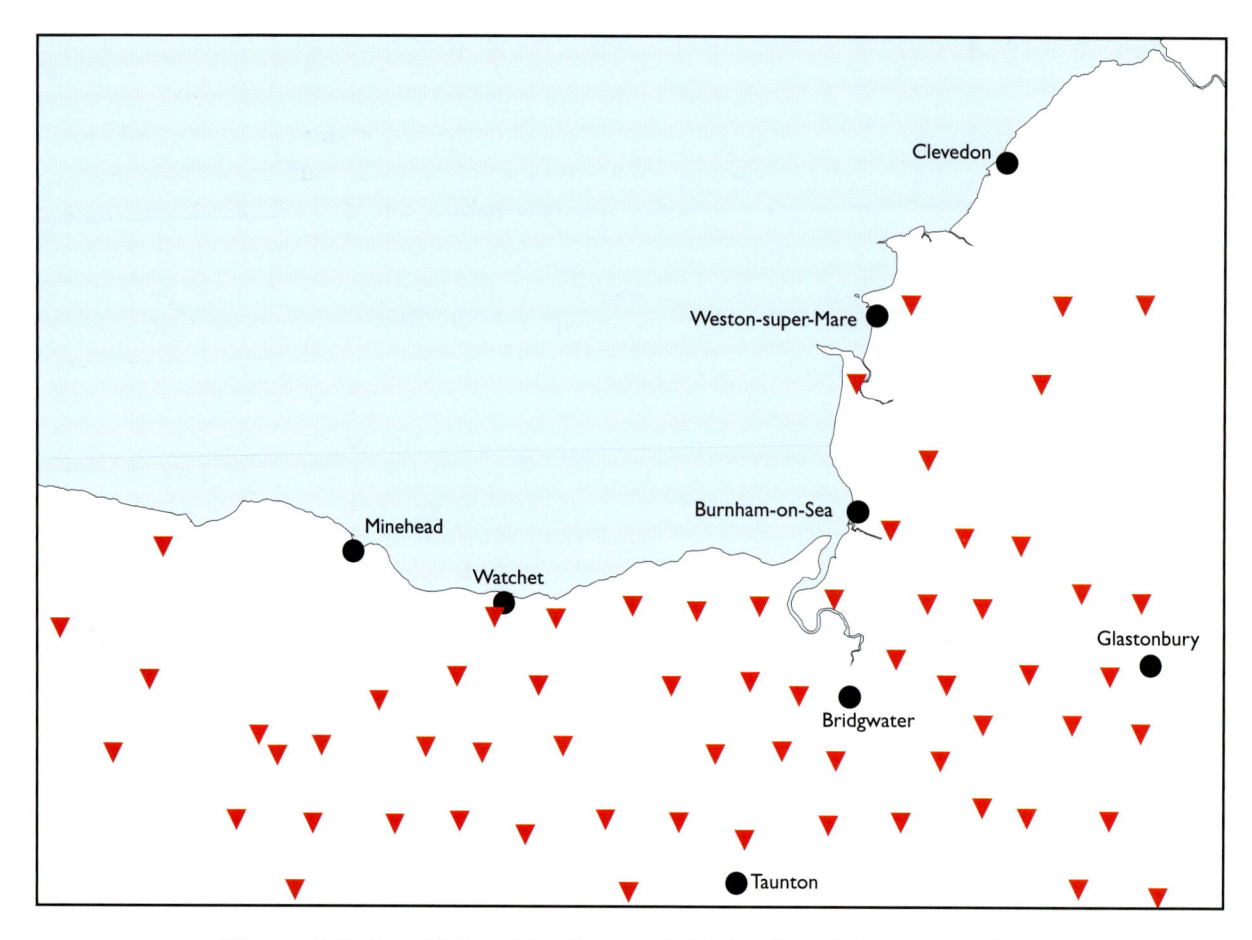

Figure 5.8: Searchlights within Somerset in Fighter Box deployment in 1942.

on Exmoor to cover the Bristol Channel. The proposed Exmoor station site at Exe Plain near Simonsbath did not provide the cover expected and was abandoned (Air Historical Branch 1950a, 60). Other sites investigated included Porlock Common, Brendon Common and Luckott Moor (TNA AIR 2/2685, BRS/4/8/1 of 2 March 1939).

After the declaration of war in September 1939 enemy aircraft started penetrating further than anticipated over the western areas of England and the Irish Sea so on 2 January 1940 the Prime Minister allocated the highest priority to closing the gaps in the radar coverage between Weymouth and Torquay at both high and low level with second priority out of a total of nine being provision for both high and low level over the Bristol Channel (Air Historical Branch 1950a, 85). In February 1940 various sites covering the Bristol Channel were examined including a possible Chain Home Low station at Countisbury Hill near Lynton in Devon. This was never built as a more suitable site had been identified near Porthcawl on the south Wales coast (TNA AVIA 7/256).

The German occupation of Denmark and Norway in April 1940 radically changed the requirement for radar cover, with an urgent need to cover the north-eastern coast of Britain (Air Historical Branch 1950a, 109). Radar was also being deployed to Middle East Command to cover areas such as Malta and the Suez Canal (Air Historical Branch 1950a, 103), which created additional demands for equipment and resources, particularly after Italy entered the war on 10 June 1940. This delayed the implementation of the plans for the South West. On 25 May 1940 as the Germans advanced towards Dunkirk, a new priority list for radars included at third place the provision of cover from the Lizard to the Bristol Channel, after the defence of London and the Channel approaches in

Air Defence

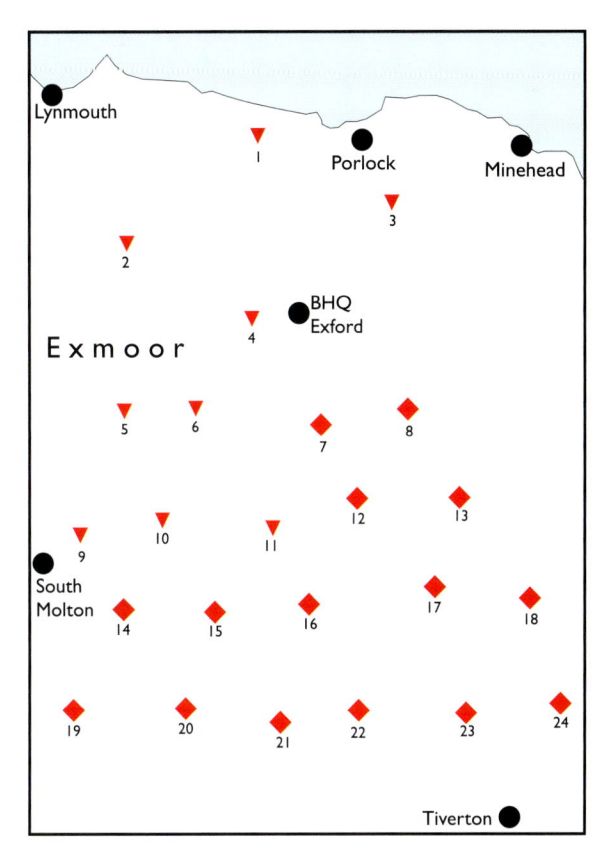

Figure 5.9: *Typical searchlight battery deployment in the 'fighter box' configuration in April 1942. 540 Battery of 88 Searchlight Regiment RA with 24 searchlight sites of which 15 had searchlight control (SLC) radar (shown by diamonds). This was the EX H area of the Exeter sector. Sites 1–4 formed part of the 'indicator belt' and the 'orbit point searchlight' was site 24 (locations from TNA WO 166/788).*

first place and Dover Strait to the Humber in second (Air Historical Branch 1950a, 109).

As already mentioned, the absence of radar cover inland meant that reliance was placed on the Observer Corps during the day and that tracking aircraft at night often depended on searchlight sightings, which at that time were still dependent on inefficient sound locators, and sometimes only on 'sound plots' by observers. However, radars were also being developed to control anti-aircraft guns (gun-laying or GL radars) enabling them to engage targets in poor visibility or at night. By June 1940 the first GL Mark 1 radars were deployed to most HAA sites but these only gave the range of the target up to about seven miles (11km) and not accurate elevation. This performance was improved by October 1940.

As a temporary measure in November 1940, a network or 'carpet' of gun-laying (GL) radars was established across southern England to track raiders inland (Figure 5.10 on the next page). Three GL radar-equipped AA gun sites around Bristol and Avonmouth, together with isolated GL radars deployed to new sites near Banwell and Wells, were connected by land-line to the Colerne Fighter Sector HQ. This gave some capability for tracking enemy aircraft over the eastern end of the Bristol Channel and its approaches from the south-east. Other radars in the 'carpet' were at South Brewham (later redeployed to Kilmington in Wiltshire) and Rode (TNA WO 166/2076, letter of 8/11/1940). This was at a time when the *Luftwaffe* had turned from the London Blitz to attacking ports; the first attack on Bristol with 134 aircraft was on 27 November 1940 (Collier 1957, 503).

By 1942 the list of GL equipped gun sites included 22 sites around Bristol, four at Weston-super-Mare and two at Yeovil. After the so-called Baedeker raids on Exeter and Bath in April and May 1942, three additional GL radars were deployed: one to Henlade (SHER 22513), one of the two new temporary gun sites at Taunton, and two to the Bath sites (TNA WO 33/1708). On 26 June 1942 this Taunton site with its GL radar engaged (unsuccessfully) aircraft on their way to attack Weston-super-Mare in another Baedeker Raid.

The problem of directing night fighters onto their targets was considerable. By day a fighter within three miles (5km) of an enemy could normally find its target but on a moonless night the fighter might not see the enemy until they were 300 yards (275m) apart. The night fighters were equipped with aircraft interception (AI) radars, which had a range of about three miles (5km) and therefore needed accurate guidance to get into AI radar-range of the target, which neither the Observer Corps nor searchlights could achieve (Crowther and Whiddington 1947, 28).

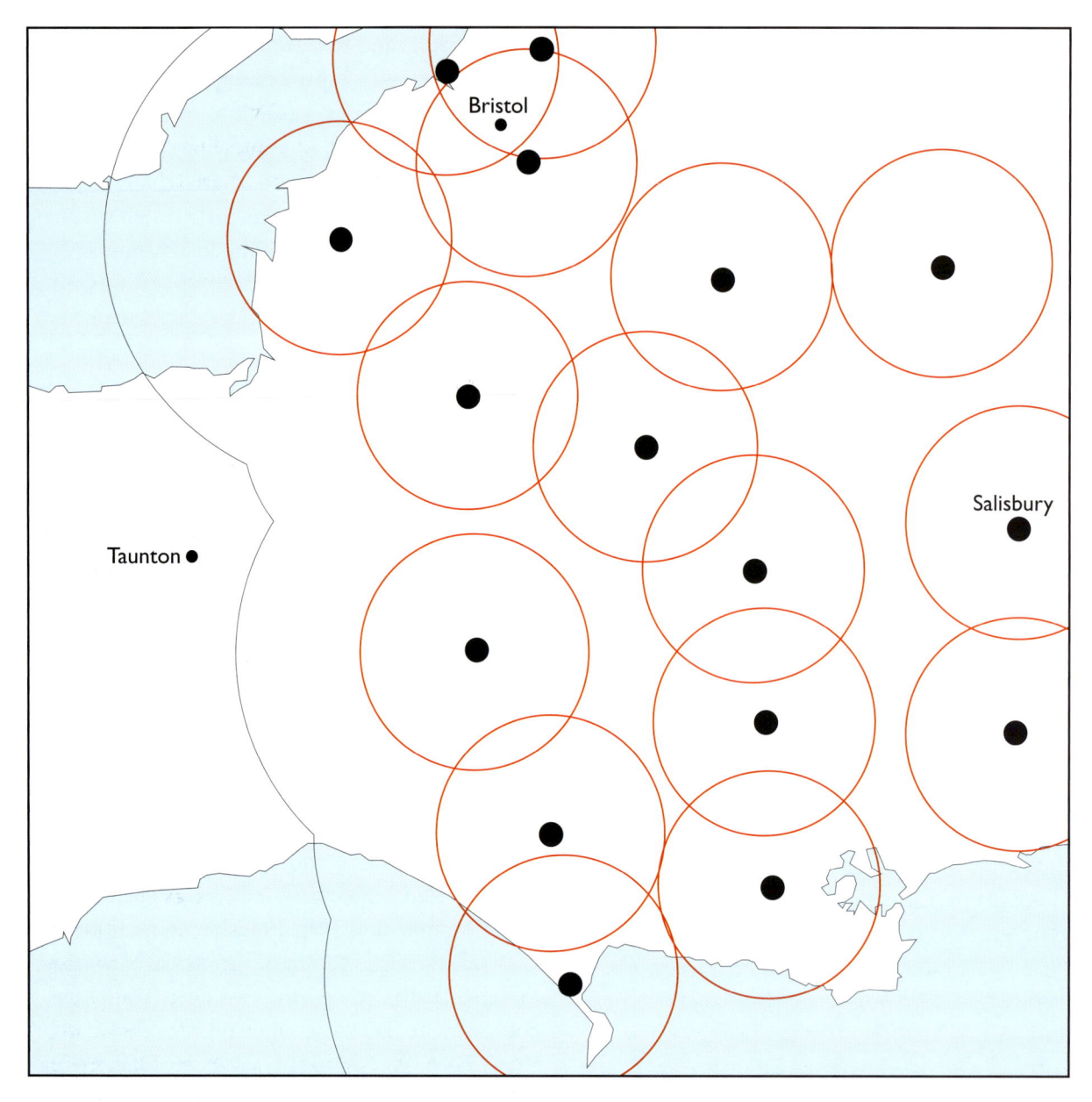

Somerset and the Defence of the Bristol Channel

Figure 5.10: Deployment of Army gun-laying (GL) radars as a 'carpet' to provide inland cover. The western edge of the maximum range (18 miles, 29km) at which the radar could first see an aircraft is shown; within the red circle (8-mile, 13km, range) the radar could accurately track the aircraft and report its position to the RAF sector.

In 1941 a new Ground Controlled Interception (GCI) system using radars to direct night fighters onto enemy aircraft was deployed. The GCI radar stations were warned of approaching enemy aircraft from Chain Home radar plots passed through the filter rooms via group and sector HQs. The GCI radars could then pick up raiders at about 90-miles (145km) using their height finding radar and could start controlling fighters at a maximum range of approximately 60 miles (95km) on their main radar where both the raider and fighter were visible on a single screen with an outline map (the plan position indicator or PPI). The use of identification friend or foe (IFF) a device based on a transponder in the aircraft which re-transmitted the radar signal illuminating it to produce a distinctive spot on the radar screen, enabled the GCI controller to distinguish the RAF night fighters on the PPI. IFF was also essential to enable GL and SLC radars to identify friendly aircraft and had a special facility to allow aircraft in distress to alert the radar operator so that its position could be passed to air-sea rescue units.

The GCI radar site had direct VHF radio telephone (RT) links to the night fighter and was able to navigate it into a position where it was able to identify the raider on its aircraft interception (AI) radar and close to attack the raider from behind. It was also important to prevent the fighter being silhouetted against the moon, sea or sky.

The initial deployment of the first six GCI radars in Britain included stations at Avebury in Wiltshire and Sopley in Hampshire but these only covered Somerset and the Bristol Channel east of a line from Burnham-on-Sea to Yeovil (Air Historical Branch 1952, 190–1). By March 1941 a site at Wrafton in north Devon to cover the western end of the Bristol Channel was planned to open in May but in April the top priority on a new list of 14 radars which 'were to be erected on coastal sites where their ability to see low-flying aircraft could be utilised against mine-laying and cloud flying raiders in daylight' was at Weston-super-Mare with Wrafton moved to priority six. At about this time the mobile GCI from Avebury was moved to Exeter where 'it would cover the route taken by aircraft crossing the coast at Lyme Bay and flying north over Somerset to the Irish Sea' (Air Historical Branch 1952, 202). In June 1941 a mobile GCI station was set up on Mark Moor, East Huntspill (Dobinson 1999, appendix 3), about ten miles (16km) south of Weston-super-Mare and presumably this site was selected on open flat ground as the hills near Weston-super-Mare would have screened the radar. The site for RAF Huntspill (SHER 44777) was reconnoitred by a Miss Francis in May 1941 who suggested using the road as all the fields were wet. In the event a field to the south of the road was used with the mobile cabins set out in a north–south line. The site was to be set up on 4 June and be operational a week later (TNA AVIA 7/1427). There were plans in November to provide accommodation in huts and a fully permanent station was envisaged. By this time GCI stations (Figure 5.11) were sited at Exminster and Hope Cove in south Devon, Wrafton in north Devon, Sturminster Marshall in east Dorset and Sopley in south-west Hampshire and which provided overlapping cover over the approaches to the Bristol Channel.

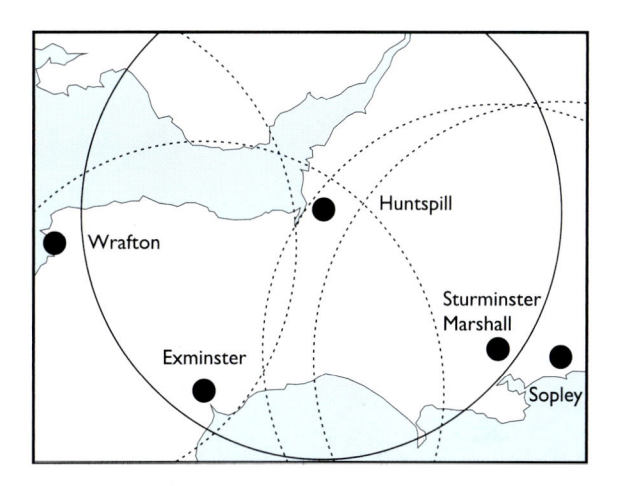

Figure 5.11: *GCI radar coverage from Huntspill (solid circle) and adjacent radar stations in November 1941.*

Eventually in January 1942 it was decided to move Huntspill GCI to a new location at Long Load approximately 14 miles (22km) to the south and permanent buildings were being built there in November (SHER 56972). However, the programme was curtailed in December (Dobinson 2010, 485–487) and construction appears to have been abandoned with the operations block partly built.

On a list dated 28 January 1943 Long Load was entered as 'operational' with an 'Intermediate Mobile' equipment which was expected to remain there as a long term solution (Air Historical Branch 1952, 284). It is likely that a fixed aerial was in position, as that was to have been the first construction, but the rest of the site was developed in temporary huts. By 1943, the GCI stations were becoming increasingly successful and each site was provided with direct communications to the local ROC centre; Long Load was connected to the ROC Group HQ at Yeovil. Aerial photographs taken

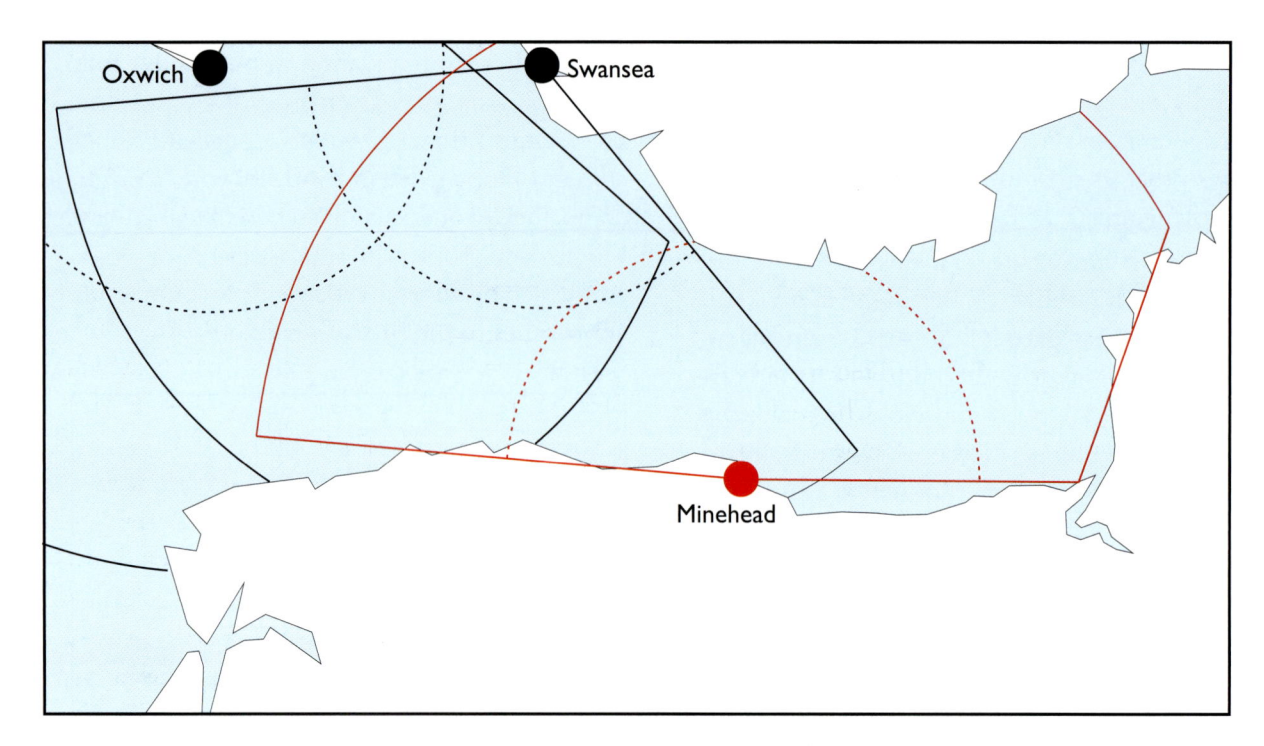

Figure 5.12: *The surface coverage against shipping of the Minehead CD/CHL radar together with adjacent radar stations in 1942. When visibility exceeded 20,000 yards (18.3km), Army radars might be permitted to be switched off and the inner (dashed) lines indicates this range. The Plan Position Indicator of Army radars covered a maximum range of 25 miles (40km) which is shown by the continuous line (after TNA WO 6114 and Air Historical Branch 1950a, 139).*

in January 1947 show the roofless operations block, the shadow of the aerial, completed standby-set house and wooden huts.

Finally it should be noted that just as the RAF Y-Service intercepted German ground to air wireless traffic (see on page 70 below), the *Luftwaffe* did exactly the same and GCI radio traffic between the radar site and the fighters was sometimes intercepted, allowing coded instructions to be sent to the intruder telling him to take violent evasive action to shake of the RAF night fighter tailing him (Air Historical Branch 1952, 211).

CHL/CD radars

Another development was the Chain Home Low (CHL) radar which could be used to locate both low-flying aircraft and ships. In the air defence role, the CHL radars were each normally associated with Chain Home sites to fill in gaps in the low level coverage of the CH stations. The CHL radars had an average range of about 30 miles (48km) depending on the radar site and the height of the aircraft. An example is the CHL station which was established in July 1941 on the cliffs at Beer Head in Devon near to the CH station which had been opened at Branscombe in October 1940. The new CHL improved low level coverage over Lyme Bay, enabling detection of low-flying enemy aircraft making northward toward the Bristol Channel and beyond (Passmore and Passmore 2008, 17).

In May 1942 a Coast Defence/Chain Home Low (CD/CHL), radar was established on North Hill, Minehead (Figure 5.12) which was taken over by 558 Regiment Coast Artillery (TNA WO 166/7178). The site was on high ground (732 feet, 225m, above sea level) and had excellent coverage northwards over the Bristol Channel. Army-controlled surface-watching radar stations were employed primarily in the detection of surface vessels and their movements. In addition stations could be ordered to supply information on aircraft observed and, if specially ordered, might be placed under direct control of the Navy. The stations reported through Army Plotting Rooms, which collated the information and passed it to the Army, Navy and RAF (TNA WO 166/6114).

An Admiralty chart dated 11 December 1942 ('British Isles: R.D/F Home Chain–Surface Watching) shows the air coverage of Bristol Channel radar stations. Minehead CD/CHL station is marked with the letter 'S' indicating that its primary role was anti-shipping as the air approaches to the Bristol Channel were then adequately covered by other radars. All the CD/CHL radar sites were later transferred to the RAF and at the same time 'operational control' of the sites passed to the Admiralty. In January 1944 Minehead was returned to GHQ Home Forces and thereafter its use is not clear (Dobinson 1999, 144).

In May 1944 a mobile high power Chain Home Extra Low radar was moved from Bolt Tail on the south Devon coast to Flat Point to the west of Ilfracombe in the surface watching role to guard the Bristol Channel but this was removed at the end of July 1944 (Air Historical Branch 1950a, 638).

Radio Counter Measures

The RAF was aware of the possibility of the use of radio beams by the *Luftwaffe* to guide bombers accurately to their targets. Beams were first identified on the night of 22–23 June 1940 by a specially equipped aircraft from Boscombe Down. The accuracy of the beams was such that a special RAF unit, 80 (Signals) Wing, controlled directly by the Air Ministry, was set up in August 1940 to develop and deploy measures to minimise the effectiveness of the beams. A 'Wireless Intelligence and Development Unit' provided airborne support. The activity was called Radio Counter Measures or RCM (Brettingham 1997, 10).

Both the *Luftwaffe* beam guidance systems and the RAF radio counter measures against them were novelties in aerial warfare and throughout the war there was an on-going battle of technology and tactics between the two air forces. Radio counter measures is a highly technical subject and the following discussion is therefore very broad-brush and greatly simplified. Only those aspects which affected the Bristol Channel or whose sites were located in and around Somerset are considered. No attempt is made to recount the history of radio counter measures or describe all the technical, organisational or operational changes that occurred.

Figure 5.13 on the next page gives a summary of the main German navigation systems, their British code names and code names of the counter measures used against them and the main sites in Somerset where these counter measures were deployed.

Knickebein

The original *Luftwaffe* system codenamed *Knickebein* ('crooked leg') consisted of two narrow beams which intersected over the target; the main beam was transmitted from France and the other from the Low Countries. The bombers from France flew along the main beam until they crossed the point of intersection of the second beam, which indicated their arrival in the target area. The system was accurate to within roughly a square mile (1.5km), which made it highly suitable for the mass bombing of urban areas by night or in poor weather (Richards 1953, 193; Jones 1978, 97–99. An important feature of *Knickebein* was that it used the Lorenz blind landing system with which all German bombers were equipped and with which all their crews had experience (Air Historical Branch 1950b, 5).

The RAF counter measure first used was simple jammers to swamp the beam signals. The system was code named 'Aspirin'. One of the first Aspirin sites was established on 10 August 1940 in Glastonbury Police Station

German Navigation System	British Code Name	British Counter Measure	RCM Stations in or near Somerset
Knickebein	Headache	Aspirin	Fairmile (Devon) Shipham Porlock Glastonbury Templecombe
X-Gerät	Ruffian	Bromide	Shipham Porlock
Y-Gerät	Benito	Benjamin/ Domino	Shipham Porlock Templecombe Gittisham Hill (Devon)
Medium Frequency Beacons	–	Meacon	Highbridge (Rx) – Lympsham (Tx) Honiton (Rx) – Fairmile (Tx) Kington Magna (Rx) – Templecombe (Tx)

Figure 5.13: *Luftwaffe Bomber Navigation Systems (Tx = transmitter, Rx = receiver)*

using an old hospital diathermy machine, which the police switched on when orders from 80 Wing were received by telephone. Other jammers were sited at the police stations in Newton Abbot in Devon and Wimborne Minster in Dorset. As improved jamming equipment became available Radio Counter Measures sites were established at five sites across southern England including Templecombe in Somerset, which became operational during July 1941. Other sites were established at Shipham and Porlock in Somerset, Fairmile, Ivybridge and Newton Abbot (Devon) and Delabole (Cornwall) allowing the diathermy equipment to be withdrawn from police stations. Glastonbury was closed on 20 January 1941. The Shipham and Porlock sites were located on high ground, which gave good cover over the Bristol Channel (TNA AIR 41/46).

This jamming had some successes but it was always necessary to first detect the narrow beams set on a target, which were only switched on before an attack and then to measure the frequency being transmitted. It was discovered that ground 'watcher' stations could receive the beams but airborne investigation capability was still important to measure their alignment. Watcher stations in the South West in 1940 were sites at West Prawl (Devon), Coverack (Cornwall) and Portland (Dorset). Depending on which beams were radiating and their directions, the best placed Aspirin stations were then ordered to transmit on the appropriate frequency when the enemy came in range. Knowing where the enemy aircraft were depended on Observer Corps, searchlights and, later, the inland radars.

The RAF Y-Service produced invaluable minute-by-minute information on the activities of raiders by monitoring their aircraft radio communications and locating their positions by directional finding fixes (see below).

In the autumn of 1940, bomber losses in daylight raids during the summer led the *Luftwaffe* to resort to night raids as the RAF fighters were significantly less effective at night. The Germans increasingly realised the effectiveness of RAF counter measures against *Knickebein* and came to rely on periods of bright moonlight for large scale attacks as individual aircraft could navigate to the target area and see their target.

The RAF 'Y-Service' operated a number of intercept stations listening to both transmissions from aircraft and locating beams after they were switched onto a particular target. The main 'Y-Service' sites in southern England were at Kingsdown in Kent, Shaftesbury in Dorset and Strete in south Devon. These were called Home Defence Units (HDU) to conceal their real mission. HDU dealt primarily with *Luftwaffe* aircraft VHF voice communications, primarily in fighters, while aircraft HF communications, primarily in bombers, using wireless telegraphy (WT, ie Morse code) were monitored by RAF Cheadle. Reports from pathfinder aircraft when targets had been marked and requests from German DF fixer stations for their position before the return flight (if the MF beacons were being 'meaconed', see page 72) provided invaluable immediate intelligence for the air defences, Radio Counter Measures and decoys, as will be explained later. In addition throughout the war 'wireless investigation aircraft' identified enemy navigation aids and tested the counter measures deployed against them.

These sources, together with information (code-named Ultra) from code-breakers at Bletchley Park, often gave the British valuable information about enemy plans for raids and, in particular, their targets for the night, allowing RCM to be instigated. This is a huge subject and, as there were no known Y-Service stations in Somerset, a single example of how the information from Bletchley Park often allowed air defences and Civil Defence services to prepare for air raids will be noted.

The war-diary of Gloucester Sub Area based in Bristol relates that on 21 January 1941, warning was received at 1530 hours from the Regional Commissioner that aerial attacks were expected in the Temple Meads area of Bristol at 1830 hours. The bombers arrived at 1850 hours and the attacks lasted most of the night (TNA WO 166/1266). The source of information was a closely guarded secret and it may be assumed that those on the Ultra list with a 'need to know' had significantly better information than that on more general release. Nevertheless such intelligence was not always available. It was not possible to intercept all wireless traffic and to then break the cipher in time for it to be of immediate value.

By the end of 1941, the British had identified 11 *Knickebein* stations between Stavanger in Norway and Morlaix on the Brest peninsula in north-west France and also a station at Lörrach in southern Germany. About a quarter of these stations were to the south of the Bristol Channel and on the routes for the south Wales ports or the industrial Midlands (Hinsley 1979, 555 and appendix 11). Throughout the war the *Luftwaffe* continued to use *Knickebein* and refine it against RAF counter measures.

X-Gerät

In August 1940, the Germans started to deploy an improved and more accurate system (the *X-Gerät*) with multiple cross beams to enable the aircraft position and ground speed to be computed and the exact bomb release point to be indicated. The system was only fitted in the specialised pathfinder aircraft of KG 100 (*Kampfgeschwader* – roughly the equivalent of an RAF bomber group), which dropped incendiary bombs on the target to cause fires enabling the main bomber force to find the target. Stations in the Brest (Morlaix) and Cherbourg peninsulas transmitted the beams to the targets and cross beams were transmitted from the Pas de Calais. This gave good coverage over the southern part of the UK and well into the Midlands. The RAF code-named the beams 'Ruffian' and counter measures were code-named 'Bromide'. It took time to identify the features of the new system and to develop counter measures (Hinsley 1979, appendix 11).

The first major use of *X-Gerät* for pathfinding was on 14 November 1940 when 469 bombers made the now-infamous attack on Coventry. Ironically the first two Bromide counter measure transmitters had been installed at Birdlip in Gloucestershire and at Hagley near Birmingham during early November 1940 but played no part in jamming the pathfinders' *X-Gerät*.

By December 1940 London had ceased to be the main nightly target but raids continued on ports and inland targets with varying success due to counter measures against *X-Gerät* and the development of decoy fires (see below on the facing page). From January 1941 the *Luftwaffe* only attacked inland targets on moonlit nights but their main attention was given to port cities like Plymouth, Bristol, Swansea, Cardiff and Hull where beams could still be deployed with minimum interference from radio counter measures (PRO 2001, 95, para 49). In 1941 Bromide jammers were deployed to the Porlock and Shipham RCM sites to meet this threat by giving cover against *X-Gerät* for the Bristol Channel and northwards beyond.

Y-Gerät

A third development was the *Y-Gerät* or 'Wotan' with a single beam. The position of the aircraft along the beam was measured using radar techniques. Six stations were set up along the French coast between the Brest peninsula and Calais. The British referred to *Y-Gerät* by the codename 'Benito' and the associated counter measures were called 'Benjamin' and 'Domino'. The counter measures equipment was deployed after May 1941 to the RCM sites including the sites at Porlock, Shipham, Templecombe and Ivybridge giving cover over the south-west peninsula, including the Bristol Channel (TNA AIR 41/46).

Luftwaffe medium frequency radio navigational beacons

In addition to the bomber guidance systems, the *Luftwaffe* used radio navigational beacons, for example, to assist bombers returning from raids over the Britain to find their base or for maritime reconnaissance aircraft. The beacons radiated signals on medium frequencies that enable the aircraft to take bearings on two beacons and establish their position accurately. The beacons started up just before the outbreak of war and 50 were operational by March 1940. The RAF countered this system by setting up sites that received the beacon signal which was then fed down a high quality telephone line to a distant transmitter site, where the signal was re-radiated. To aircraft flying over the UK, these signals were considerably stronger than those from the correct sites and caused major navigation errors for the aircraft.

These counter measure sites were code named 'Meacon' – derived from 'masking of beacons'. There were three pairs of sites in the South West. Beacon signals were received in Somerset at Highbridge and re-radiated from a transmitter site covering the Bristol Channel at Lympsham. Other sites in Devon were at Honiton (receivers) and Fairmile (transmitters) together with Kington Magna in Dorset (receivers) with the transmitters at Templecombe in Somerset (TNA AIR 41/46).

The 'meaconing' of the beacons was not always successful due to German countermeasures, including frequency and call-sign changes. However, examples of the successes include a *Luftwaffe* aircraft landing at RAF Chivenor near Barnstaple believing that it was in France and, on 21 October 1941 a Dornier 217 aircraft returning from a shipping reconnaissance over the Western Approaches to an airfield near Paris was misled by meaconing from Templecombe into mistaking the Bristol Channel for the English Channel and flew on over southern England believing it to be over France. Further successful meaconing from Newbury caused it to fly in an easterly direction until it crossed the north coast of Kent and, finally running out of fuel, landed at Lydd. An added bonus was that the aircraft was equipped with a complete model of a new version of the *Knickebein* receiver (Air Historical Branch 1950b, 35–6). On 24 July 1941, another *Luftwaffe* Ju 88 was deceived by the Lympsham Meacon, landed by mistake at Lulsgate Bottom and was captured (Price 1977, 129).

Control of BBC transmissions

The first radio counter measure to be deployed after the declaration of war in 1939 was intended to prevent intrusions by enemy propagandist announcers into the gaps between BBC programmes which were a feature of broadcasting at that time. BBC announcers also gave their names before making announcements so that the public became familiar with their voices and mannerisms (Air Historical Branch 1950b, 8).

To prevent the *Luftwaffe* using British high power (over 500 watts) transmitters as navigation aids, all transmitters used by the armed forces, the GPO, civil aviation, Home Office and BBC were put under the control of the RAF so that during enemy raids broadcasting could be suspended and stations closed down. The BBC medium-wave broadcasting stations across Britain were split into groups of four with each group transmitting a synchronised signal on the same frequency making it difficult for enemy aircraft to identify where the transmission was coming from.

These stations included the BBC transmitter at Washford Cross (Figure 5.14; Wilson 1996) near the west Somerset coast which was grouped with Moorside Edge, Droitwich and Brookman's Park on the south Home frequency of 668 kHz. When enemy aircraft flew near one of the transmitters in any group, its signal would have been significantly stronger than the other synchronised transmitters and could have been used for navigation purposes. In order to prevent this Fighter Command and later 80 Wing would order the transmitter to be switched off (Air Historical Branch 1950b, 302). When transmitters were switched off, programmes continued to be broadcast from local low power transmitters at sites including Bristol, Exeter and Taunton (Collier 1957, 158). As the war proceeded, more groups of BBC transmitters were formed.

Similar measures were taken with the GPO wireless telegraphy transmitters at Portishead and at 19 other sites across Britain. In 1943 two Admiralty seaborne radio beacons including Scarweather Beacon off Swansea in the Bristol Channel were included in the system. Ireland operated a 1000 kW transmitter at Athlone but it proved difficult to arrange for it to be switched off during raids over Britain. By 9 December 1939 'spoiler' transmitters were erected by the BBC at three sites all under the control of Fighter Command including a 2 kW transmitter at Clevedon. The system was abandoned on 3 February 1941 as the Irish government had set up spoilers of their own (Air Historical Branch 1950b, 3002).

Figure 5.14: *The front of the main building at Washford Cross BBC transmitter station (Somerset County Council HER, 1983).*

In May 1944, the Washford and Brookman's Park (Hertfordshire) transmitters were held ready each night between 2330 hours and 0600 hours for counter-measures against German instructions to aircraft being broadcast from the Calais area. The operation was controlled by 80 Wing RAF through the RAF Y-Service radio intercept station at Kingsdown in Kent. If an air raid was expected, control of the two BBC transmitters could then be switched over to the RAF allowing them to jam any German transmissions. The procedure was called 'Operation Bareback' (TNA AIR 41/46).

Bombing decoys

Decoy sites (known as QL sites) used lights to simulate the reduced lighting used at depots, factories, aerodromes, railway marshalling yards and docks. They were designed to deceive *Luftwaffe* pathfinder aircraft, particularly if their navigation aids were being jammed, into dropping their target-marker incendiary bombs on the decoy lights, which were sited in open countryside. A second series (QF sites) of adjacent decoys was equipped with a variety of devices to simulate fires caused by the incendiary markers and thus persuade the main bomber force that this was their target. Generally, QL and QF sites were controlled from the target that they were to protect. The decoys were most effective when visibility was poor on dark nights, particularly with thin cloud or mist and were least effective on bright moonlit nights or when the ground was snow-covered.

Potential targets in Somerset that received QL and QF decoys included the Army Supply Reserve Depot at Norton Fitzwarren (SHER 44685, decoying SHER 44543), Westland's aircraft factory at Yeovil (SHER 57008, decoying SHER 55404) and the Royal Ordnance factory at Puriton near Bridgwater (SHER 12715, decoying SHER 12502). The Bristol Channel defences included QF sites to protect Avonmouth oil refineries (2), Bristol (16), Swansea (17), Cardiff (5), Newport (10) and Milford Haven (6) (Dobinson 2000, 241–89; Schofield *et al.* 1998, 271–86).

After the devastating night raids on Coventry on 14–15 November 1940, a series of massive Special Fire (SF) sites was rapidly developed to simulate the extensive fires resulting from similar mass raids on urban targets. These SF sites, or Starfish as they were later called, were controlled directly by 80 Wing, which was provided with 'the best possible information' from both RAF Y-Service and Bletchley Park. Between these two sources the *Luftwaffe* target for that night was often known in advance.

As mentioned above, the RAF Y-Service was able to follow and report the progress of an attack by monitoring bomber communications, both in flight and from their bases, as well as 'fixing' aircraft positions by using DF. This was then then combined with information from Fighter Command including radar plots, searchlight reports and Observer Corps reports. Local Starfish controllers reported the position and size of any fires produced. Taking all this information together, 80 Wing were able to decide which were the appropriate Starfish to be fired and when this should take place. Bristol got its first SF site by 27 November 1940 and a few days later on 2–3 December, two Bristol sites became the first in Britain to be used successfully during an attack by attracting a total of 66 HE (high explosive) bombs. By the spring of 1941 Bristol had five sites which were extremely successful on a number of occasions.

In 1942 after the Baedeker raids on Bath and Exeter the QF decoy protecting the Army Supply Reserve Depot (SHER 44543) at Norton Fitzwarren was moved to Castlemans Hill (SHER 44684) to the south-west of Taunton and made into a 'Temporary Starfish' to protect both Taunton and the depot. In that position it would have also given protection to the Hydrographic Office (SHER 15632). The site was closed in 1944 but later in the year, when the *Luftwaffe* developed and used more sophisticated and numerous target marker flares, 'minor Starfishes' were set up to mimic these flares should any markers be dropped near a Starfish site (Dobinson 2000, 194–95). Even as late as March 1944 the QL decoy site at Bleadon protecting Weston-super-Mare aerodrome and the shadow aircraft factory attracted significant numbers of HE and incendiary bombs during an attack on 27–28 March (Dobinson 2000, 195).

After the war the Air Historical Branch (AHB) estimated that out of the total number of bombs dropped on Britain, the 'war average' of those that were diverted by decoys was 5% but this was thought to be a very conservative estimate with the true figure being nearer 10%. Starfish sites attracted 101 recorded attacks. The AHB survey found the most successful sites were those at Portsmouth, Plymouth, Bristol, the Humber and Middlesborough. Dobinson suggests that on the basis of the 5% wastage of bombing decoys, casualties saved would be 3160 injured and 2596 dead (Dobinson 2000, 212–13). Perhaps the refusal of the Ministry of Defence to release files before 1979 is some indication of the success of the techniques used and their possible application in the Cold War (Dobinson 2000, x).

Camouflage and concealment

In addition to decoy sites, important targets were camouflaged to make them less visible to daylight raiders. For example, the water-storage lake for the new Royal Ordnance Factory (ROF, SHER 12502) at Puriton was created as a linear feature (the Huntspill river, SHER 11684) that could also be used to drain the levels in winter rather than a more conspicuous simple lake. As the Hydrographic Office (SHER 15632) was built on one side of Creechbarrow Hill, the 'disruptive camouflage painting' with irregular patterns in green, black and brown attempted to break up the straight edges of the building and merge it into the landscape. Westland's aircraft factory at Yeovil (SHER 55404) was camouflaged with bands of disruptive painting to make it appear from the air like rows of terrace houses.

An ambitious scheme was implemented to conceal the newly built Army Supply Reserve Depot at Norton Fitzwarren (SHER 44543). The immediate surroundings of the depot (Figure 5.15) were described in 1941 as 'open country broken up by modern housing estates ... a combination of "housing" and "rural patterning" was obviously appropriate.' The scheme was 'to apply a disruptive tree patterning and to simulate houses and other buildings over parts of the main buildings. The establishment area to be broken up further by ground patterning which will be in harmony with the small woods and clumps of trees in the adjacent surroundings' (TNA WO 227/51).

Mobile smoke screens were deployed to hide key targets like Avonmouth. On 25 June 1941, Pioneer Corps soldiers arrived at Shirehampton to set up and operate a smoke screen over Avonmouth docks. The operation was the responsibility of the Ministry of Home Security

Figure 5.15: *Aerial photograph of the Supply Reserve Depot at Norton Fitzwarren, taken on 6 January 1944 to assess the camouflage scheme (TNA WO 227/51).*

through the Smoke Controller in the Central Smoke Operations Room in London. Two types of smoke generator were used: the old 'No. 24 Mark II static' or 'smoke pots' and the new Haslar mobile equipment. The 'smoke pots' had a burn time of five hours and were used in pairs to cover up to ten hours of operation. The Haslar was a mobile oil burning installation which produced biscuit coloured smoke comparable with a London smog.

By mid 1941 the Avonmouth smoke screen was laid out with an outer ring some 1500 yards (1.4km) from the target consisting of Haslar generators spaced at 85 yard (78m) intervals and an inner ring of 1000 yard (915m) radius with pairs of Mark II generators at five to ten yard intervals. Generators were deployed each night only to the upwind sector within a 60° arc on either side of the predicted wind direction, as advised by a small meteorological staff. The equipment was first used early on the morning of 5 July 1941 and by September some 2510 Mark II generators were installed.

On 24 February 1944 in response to renewed bombing attacks and in preparation for the Normandy landings, 24 'Esso Smoke Generators' of the 79 Chemical Smoke Generating Company of the US Army were deployed at Avonmouth. By the autumn of 1944 the screens had become redundant and the manpower was deployed elsewhere. In general, the use of smoke screens to protect individual targets appears to have produced satisfactory results (John Penny, pers. comm.).

Conclusion

The air war over the Bristol Channel and its approaches over Somerset was a part of the war where technology was exploited to the full with scientific developments that were at that time state of the art, particularly in the fields of radar and what is now called electronic warfare including radio interception, code and cipher breaking, direction finding position fixing and a wide range of Radio Counter Measures. In stark contrast, First World War weapons like the Lewis gun and the 3-inch AA gun continued to give good service.

Developments in radar, in not only identifying enemy aircraft well beyond the shores of Britain, but in ground control interception using fighters with airborne radar to destroy enemy aircraft at night, was vital for defending the Bristol Channel ports against air attack. Radar technology was harnessed to AA gun-laying, searchlight direction and maritime surveillance using CD/CHL radars, but at the same time, observers still scanned sea and sky with their naked eye or binoculars and, despite the modern air defence communications, were still equipped with flares or pyrotechnics should communications fail. Somerset had its part to play in the rapid deployment of new effective radio counter measures against enemy bomber navigation aids and extensive deception measures including camouflage and decoys to minimise the effectiveness of bombing raids.

The threat from the air has also to be seen in terms of enemy reconnaissance, anti-shipping mine-laying and the potential for invasion. The proven ability of the *Luftwaffe* to land fighting troops by glider, parachute or aircraft almost anywhere with the minimum of warning brought a dimension to warfare which was a far more significant threat to the southern coastline of the Bristol Channel than seaborne invasion. Two air threats never materialised in the South West: both sides had invested heavily in protection and defence against the possibility of air-delivered chemical warfare and the German preparations to attack Bristol and Plymouth with V1 flying bomb (basically a first generation cruise missile) could have had a devastating effect on the preparations, launching and support for operation Overlord. The chemical weapons were never used and the threat of the V1 vanished soon after D-Day.

General Karl Koller, Chief of the German Air Staff at the end of the war stated that: 'The campaigns in Poland, Holland, Belgium, France and Norway had proved unequivocally how important air supremacy is in modern war' (PRO 2001, 407). Thanks to the achievements of the British air defences, the *Luftwaffe* never achieved air supremacy over the Bristol Channel or indeed over the British Isles. Without air supremacy, any invasion attempt would have been doomed to failure. The German bombing campaign was frustrated by Fighter Command by day but, at night, radio counter measures and bombing decoys were the only effective defence until the development of GL, GCI and AI radars. Despite the heavy bombing raids on Bristol Channel ports, the air defences did much to minimise and mitigate their effects and were therefore a vital part of winning this local part of the war.

Chapter 6

Other military uses of the Somerset coast

IN RESEARCHING maritime Somerset the authors kept coming across mentions not only of military sites and establishments along the coast of Somerset but also of a number of military activities and experimental work that took place in the area on or near the coast. This chapter attempts to bring these together to give some idea of how involved the Services were on the coastline and how varied these activities were beyond the purely defensive measures to secure the coast.

Military use of seaside holiday accommodation

On the outbreak of war, the Somerset holiday resorts offered safe accommodation for those who wished to avoid the expected bombing and evacuees were sent to Somerset. During the German offensives in May 1940 the population of Britain began to understand the magnitude of the crisis they faced and appeared to be prepared to make sacrifices and expected the same from others, On 15 June 1940 the Ministry of Information reported from Bristol, 'strong resentment expressed in Bath for paid holidays for 4000 evacuated (Admiralty) civil servants. Similar criticism of joy riding holidaymakers from Taunton and district; disgust expressed by local inhabitants.' Nevertheless on 31 July in the midst of the preparation of beach defences and the emplacement of the Coast Artillery battery at Minehead, another report from Bristol noted that, 'Complaints from Minehead that potential holidaymakers have the impression that the South West resorts are dangerous areas.' On 5 August Bristol again reported, 'No grumbles about the absence of bank holiday. Holiday resorts on the Bristol Channel coast complain about the mention of the Bristol Channel in Home Security bulletins and say their trade is thereby being ruined' (Addison and Crang 2010, 177, 287, 302). The reports were prepared daily in 'telegraphese' to get them to London by early afternoon.

After the evacuation from Dunkirk and the fall of France in June 1940 the Army urgently required accommodation, particularly for troops deployed on coast defence duties. Beach huts at Dunster Beach and holiday camps at St Audries Bay and Berrow were requisitioned. At Dunster Beach there were 185 huts but no other infrastructure other than two small shops, toilets and a few outside water taps. The 18 feet by 14 feet (5.5 by 4.3m) beach huts were stripped of any internal partitions and equipped with beds and a solid fuel stove to typically accommodate four men (at the then regulation space of 60 square feet (18.3m^2) per man, War Office 1940) but this was increased to eight when accommodation was short and soldiers then slept with their feet towards the stove in the centre. Ancillary buildings like cookhouses, ablutions, latrines, bath houses and coal yards were built. Nissen huts and Romney shelters were erected, the latter used for messes.

Both Dunster Camp, as the Army named the site, and St Audries Camp were each capable of accommodating a basic infantry battalion of about 600 men (author's, DH, recollections;

Figure 6.1: The surviving Army bath house at Dunster Beach camp (David Hunt, 2008).

Concannon 1995, 37). When more space was needed, accommodation at Dunster Hall and Lower Marsh Farm was requisitioned (TNA WO 166/1924). After the war the chalets were returned to their owners and the site improved. Most Army buildings were removed but several remain in use (Figure 6.1) while a few concrete hut bases indicate the sites of others.

Smaller establishments, such as hotels, were also used. In Minehead, the Royal Armoured Corps Armoured Fighting Vehicle Range (tank gunnery) had its headquarters at the Conway Hotel on The Avenue and the 8 Corps Junior Leaders School and Vehicle Maintenance School were at the Metropole Hotel (TNA WO 166/11001, 24/10/1943). At Burnham-on-Sea, hotels were used both for accommodating soldiers and, from 1 May 1943, the Manor Hotel was used as the HQ of Somerset Sub District (TNA WO 166/11001). As mentioned above (on page 14), the Resident Naval Officer, Watchet established his headquarters at the Langbury Hotel at Blue Anchor.

Many service personnel were billeted with civilian families or in holiday accommodation. The war-diary of the 10th Battalion of the Somerset Light Infantry recorded (10 Oct 1940) that the battalion was guarding the beaches between Burnham-on-Sea and Brean, with its HQ in Naish House in Burnham-on-Sea, and its A and B Companies at Berrow, C Company at Brean, and D and HQ Companies at Burnham-on-Sea, with all companies in billets (TNA WO 166/4661). The battalion strength in December 1940 was about 948 all ranks. The total military population (see page 40) was then nearly 2000 men in an area with a civilian population of *c.*3800 and that presumably had already taken evacuees.

On operations, use was made of village halls, public houses (often for HQs, presumably because they may have had a telephone) and farms to provide soldiers with accommodation. The war-diary of the 9th Somerset Light Infantry shows that it deployed from St Audrey's Camp during the 'Cromwell' invasion alert between 7 and 9 September 1940 (see page 45) to guard the area between the west Somerset coast and the Brendon Hills. The war-diary lists billets in village halls at Dunster, Withycombe, Roadwater and Old Cleeve together with the White House Inn (Exford), Railway Hotel (Washford), Red Lion (Timberscombe), Butcher's Arms (Carhampton), Higher Marsh Farm (Dunster), St Decuman's vicarage and Parsonage Farm. At other locations the soldiers used bivouacs or sheltered in woods. Battalion HQ was located at the BBC Transmitting Station at Washford Cross (TNA WO166/4660).

In the preparations for D-Day, American forces were stationed in the area of the Somerset coast. This has not been researched in detail but Wakefield (1994) identifies the locations of a number of US formations and units from the 'First US Amy Station List' dated 31 May 1944. The HQ of First Army was accommodated in Clifton College in Bristol. The 1st Engineer Brigade (Support) and its 519 Port Battalion were also located in Bristol. The latter unit had four US Port Companies (302, 303, 304 and 305) in Bristol and there were also several logistic units.

Weston-super-Mare was the base for the HQ of 49th Anti-aircraft Artillery (AAA) Brigade, with the HQ of 16th AAA Group under its command including 197th AAA AW Battalion. Also at Weston-super-Mare were 115th AAA Gun Battalion and 457 AAA AW Battalion M.

Eighty-Sixth Ordnance Battalion was located at Brean together with 507th Ordnance HM Company Field Artillery. Further west, 186 and 187 Field Artillery Battalions were located at St Audries together with the HQ of 187th Field Artillery Group. A large US fuel depot with a network of railway sidings was established at Walrow to the east of Highbridge as part of the D-Day preparations (SHER 15405). Further research will be needed to establish the full pre D-Day deployments of American forces in Somerset.

Ranges

The lonely beaches and clear views out to sea offered the military a number of opportunities for ranges and test facilities along the Somerset coast. The safety areas up to and beyond the targets were normal cleared of livestock and entry was restricted while firing was proceeding. Clearing the safety areas for inland ranges required resources and could interfere with agriculture so that firing out to sea was a simple alternative.

Rifle ranges

The danger area of a typical 600-yard (550m) rifle range would be about 1000 yards (900m) wide and extend perhaps 1.5 miles (2.5km) behind the targets (War Office 1914, para 17). An early 700-yard (640m) rifle range at Blue Anchor beach was sited to fire eastwards along the shore line, past the Blue Anchor Inn and onto targets on the cliffs. The Ordnance Survey 6-inch maps show the firing points at 100 yard (91m) intervals, flag staffs for warning flags when firing was in progress and iron 'mantlets' to protect those marking the targets. At Lilstock and Sand Bay 600-yard (550m) rifle ranges fired seawards with targets on the cliffs, while at Uphill a range used a nearby hillside as stop butts and at Berrow a 600-yard (550m) range fired northwards along the edge of the beach. South of Clevedon there was also a range at Gullhouse Point.

During the war, when safety regulations were somewhat more lax, Home Guard rifle and spigot mortar practice took place in Porlock Bay while rifle firing also took place westwards along the shore near Minehead gas works. The Bridgwater Home Guard used the disused Cannington rifle range. At Brean Down six open, semi-circular brick emplacements survive overlooking Weston Bay. These do not appear to be tactically sited, or to offer any protection against even small arms fire, and are therefore unlikely to be anti-invasion defences. It is possible that may have been used by the

Figure 6.2: *Pre-war anti-aircraft gunnery training at Doniford with the 3-inch AA gun (courtesy Vernon Stone from a postcard by HH Hole).*

RAF air navigators' school at Weston-super-Mare before it was moved to South Africa in August 1940. It is believed that targets were towed past the firing points at about the same height to present target aspects that might be encountered in air combat.

Anti-aircraft gunnery ranges

The development of AA artillery between the wars and the use of the Territorial Army for AA units resulted in an AA practice camp being set up at Doniford near Watchet in 1925 (Figure 6.2; Dobinson 2001, 72). Firing live ammunition required a site on the coast where inshore waters could be kept clear of shipping and aircraft for a distance of about seven miles (11km). Firing points for the 3-inch gun were established on the coast, with a tented camp at Liddymore to accommodate the soldiers training there. A larger hutted camp was established at Doniford from 1934 (Figure 6.4 on page 82). Targets were towed by aircraft from RAF Weston Zoyland. General Sir Frederick Pile (1949) noted that practices were fired at air targets towed at some 60 mph, which was 100 mph slower than any German aircraft. A small grass airstrip was provided at Doniford, which allowed target towing aircraft to land.

From 1937, the 'Queen Bee' radio-controlled target was also used (Figure 6.3 on the next page). This was based on a Tiger Moth aircraft and was launched from a catapult at the west end of the range firing point. The unmanned aircraft, which was equipped with floats, was then landed on the sea and recovered by launch into Watchet Harbour before being lifted by crane onto a truck to be returned Doniford. The initial Queen Bee launch took place from the cruiser HMS *Neptune* on 29 July 1935 and the first land launch was made on 3 July 1937 (Berryman 2006, 127–8).

Before the outbreak of the Second World War, Doniford was also used for the new 3.7-inch AA gun and the 4.5-inch gun, which was based on a modified naval gun. When

Figure 6.3: Pre-war view of the 'Queen Bee' target plane on the catapult at Doniford (courtesy Vernon Stone from a postcard by HH Hole).

the performance of the 3.7-inch AA gun was upgraded, it could no longer be fired at Doniford as the safety area was insufficient (Cooper 2004, 25). The range was then used for the 40mm Bofors light anti-aircraft guns. The range danger area shown on maps and charts suggests that firing could also have taken place from the St Audries area.

During the war, the School of Anti-Aircraft Artillery (SAAD) (Radar Wing) was based at Doniford Camp with the main SAAD located at Manorbier in Pembrokeshire. In 1942 the site was listed as 'AA Practice Camp 8 Watchet' with 'The School of Anti-Aircraft Defence Wireless Wing Watchet' also listed at Doniford. In 1945, the range was described as 'Army Range A201 Watchett [sic] AA (H & L)' suggesting that it was still possible to fire both heavy and light AA guns there (map SD559: Armament Training Areas, edition of May 1945, TNA AIR 10/4182; see Figure 6.6 on page 84)

A radar set is known to have been employed at the Doniford ranges, but it is not clear whether it was a training radar, GL radar for use on the ranges, range safety or in an experimental role, as little is known of it beyond its existence (Stafford 2006, 178). It is known that in 1941 GL Mk II radar trials were carried out at Watchet (TNA WO 291/14). In July 1947, the range became the RAF Regiment Light Anti-Aircraft Gunnery School for the Bofors L40/70 gun, an improved version with radar control. The facility closed in February 1957 although the camp continued to be used by the Army until at least 1967 (author's, DH, recollection). It is now a caravan park and holiday camp where a few of the Army buildings are still in use. Another site was an Army 'anti-aircraft (machine gun) range', which fired out to sea, listed in 1944 at Wains Hill, Clevedon (TNA AIR 10/4182).

In 1940 anti-aircraft rocket projectiles were introduced which, for reasons of security, were referred to as 'unrotated projectiles' or UPs. The defences of Bristol included so-called Z batteries, which was the title given to units equipped with UP projectors (as the launchers

Figure 6.4: Doniford Camp with tented accommodation for pre-war summer exercises (courtesy Vernon Stone from a postcard by HH Hole).

were called). By October 1942 some of these Z sites were manned by the Home Guard and a practice camp for firing the rockets over a temporary range was set up at Redcliff Bay to the south-west of Portishead. The range safety area was a sector 14,000 yards (13km) long running parallel to the coast roughly from south-west of the launch site up to a height of 14,000 feet (4300m). A deployment report for the Bristol area Z sites dated 15 October 1942 lists 16 twin UP projectors deployed at Watchet, presumably for training purposes using the Doniford anti-aircraft range (John Penny, pers. comm.).

On 12 December 1942 a report lists six UP projectors deployed at Pawlett while ten remained at Watchet. The safety area of the bombing and air gunnery range at Steart would appear to have allowed UPs to have been fired into it from Pawlett. Vernon Stone, the current Harbour Master of Watchet, was told that the Watchet site was between the harbour and Helwell Bay and that firing had taken place on the site. RAF aerial photographs taken in 1946 show two parallel lines each of ten structures, similar to shelters used at other Z sites, in the Helwell Bay area which another local resident identified as the launcher site. The last report of UP projectors being located at either of these two sites was on 8 July 1943 (John Penny, pers. comm.).

Tank and anti-tank gunnery ranges

North Hill, Minehead had long been used by Volunteers and later by Territorials for annual camps and training. During the Second World War, the expanses of open moorland and the proximity of the sea were ideal conditions for a tank gunnery range. Range training needs to ensure that the tank crew can not only fire on targets while stationary but also when on the move. Targets may be fixed infrastructure like buildings or bunkers but are more likely to be other tanks on the move. The crew have to learn to make the best use of the terrain to move swiftly and to minimise their exposure to enemy observation and fire.

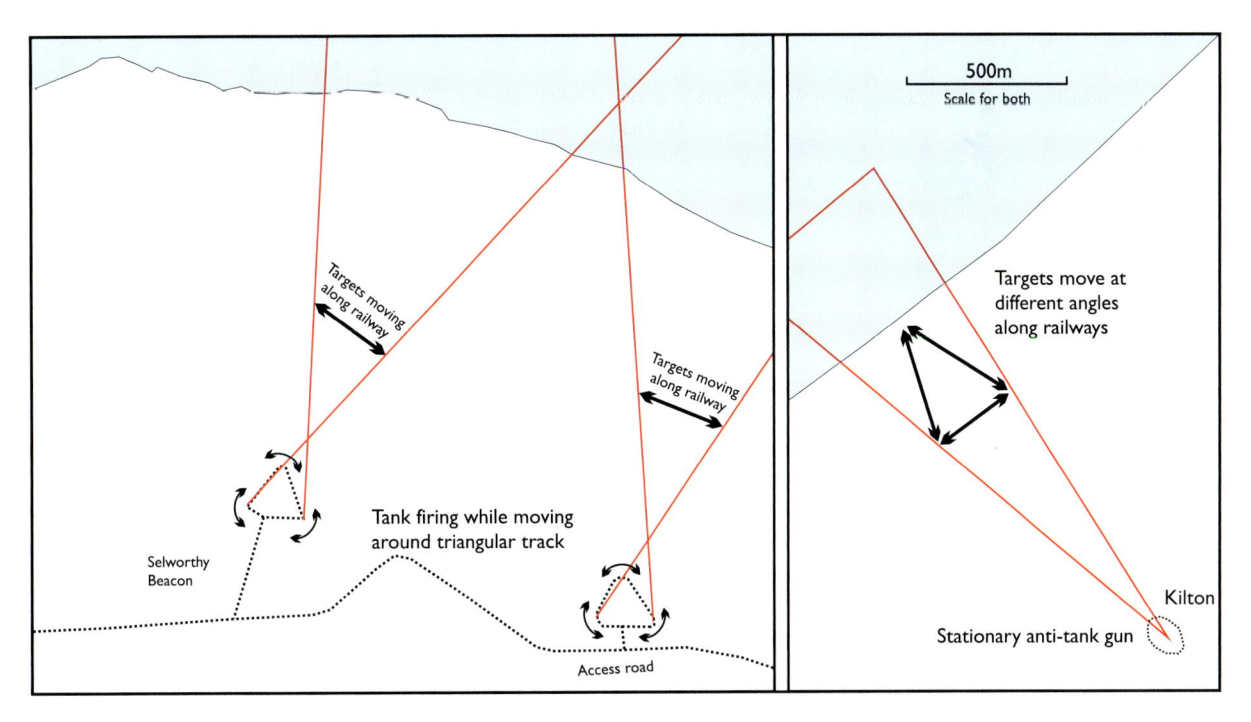

Figure 6.5: Comparison between the tank gunnery ranges at North Hill Minehead (two out of three shown) and the anti-tank range at Kilton. Both involved the use of target tanks pulled along railways protected by earth banks but at North Hill the firing tank was also moving.

To practice firing on the move against moving targets, ranges employed a triangular track some distance from a target moving along a small railway (Figure 6.5). The tank drove round the triangular track so that it was presented with targets which were advancing, withdrawing or crossing its path. Three of these ranges have survived on North Hill and a key feature of all of them is the use of the sea as the safety area. The range was used by American forces in the build-up to D-Day and a large area of Exmoor was also used for artillery field firing (TNA AIR 10/4182).

The increasing use of towed and self-propelled anti-tank guns required another form of gunnery range, an example of which is known at Kilton. As towed anti-tank guns cannot fire on the move and self-propelled guns are not normally equipped to do so, the gunnery training was restricted to firing from fixed positions on moving targets that typically might occur in a defensive position. The Kilton range consisted of a triangular target railway with winch houses which presented the guns with advancing, withdrawing and crossing targets from their static firing point. The range, which was built in 1942, was extensively used by US forces in preparation for D-Day (Figure 6.5; Riley 2006, 153-4).

In the autumn of 1940, 58 Medium Regiment Royal Artillery was moved to Dunster Camp (see page 77) to train gunners on the 6-pounder guns recovered from First World War tanks, which had been issued for use on stop lines in the South West. The beach offered excellent opportunities to fire out to sea, but most of the firing is likely to have been at targets within 600 yards (550m) as this was the practical limit placed on these guns. Nevertheless, the guns are believed to have a maximum range of over 8000 yards (7.5km) and the safety area would probably exceed that. The trained gunners were then deployed to man 6-pounder guns on stop lines. In 1941 the guns were withdrawn from the stop lines and were deployed to the beaches where they were manned by Home Guard or other soldiers (see Watchet defences on page 33).

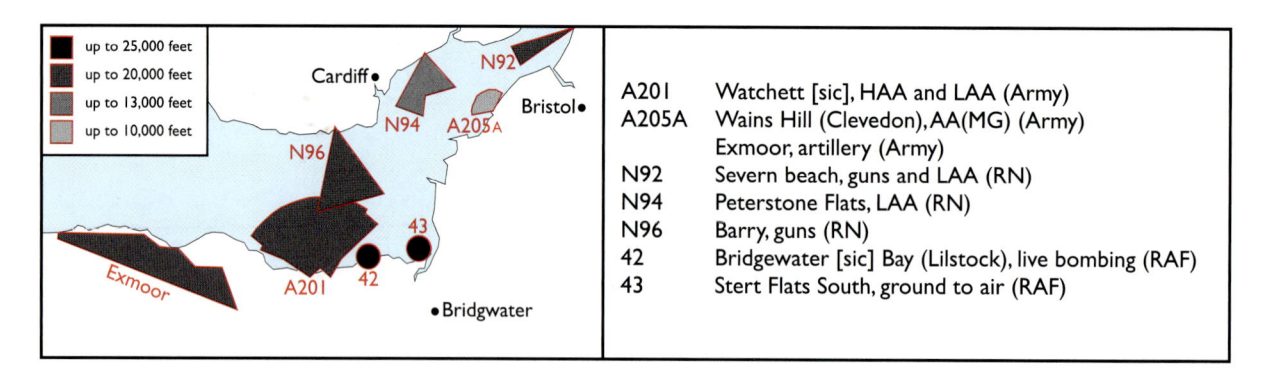

Figure 6.6: Firing ranges in Somerset and the Bristol Channel in May 1945 (TNA AIR 10/4182).

In November 1941, 954 Defence Battery of 11 Defence Regiment RA, which was then based at Brymore near Cannington, opened an anti-tank gunnery range at Stert Flats. Work appears to have started on this range on 11 August 1941 but no other details are known. The battery had been equipped previously with lorry-mounted 4-inch naval guns but these were returned to the Royal Navy and the battery then appears to have been equipped with towed anti-tank guns including 8-pdr QF Hotchkiss 6-cwt guns (TNA WO 166/2040). The regiment became 176 Field Regiment RA in January 1942.

Air gunnery and bombing ranges

During the Second World War there was an urgent need for bombing and air gunnery ranges. Across the UK, about 103 ranges were constructed in coastal areas with 108 on inland sites. These normally consisted of several bombing targets together with air-ground or air-sea targets. The demands of ranges for US Forces and for D-Day preparations resulted in a programme in 1943 to expand existing ranges. Local byelaws allowed farmers access to coastal land when the ranges were not in use to minimise the disruption to agriculture and red flags were flown when access was not permitted (Smith 1989, 187). As the majority of the Bristol Channel shipping moved along the swept lanes near to the Welsh coast, this allowed the use of the Somerset coastal area for both air gunnery and bombing practice ranges.

Lilstock range

A wartime bombing range was established in the sea to the north of Lilstock. In 1945 it was known as 'RAF Bombing Range 42 Bridgwater Bay' and came under Technical Training Command but was parented by RAF Weston Zoyland (Roger JC Thomas pers. comm. quoting TNA AIR 10/4182). Later RNAS Yeovilton assumed responsibility and it became known as the 'Lilstock Royal Navy Range'. It was used as a practice bombing range for fixed-wing aircraft using inert ordnance until 1995 when it was redesignated as a helicopter gunnery range. Wartime Admiralty charts show a group of some three targets about 250m apart at about ST 176 472 to the north of Lilstock. One appears to have been a raft and moored target floats were to be seen on occasions in Watchet harbour.

A large concrete arrow (SHER 22854) on the cliff top, visible on post-war aerial photographs (Figure 6.7 on the facing page), was used to indicate the target area to approaching aircraft. Another large arrow on Brean Down (SHER 12365) also points towards the targets, although Crowther and Dickson (2008, 262–63) list Brean as a separate range; to date, no evidence to support this has been found.

Bombing ranges had two or more 'quadrant towers' of a standard pattern overlooking the target area. These were equipped for observers to take cross bearings and accurately locate the point of impact of the practice bombs and then to radio the results to the aircraft. There is a single modern quadrant tower, which looks similar to an airfield control tower, on the shore overlooking the range (SHER 15476); the sites of earlier ones are recorded (SHER).

Stert Range

Another bombing and air gunnery range was established on Stert Flats with a single targets at ST 260 476 and three more at ST 245 470. Stert was designated 'RAF Bombing Range 43'. Two concrete arrows at Steart (PRN 34598) pointed out onto the range but not towards these war-time targets. A second range (Range 46 – Stert Flats South) with ground to air facilities is listed under Bomber Command but was administered by RAF Weston-super-Mare (TNA AIR 10/4182). The Defence Estates still list the 'Stert Flats Air Gunnery and Bombing Range' and even today (2009) aircraft can be seen circling over the ranges and firing anti heat-seeking-missile flares in preparation for operations in Afghanistan.

Sand Bay and Sand Point ranges

Sand Bay to the north of Weston-super-Mare was also used as an air gunnery range (Smith 1989, 195). In addition, Sand Point was also used as a range with four steel targets. Red warning cones were hoisted to indicate when firing was taking place (Hawkins 1988, 114).

Experimental sites

Birnbeck Pier and associated sites

The acquisition of Birnbeck Pier in 1941 as an outstation of the Royal Navy's Department of Miscellaneous Weapons Development (DMWD, nicknamed the Wheezers and Dodgers) has been mentioned above. It had two great advantages. It met an immediate need to find a location where the spread and fuzing of what was to become the highly effective forward firing anti-submarine mortar, 'Hedgehog', could be perfected. For this a good depth of water was required but one

Figure 6.7: *Direction arrow on the cliffs above Lilstock for the off-shore aircraft bombing range (Somerset Studies Library, RAF CPE/UK/1944 3165, 23/1/1947).*

whose bed was exposed at low water to allow for the spread of bombs to be plotted and the bombs themselves retrieved. The steamer pier at Birnbeck with its tidal range of between 19 and 36 feet (5.8–11m), collection of useful workshops and secluded position was ideal (Figure 6.8 on the next page).

Not only did the pier prove to be an effective base but there were further sites near at hand in Brean Down and Middle Hope Cove where some of the more demonstrative experiments could be held in comparative safety and security (Pawle 2009, 118–19, 141–14). The DMWD was initially primarily concerned with air defence measures for shipping, such as the development of Plastic Protective Plating (see page 54), but the majority of the work at Birnbeck was concerned with anti-submarine warfare and, later, measures in support of the D-Day landings.

From its first trials in February 1941, Hedgehog completed its land and sea trails within a year and HMS *Westcott* scored one of the first kills, U-581, on 2 February 1942 (Brown 2007, 118). The 'Expendable Noise-Maker', a device intended to confuse German acoustic-homing torpedoes, proved to be one of the more demonstrative experiments and tests were moved to Brean Down and Middle

Figure 6.8: Birnbeck Pier and Birnbeck Island with the steamer landing stage on the right and lifeboat launching ramp left. Steep Holm and Flat Holm are visible in the distance (David Hunt, 2009).

Hope Cove after a round exploded just outside Admiral Casement's office (Pawle 2009, 144–45). Trials were also carried out in the Bristol Channel of more effective illuminating flares to expose surfaced U-boats at night. Flares suspended from balloons were evaluated by observation and measurement from the pier (Pawle 2009, 157–58).

Tests of the 'Type J Parachute and Cable Rocket' (PAC), which carried a 5-ton cable up to a height of 600 feet (180m), a device that DMWD had developed to bring down enemy aircraft, were carried out in a desolate area of the Somerset coast. This is not named but the associations of DMWD with the barrage balloon cable cutting trials at Pawlett (see page 89) make this a possible site. Birnbeck was also equipped with PAC as it was hoped that bomber raids making for Bristol Channel ports might give an opportunity for live testing but the chance never occurred. The War Office asked DMWD to carry out tests to see if a cable-fired rocket could stop enemy tanks. Tests were carried out on the foreshore at Brean Down against a Valentine tank using 600 feet (180m) of exceptionally strong wire. This ensnared the tank so effectively that it took two days to get it mobile again but the system does not seem to have been developed and brought into service (Pawle 2009, 145–46).

In preparation for D-Day, DMWD embarked on a wide ranging series of experiments. Exhaustive tests were carried out with shaped charges on the concrete-filled hulk of the steamer, *Fernwood*, sunk off Weston-super-Mare, to find ways of disposing of wrecked ships used to block harbours (Pawle 2009, 148). In the autumn of 1942, work

Figure 6.9: *Surviving rails for the experimental bouncing bomb at the tip of Brean Down. Beyond them stands the remains of a Coast Artillery searchlight like that shown in Figure 4.5 on page 54 (David Dawson, 2010).*

started on a device called 'Hedgerow' which was designed to fire salvoes of mortar bombs from a landing craft to clear beaches of mines. Initial tests were carried out on Berrow Flats using German Teller mines lifted from the Western Desert. The system was first used in earnest at Salerno (Pawle 2009, 145–49).

Retarding rockets, designed to enable airdropped vehicles to land softly after parachute descent, were also tested. The system, known as 'Hajile' (Elijah reversed), was used at Birnbeck to test drop concrete bombs but was not sufficiently developed to play any role in D-Day (Pawle 2009, 174). 'Bookrest' was another beach minefield clearing device: a hose filled with plastic explosive (Pawle 2009, 260–61). A system to break up waves in heavy seas using pipes with air jets as a 'bubble breakwater' underwent some initial trials at Birnbeck but the device failed as the air compressors lacked the power and capacity to deliver sufficient air. The idea was superseded by the development of components for the 'Mulberry' harbour (Pawle 2009, 240–45).

Other experiments at Brean Down included a stores-carrying rocket designed to deliver supplies to troops ashore and a rocket grapnel designed to fire a 500-foot (150m) climbing line from the beach onto cliff tops. The major trials for this took place at Portland Bill and the system was developed and used successfully on D-Day by the US Rangers for their assault on the battery that was believed to be armed at Pointe du Hoc three miles (5km) to the west of Omaha Beach (Pawle 2009, 262). PLUTO (PipeLine Under The Ocean), which was to be vital for the supply and maintenance of the allied forces landing in Normandy, underwent initial pipelaying trials run by the staff at Birnbeck in the Bristol Channel. Birnbeck also successfully developed a long tube called 'Helter Skelter' for the Army to allow rapid disembarkation of troops from ships into landing craft. Initial tests were carried out from the side of Birnbeck Pier (Pawle 2009, 279).

DMWD were involved in the design and testing of the 'Dam Busters' bomb, the brainchild of Barnes Wallis, but this took place at Chesil Beach not in the Bristol Channel. However, tests were made using the same technique but with a rocket-propelled explosive ball to be fired horizontally from a motor torpedo boat and sent bouncing over the sea to the target and hopefully over any torpedo net defences. Initial test were carried out at Birnbeck but were transferred to Brean Down for safety and security reasons. Remains of the rails still exist at the west end of the promontory (Figure 6.9 on the preceding page). The trials were then moved to Middle Hope Cove where the beach allowed the missiles to be recovered after firing, Sea trials were carried out using an old barge called *Mary* but development never reached fruition. Other trials were also carried out on a flying-saucer bomb designed by a Norwegian (Pawle 2009, 151-54).

DMWD carried out a number of experiments at the Combined Operations Experimental Establishment (COXE) at Appledore to find ways of enabling tanks to breach the anti-tank walls that were being constructed on some potential invasion beaches. This element of the 'Atlantic Wall' was believed to be 10 feet (3m) high and 7 feet (2m) thick. The 'Great Panjandrum' was a device intended to carry a load of nearly two tons of explosives from a landing craft across a beach and place the explosives against the wall. It consisted of two 10-foot (3m) diameter wheels with 1-foot (30cm) wide rims and the explosives were carried on the axle between them. The device was propelled by rockets attached to the rim of the wheels in a similar manner to a Catherine-wheel firework, which it was hoped would propel the Panjandrum forward at speeds of up to 60 mph (95 kph).

In September 1943 unsuccessful trials were carried out at Westward Ho! and later at Instow. Two modified Panjandrums were then moved to Lilstock beach for further trials, which were supported by the Bridgwater Home Guard battalion which was responsible for that part of the coastline. A number of important observers were at the trial but both Panjandrums toppled over on the beach and remained motionless until their rocket motors burnt out. The final trials at Westward Ho! in January 1944 were spectacularly unsuccessful and the project was abandoned (Wilson 2005, 204; Pawle 2009, 221–28). It can only be speculated why these preparations were made when there were no walls of this type in the selected invasion area in Normandy. It has been suggested that the trials may have been part of the deception plan to make the Germans believe the invasion was to be elsewhere.

DMWD left Birnbeck and its on-going work was taken over by other departments until it was paid off in January 1946 but Middle Hope Cove to the north-west of Sand Bay was still in use in 1988 for Admiralty tests of underwater devices (Warlow 2000, 25). Crowther and Dickson (2008, 236) mention that the site at St Thomas's Head on Middle Hope continues to be in military use and is now operated by QinetiQ as an explosives and shock-test facility.

Tank mud trials

The Fighting Vehicle Proving Establishment carried out 'mud trials' in Somerset in March 1945 at Bristol and Clevedon. The aim of these trials was to investigate means of improving the ability of Cromwell and Sherman tanks to negotiate soils of low bearing capacity. Considerable difficulties were experienced when searching for a suitable site in the UK but eventually trials on 'sinkage' were carried out at St George's Wharf in Bristol and 'traction' trials at Kingston Seymour near Clevedon (TNA WO 194/853).

Figure 6.10: The barrage balloon hanger built at Pawlett to hold an inflated balloon for use in experimental work (David Hunt, 2009).

Pawlett experimental establishment and balloon tests

Pawlett Hams on the lower reaches of the Parrett, where the river swings in wide meanders across the low land was a lonely area and well suited to secret experiments. These were run by the Royal Aircraft Establishment, Farnborough (RAE). The initial trials were to test the breaking strain of German barrage balloon cable and to compare them with British balloon cables. The tests were carried out by aircraft with strengthened wing edges flying into the cables. The aircraft were initially based at RAF Exeter but were later moved to RAF Churchstanton on the Blackdown Hills. Other experiments included testing aircraft fitted with strengthened wings or cutters to attempt to cut or deflect German balloon cables. Experiments to test the concept of aerial minefields included suspending 'paint bombs' from a balloon. A barrage balloon was stationed at Pawlett and a balloon hangar (SHER 10688) constructed to house it. This avoided the need for a balloon crew to be constantly present to turn the close-hauled balloon into the wind or for the balloon to be deflated and re-inflated for each experiment. The hanger, which measures 100 x 70 x 80 feet high (30 x 21 x 24m), was erected in 1940-41 and still survives (Figure 6.10). An adjacent camp was constructed to accommodate personnel and provide administrative facilities (SHER 12722).

Pawlett ranges

It is claimed by ex-workers that the range on Pawlett Hams, to the east of the balloon hanger was used for the initial trials of the first 500lb and 1000lb (227 and 454kg) bombs. Other trials included the dispersion of incendiary bombs; local inhabitants tell of workers being sent over the Hams to find and extract dummy incendiary bombs and record their positions. This is said to have been in preparation for the bomber raids on Dresden. A pyramidal brick structure about 15 feet (4.5m) high was built as a target or aiming mark, which survived until it was removed in about 2000 (SHER 18121). In 1945 Pawlett Range was used for aerodynamic trials of models falling at supersonic speeds, the behaviour of which was monitored by radar and telemetry stations, possibly at Alstone to the south-east of Highbridge (see page 92). The range was closed later in 1945, forcing the experiments to move elsewhere (Kell 1955, 2).

Aircraft Torpedo Development Unit

Between March 1944 and 1949, a detachment from the Aircraft Torpedo Development Unit (ATDU) was moved from RAF Weston Zoyland to Weston-super-Mare aerodrome. The ATDU was responsible for testing air-launched torpedoes and developing their operational use. The air ranges in the Bristol Channel were used with Beaufighters and Swordfish dropping torpedoes which were filmed from chaser aircraft. Later trials used Tempest and Mosquito aircraft (Berryman 2006, 139–42).

Dunster Beach rocket tests

Secret trials of rocket projectiles are said to have been made on Dunster Beach in 1942 or 1943. These appear to have been launched from frames and possibly used a volatile fuel propellant (Concannon 1995, 48). To date no other information of these trials has been found although 58 Chemical Warfare (CW) Company Royal Engineers (RE) was based in Porlock in March 1941 and 3 Group CW RE moved into Dunster Beach Camp with 68, 69, 70 and 75 CW Companies on 25 April 1941 before moving to Kent on 16 July 1941. While at Dunster several 'projector' and '5-inch rocket shoots' were carried out by day and night. It is not known whether the shoots took place on the coastline or on Exmoor. The primary role of the group at this time was Southern Command CW Reserve (TNA WO 166/1317; WO 166/3432).

Rocket trials, for chemical-weapon delivery, were also carried out on a range on Brendon Common (Devon) with a temporary hutted camp to the north at Slocomslade (Devon) to accommodate the troops (ENPA 2007).

Smoke screen trials

On 11 November 1943, 810 Smoke Company of the Pioneer Corps moved from Avonmouth to a new training camp at Clevedon where four sections trained on the American Esso Smoke Generators. On 15 November two sections were sent to Brean for smoke trials and were accommodated at the Brean Holiday Camp. Ten days later the detachment returned to Clevedon before moving on 4 December to another training area at Denton near Newhaven in Sussex (John Penny, pers. comm.).

Before D-Day the 79 Chemical Smoke Generating Company of the US Army was deployed at Avonmouth (see page 76) and on 29 February a trial was carried out using 24 Esso Smoke Generators deployed at 100 yard (91m) spacing. The screen was ignited and burnt for an hour as a daylight observation exercise. It was overflown by an Anson from Whitchurch which reported that the screen was 'entirely satisfactory' although it could have been improved with more generators, more closely spaced, and sited slightly further away. A night test was also carried out on 8 March (John Penny, pers. comm.).

Wireless stations

The propagation of radio waves in the medium and high frequency bands is significantly better over sea water or damp soil and it is worse over dry land and desert. There are therefore technical advantages in siting such wireless stations near to the coast on flat damp land and hence a number of important wireless facilities were established along the Somerset coastline. The BBC broadcast transmitters at Clevedon and Washford have already been mentioned (on page 73). The following are further examples.

Post Office maritime radio stations

In 1920 the need for transmitting and receiving telegraph messages from ships up to 2000 miles (3200km) from the UK resulted in the GPO taking over an Army low frequency transmitter and receiver station at Devizes. The new service was a success and a new transmitter site at Portishead with its associated receivers some 25 miles (40km) away at Burnham-on-Sea was opened to meet demand. This splitting of the transmitters and receivers minimised the interference between the powerful outgoing signal transmissions and the weak signals being received and allowed simultaneous transmission and reception on all channels. The two sites were collectively known as 'Portishead Radio' although the operation and traffic handling was carried out from Burnham-on-Sea with remote control of the transmitters. The first high frequency transmitters and receivers were installed in 1926 and by 1939, 15 receivers at Burnham-on-Sea and 6 transmitters at Portishead were handling 3½ million words per year.

During the war, the threat of German direction-finding locating the positions of ships through their transmissions or establishing their destinations meant that two-way communications with ships was too dangerous and messages had to be broadcast to ships without any acknowledgement of receipt. Variations in radio propagation conditions often meant that direct calls to ships had to be made over a long period and repeated through the day and night to maximise the chances of the message being received. The Commonwealth Area System was set up with eight areas, each with a transmitting and receiving station, giving better coverage to ships in that area, compared with direct transmissions from the UK. The area stations were all interconnected through an Admiralty point-to-point wireless network.

A listening watch for distress calls and enemy-sighting reports from ships attacked by surface raiders or submarines was constantly maintained. These reports were critical for naval intelligence to locate and track the positions of submarines and surface raiders. The station also received clandestine signals from Europe and reports from the north Africa landings. A special aircraft section was established to maintain communications with maritime patrol aircraft in the north Atlantic. GPO staff from Burnham-on-Sea were also seconded to operate radio stations for other government services and radio officers were also trained to work in merchant ships in naval convoys. In 1943 the GPO staff at Burnham-on-Sea was reinforced by a Royal Navy officer and 18 telegraphists from the Naval Shore Wireless Station (HMS *Flowerdown*) near Winchester.

After the war the stations returned to commercial activities and the demand for long range communications increased vastly. The Area Scheme introduced during the war was so successful that it was adopted for all British and Commonwealth registered vessels allowing them to use naval stations around the world to relay their traffic to Portishead, however, direct calling was still used for foreign ships. In 1948 Burnham-on-Sea radio station was re-equipped and reconstructed but the advent of satellite communications reduced the need for high-frequency telegraphy (Morse) communications. The aerials were removed from Burnham-on-Sea in 1983 and the receiver service was transferred about 17 miles (27km) away to Somerton. The station eventually closed on Sunday 30 April 2000 after 80 years service. It was one of the largest communications centres in the world with 340 people were employed using both wireless telegraphy (Morse) and radiotelephones for many decades (GPO 1959; British Telecommunications 2001).

Somerset and the Defence of the Bristol Channel

Figure 6.11: RAF DF (direction finding) sites at Alstone (Somerset Studies Library, RAF CPE/UK/1924 1010, 16/1/1947).

Direction finding stations

The Radio Security Service (RSS) was established before the Second World War to monitor illicit transmissions from spies or enemy agents within Britain and to establish the locations of their transmitters. It was run by the GPO on behalf of MI5. One important initial task was to search for German navigation beacons that were (wrongly) believed to have been established in Britain. The Meacon RCM described above (on page 72) and used against German bombers was originally designed by the GPO to counter this threat. As the Germans had not successfully managed to establish a spy network in Britain, the RSS stations became increasingly involved in receiving German Secret Service traffic signals to their spies and agents in occupied Europe. Most of them were taken over by MI6 and they became an important source of intelligence for Bletchley Park. The Stockland Bristol site consisted of two direction finding (DF) stations about 300m apart, which appear to have been operated separately. Each DF station had four aerial masts set in a square with the receiver hut in the centre.

One site, 'Stockland SL' (SHER 27744) was associated with the RSS DF stations at Weatherthorpe SL in north Yorkshire, Wymondham SL in Norfolk and St Erth SL in Cornwall. The other station, to the north-west, was called Stockland A (SHER 27745) and was associated with DF stations called Sandridge A in Hertfordshire and St Erth A in Cornwall (Stan Ames pers. comm.; TNA HW 41/401). Another RAF DF station is listed at Highbridge and the grid reference indicates that it was located on the flat ground to the east of Alstone (Figure 6.11) but was listed as 'not yet operational' in 1944 (TNA HW 41/1401). The 1948 RAF air photos show at least three DF aerial sites, the largest one of which appears to have

Figure 6.12: The remains of some of the steel fixings to the rocks on the beach at the foot of the cliffs of Brean Down (Somerset County Council HER, 1995).

been a 'Marconi Adcock aerial' for working to aircraft on wavelengths of 600 to 1000m. This site consisted of four 75-foot or 100-foot (23 or 30m) masts set out north, south, east and west with a central receiver hut forming a square with a 200-foot (60m) diagonal. Four concrete anchors are visible to support each mast. Two adjacent sites have the same diamond pattern and orientation but are smaller and therefore appear to be DF stations working at higher frequencies (SHER 17888).

From 1937 the RAF ran a Medium Frequency Direction Finding (MFDF) Organisation which provided two aircraft navigation services: a Direction Finding Security Service and an Identification Service. The Security Service provided aids in the form of bearings and fixes of aircraft in flight, particularly when beyond British shores, from two or more Direction Finding (DF) stations while the Identification Service established the location and identity of friendly aircraft returning to the British Isles. These services were run from 12 separate DF sections each with two or more DF receiver stations and a medium wave transmitter. The last was used for communicating with aircraft and for passing bearings and control messages to other DF stations if landlines were unavailable (Air Historical Branch 1950b, 306). When returning to the UK, bomber and coastal aircraft made a short manual wireless transmission when they were about 100 miles (160km) from the coast to establish their identity and fix their position.

The pilots of fighter aircraft did not have time to make a manual transmission so fighters were fitted with a device called 'Pipsqueak' to automatically transmit on high-frequency radio. Later on fighters were fitted with Identification Friend or Foe (IFF, see page 66). Within Britain each Fighter Command Group had DF stations to track fighters, which continued to be developed and used to good effect throughout the war (Air Ministry 1952, 71).

On-going research suggests that the site at Alstone (SHER 17888) may have been used for MFDF purposes and it appears to have been used into the Cold War as masts are visible on 1958 air photographs but had gone by 1960.

Coastal aerodromes

In 1939 the RAF contracted flying training at Weston-super-Mare to a civilian flying school run by Straight Corporation, the owners of Weston Airport. The school was named No 39 Elementary and Reserve Flying Training School. On the outbreak of war the flying training was moved to other sites and Straight Corporation were contracted to run No 5 Civil Air Navigation School to train RAF navigators. The Bristol Channel provided an ideal training area, well away from interference from enemy aircraft. On 1 November 1939, the RAF took control of the school which was redesignated as 5 Air Observer and Navigation School but in August 1940, the school was transferred to Oudtshoorn in South Africa (Berryman 2006, 132). As mentioned on page 80, a small airstrip on the coast at Doniford was established in the 1920s for use by the target towing aircraft from RAF Weston Zoyland serving the Doniford AA ranges (Ashworth 1990, 259).

Barrage balloon gas

The hydrogen gas for balloons in the Southern Barrages (Eastleigh, Southampton, Portsmouth and Gosport) and the Western Barrages (Bristol, Avonmouth, Plymouth and Cardiff) was manufactured at the Imperial Chemical Industries (ICI) plant at Weston-super-Mare gas works. The gas was delivered compressed into cylinders each containing 575 cubic feet (175m^3) of gas at a pressure of 200 atmospheres (61 kPa). The standard LZ (Low Zone) balloon used throughout the war needed some 30 cylinders of gas to supply the 19,000 cubic feet (5800m^3) required to inflate it and about two cylinders a day to keep it topped up. The LZ balloon was flown from a mobile winch and was designed for a maximum altitude of 5000 feet (1500m) (John Penny, pers. comm.).

Conclusion

A surprising number and wide range of military activities took place on or near the Somerset coastline, many unrelated to the defence of the Bristol Channel ports, or of Bristol as a manufacturing centre, or of the Somerset coast. Some of the experimental work was of great significance, particularly in the Battle of the Atlantic. While archaeological remains survive at some sites, many activities appear to have left no discernable traces and often the exact sites involved cannot be located with accuracy.

Equally there are some surviving remains whose purpose is unclear. An example is the series of iron and concrete structures set into the rocks at the foot of the cliffs near the high water mark on the beach on the south side of Brean Down (Figure 6.12 on the preceding page). They appear to be evidence of Second World War activity (although they could be earlier or later) but so far no documentary evidence or local inhabitants with knowledge of the site has been discovered. Rather than risking new theories which might so easily become adopted as the truth and refined far beyond what the very limited evidence will sustain, the authors have avoided guessing their nature and purpose. All these sites form part of the archaeology and history of the Somerset coastline and deserve full record and further research.

Chapter 7

Conclusion

IT MAY BE thought that there must be little more to add on the subject of the Second World War. By concentrating on the theme of maritime Somerset and its part in the war, it has been a constant surprise and pleasure at the ways in which the evidence has delivered a different perspective from that presented in other forms of study. The national imperatives – keeping the sea lanes open for vital imports of food, fuel and military supplies and cash earning exports, keeping the nation safe from invasion and retaining the ability to project and supply military expeditions to other theatres of war – apply throughout the war and apply to the role of Somerset.

In arriving at the conclusions presented here, evidence from a far wider range of sources has been used than will be evident from the references given. Surviving archaeological and documentary evidence is far from complete but further work will undoubtedly uncover more. Time has also moved beyond the range of much reliable anecdote and personal memory, so much so, as is noted in the introduction, that memories, for example at Watchet of HMS *Iliad*, have been overlaid by later activity associated with the Doniford and Lilstock ranges and at Minehead have become unconsciously distorted in the retelling. In particular, it is no longer possible to engage with those of middling rank in all three services who were involved in decision-making at a regional level. Even the detailed topography of stretches of the Somerset coastline has changed in the last 60 years, sometimes quite dramatically. For example, the breach in the shingle bar between Porlock and Bossington has flooded the area behind, and substantial coastal erosion between Dunster Beach and Blue Anchor Bay has destroyed some defences and threatens to overwhelm surviving structures. However, where possible all sources of evidence have been compared, including evaluation of air photos, and overall findings have been tempered with military experience and judgement.

Much of the fascinating and much more complex detail that has emerged from such an approach will have to await further publication. This applies for example to the perceived threat of invasion in West Somerset where archaeological evidence not only confirms the documentary sources but clearly indicates that the ways in which the threat was met were much less simple that might otherwise be thought. It was said that: 'If there are three courses of action open to an enemy, he will choose the fourth!' The impossibility of deciding what the threat was, where and when it might materialise and what its objectives might be made the task of planning defences exceptionally challenging.

Most people seeing pillboxes along the beach assume that they were built to meet a seaborne invasion yet the documentary evidence clearly shows that the main perceived threat was troop-carrying aircraft landing on the beaches, or on the high ground behind them, and even off-loading light air-portable tanks. No matter how improbable the airborne threat appears today and how deep ideas of a seaborne invasion have become embedded in communal consciousness, the evidence for the perception of the airborne threat in 1940 is firm.

Post-war access to German plans for invasion shows us how wrong the British planners were but contemporary documentary evidence shows that these threats were not dreamt up locally but formed part of the national strategy and were, ordered, resourced and controlled through the Field Army chain of command. In retrospect it should be understood that no one could know (nor if they had would they have been believed) that the Germans had no plan of invasion prepared in June 1940 and later when the German command had started implementing plans for the seaborne invasion of south-east England (Operation Sea Lion) that this was effectively their only plan. The enemy had shown great flair and success in delivering the *coups de main* that felled Czechoslovakia, Poland, Denmark, Norway, the low countries and France, and later Greece and Crete. Steps had to be taken to apply that experience. Rearming the Severn defences to counter an invasion force spearheaded by heavy warships based on Brest, taking measures to contain airborne landings on Exmoor and elsewhere in the South West and even having half an eye on the three hundred year old threat from an enemy based in France – the invasion of Ireland as a step to defeating Great Britain – all were sensible considerations that demanded planning and resources.

Standing back from the detail it can be seen that Somerset made a surprisingly important contribution to the maritime activities that led to victory in the Second World War. The county lent to the war effort modest but important port facilities especially the Port of Bristol Authority's dock at Portishead. Somerset boats and crews served in the Bristol Channel and wherever in the world they were sent or taken. On land, the southern flank of the Bristol Channel along the Somerset coast was defended against both airborne and seaborne invasion, which could have halted all maritime activities and threatened the major port facilities at Bristol and Avonmouth. Within the county of Somerset and the neighbouring counties, the air defence system minimised the threats of enemy air reconnaissance and destruction of ships, ports and installations. It was a system that underwent rapid technological change and became more sophisticated and dependent on what are now called electronic warfare measures. Enemy aircraft on reconnaissance, bombing, anti-shipping or mine-laying missions were harassed and attacked, while the warning systems ensured that essential work suffered the minimum interruption. Along the Somerset coastline the military were able to train effectively and carry out firing exercises with anti-aircraft guns, artillery, tanks and anti-tank weapons and small arms while air gunnery and bombing ranges were used extensively by the RAF and Fleet Air Arm.

Important experimental work could also be carried out in a relatively safe and secure environment, in particular the design and testing work of the Royal Naval Department of Miscellaneous Weapons Development at HMS *Birnbeck* in producing effective solutions in anti-submarine warfare and in support of the Allied invasion of mainland Europe. There were also important communications facilities particularly the GPO maritime radio stations at Portishead and Burnham-on-Sea, while along the Somerset coast local men and women served in the Home Guard, Observer Corps, Coastguards, Royal Naval Auxiliary Patrol, and Civil Defence. Larger numbers of other uniformed men and women from across the UK and wider afield also served in Somerset and carried out their duty to King and Country.

Sources

The National Archives

All of the following should be prefixed 'The National Archives (TNA): Public Record Office (PRO)' to produce a full citation.

AIR 2/2685. Radar and Radio Counter Measures: RDF stations, siting. 1937–40.

AIR 10/4182. Map with list appended showing notifiable firing ranges in the United Kingdom, May 1945.

AIR 41/46. No 80 Wing Royal Air Force Historical Report 1940–1945. 1946.

AVIA 7/256. Royal Radar Establishment: Extension of RDF chain. 1938–40.

AVIA 7/1427. Operational GCI station Huntspill: installation. 1941–42.

HW 41/401. Government Code and Cypher School: Lists and locations of Y stations. Oct 1941–Aug 1945.

WO 33/1708. War Office: Location and frequencies of GL and CD/CHL sets in Great Britain. 1942.

WO 166/11. General Headquarters: Royal Artillery, coast defence (RA CD). Nov 1939–Dec 1941.

WO 166/57. HQ Southern Command war-diary: General Staff. Jul–Dec 1940.

WO 166/298. HQ VIII Corps war-diary: General Staff. Aug 1940–Dec 1941.

WO 166/299. HQ VIII Corps war-diary: Adjudent and Quartermaster. July 1940–Dec 1941.

WO 166/303. HQ VIII Corps war-diary: Commander Medium Artillery. July 1940–Feb 1941.

WO 166/1243. HQ Southern Command war-diary. Oct 1940–Mar 1941.

WO 166/1251. HQ Western Area war-diary. Dec 1940–Dec 1941.

WO 166/1252. HQ South Western Area war-diary. Aug 1939–Jan 1941.

WO 166/1266. HQ Bristol Sub Area war-diary. Jan–Dec 1941.

WO 166/1275. HQ North Devonshre Sub Area war-diary. Jul 1940–Dec 1941.

WO 166/1314. HQ Severn Sub Area war-diary. Dec 1940–Dec 1941.

WO 166/1317. Somerset Sub Area war-diary. Jul 1940–Jun 1941

WO 166/1757. 20 Coast Group/558 Coast Regiment war-diary. Nov 1940–Dec 1941.

WO 166/1842. 365 Coast Battery war-diary. Jun–Aug 1940, Feb–Sep 1941.

WO 166/1862. 400 Coast Battery war-diary. Dec 1940–Mar 1941.

WO 166/1924. 58 Medium Regiment, Royal Artillery war-diary Aug–Dec 1939, June 1940–Nov 1941.

WO 166/2038. 952 Defence Battery (Mobile) war-diary. Sept 1940–Jan 1942.

WO 166/2040. 954 Defence Battery (Mobile) war-diary, Jan–Nov 1941, Jan 1942.

WO 166/2060. Plymouth Fixed Defences war-diary. Aug 1939–Jan 1942.

WO 166/2076. HQ Anti-Aircraft Command war-diary: General Staff. Nov–Dec 1940.

WO 166/3292. 447 Searchlight Battery war-diary. Aug 1939–Apr 1941.

WO 166/3432. 3 Chemical Warfare Group war-diary. Sept 1940–Dec 1941.

WO 166/3937. 930 Port Construction and Repair Company war-diary. Mar–Dec 1941.

WO 166/4660. 9 Somerset Light Infantry (Prince Albert's) war-diary, Jul 1940–Dec 1941.

WO 166/4661. 10 Somerset Light Infantry (Prince Albert's) war-diary, Oct 1940–Dec 1941.

WO 166/6114. HQ VIII Corps war-diary: General Staff. Jan–Dec 1942.

WO 166/6775. HQ South Somerset Sub Area war-diary. Jan–Dec 1942

WO 166/7178. 558 Coast Regiment war-diary. Jan–Dec 1942.

WO 166/7881. 540 Searchlight Battery war-diary. Jan–Oct 1942.

WO 166/10824. HQ Somerset and Bristol Area war-diary. Jan–Apr 1943.

WO 166/10904. HQ South Western District war-diary. Jan 1940–Dec 1943.

WO 166/11001. Somerset Sub District war-diary. May–Dec 1943.

WO 192/155. Flatholm, Bristol Channel 1737–1944 fort record book. 1895–1944.

WO 192/316. Cardiff, south Wales Lavernock Battery fort record book. 1916–1956.

WO 192/317. Cardiff, south Wales Lavernock Battery (1901–1955) fort record book. 1918–1955.

WO 194/853. Committee on Mud Crossing Performance of Tracked Armoured Fighting Vehicles (AFVs) – CMCP: Comparative trials on Somerset coastal sites, various AFV tracks in soft ground conditions (Part 1 – Final). Jan–Dec 1945.

WO 199/92. HQ Home Forces, beach defence, coast watching: enemy agents landing on coast. Apr 1941–Jun 1944.

WO 199/392. HQ Home Forces, communications. Jul 1940–Aug 1944.

WO 199/523. HQ Home Forces, formation of coast batteries. Jun 1940–Aug 1941.

WO 199/544. HQ Home Forces, civil liaison: Keeps and fortified villages, nodal points and anti-tank islands. Sep 1940–October 1942.

WO 199/1110. Home Forces Coast Defence Committee Minutes. Jan–Dec 1941.

WO 199/1111. Home Forces Coast Defence Committee Minutes Jan–Nov 1942.

WO 199/1624. HQ Southern Command: Beaches, suitability for tank or other landings: VIII Corps. 1941.

WO 199/1638. HQ Southern Command: Coastal defence. Jul 1940–Mar 1942.

WO 199/1779. HQ Southern Command: Pillboxes, suitability in defence. Jul 1940–Sep 1944.

WO 199/1803. HQ Southern Command. Works Services: Progress report, Taunton line. Jul–Nov 1940.

WO 199/1812. HQ Southern Command. Works Services: Matters connected with defensive works. Aug 1940–May 1941.

WO 208/2969. Notes on the German preparations for Invasion of the United Kingdom (second edition). Jan 1942.

WO 227/51. Royal Engineers Camouflage Development and Training Centre. Appendix D: 1st degree concealment of a supply depot illustrating a housing scheme (Supply Research [sic] Depot, Taunton, Somerset). Jan–Dec 1944.

WO 291/14. Air Defence Research Development Establishment: Analysis of readings taken at GL mk II trials at Watchet. 1941.

Somerset Record Office

C/S/5/3. Somerset County Surveyor, war measures: Plans for road blocks and map showing positions. 1940.

Bibliography

Addison, P and Crang, J A (eds). 2010. *Listening to Britain: Home Intelligence Reports on Britain's Finest Hour, May-September 1940*. London: Bodley Head.

Air Historical Branch. 1950a. *The Second World War 1939–1945. Royal Air Force Signals: Vol IV, Radar in Raid Reporting*. London: Air Ministry. Reprinted by Military Library Research Ltd, 2 vols, 2008. Original available in TNA AIR 10/5519.

Air Historical Branch. 1950b. *The Second World War 1939–1945. Royal Air Force Signals: Vol VII, Radio Counter Measures*. London: Air Ministry. Reprinted by Military Library Research Ltd, 2008. Original available in TNA AIR 10/5206.

Air Historical Branch. 1952. *The Second World War 1939–1945. Royal Air Force Signals: Vol V, Fighter Control and Interception*. London: Air Ministry. Reprinted by Military Library Research Ltd, 2008. Original available in TNA AIR 20/12426.

Ashworth, C. 1990. *Action Stations 5: Military Airfields of the South-West*. Wellingborough: Patrick Stephens, 2nd edition.

Babington Smith, C. 1957. *Evidence in Camera: The Story of Photographic Intelligence in the Second World War*. Harmondsworth: Penguin.

Barnett, C. 1991. *Engage the Enemy More Closely: The Royal Navy in the Second World War*. London: Hodder and Stoughton.

Barrett, J. 1992. *Flat Holm during World War 2*. Privately printed.

Berryman, D. 2006. *Somerset Airfields in the Second World War*. Newbury: Countryside Books.

Binding, H. 2007. *The Book of Carhampton and Blue Anchor*. Tiverton: Halsgrove.

Brettingham, L. 1997. *Royal Air Force Beam Benders: No. 80 (Signals) Wing, 1940–1945*. Leicester: Midland Publishing.

British Telecommunications. 2001. *The Story of Portishead Radio: Long Range Maritime Radio Communications, 1920–1995*. Online publication at http://jproc.ca/radiostor/portis1.html Accessed 5 September 2008.

Brown, D. 1999. *Somerset v Hitler: Secret Operations in the Mendips 1939–1945*. Newbury: Countryside Books.

Brown, D K. 2007. *Escorts: Ships, Weapons and Tactics in World War II*. Barnsley: Seaforth Publishing.

Brown, H G. 1945. *English City: The Growth and the Future of Bristol*. Bickley: JS Fry and Sons Ltd.

Butler, J R M. 1957. *Grand Strategy: Volume 2, September 1939 – June 1941*. London: HMSO.

Bykofsky, J and Larson, H. 1990. *The Transportation Corps: Operations Overseas.* Washington, DC: Office of the Chief of Military History.

Churchill, W S. 1949. *The Second World War: Volume 2, Their Finest Hour.* London: Cassell.

Collier, B. 1957. *The Defence of the United Kingdom.* London: HMSO.

Concannon, B. 1995. *The History of Dunster Beach.* Solihull: Monkspath Books.

Cooper, A J. 2004. *Anti-Aircraft Command 1939–1945: The Other Forgotten Army.* Fleet Hargate: Arcturus Press.

Costello, J and Hughes, T. 1977. *The Battle of the Atlantic.* London: Collins.

Crowther, J G and Whiddington, R. 1947. *Science at War.* London: Department of Scientific and Industrial Research.

Crowther, S and Dickson, A. 2008. *Severn Estuary Rapid Coastal Zone Assessment Survey National Mapping Programme.* Gloucester: Gloucestershire County Council. Online publication at http://www.gloucestershire.gov.uk/index.cfm?articleid=16998 Accessed 1/8/2010.

Dobinson, C. 1996. *Twentieth Century Fortifications in England, Volume VI: Coast Artillery, 1900–56.* Unpublished Council for British Archaeology report for English Heritage.

Dobinson, C. 1999. *Twentieth Century Fortifications in England, Volume VII: Acoustics and Radar.* Unpublished Council for British Archaeology report for English Heritage.

Dobinson, C. 2000. *Fields of Deception: Britain's Bombing Decoys of World War II.* London: Methuen.

Dobinson, C. 2001. *AA Command: Britain's Anti-Aircraft Defences of World War II.* London: Methuen.

Dobinson, C. 2010. *Building Radar: Forging Britain's Early-Warning Chain, 1935–1945.* London: Methuen.

ENPA. 2007. *Historic Environment Review.* Dulverton: Exmoor National Park Authority.

Farr, G. 1967. *West Country Passenger Steamers.* Prescot: T Stephenson and Sons.

GPO. 1959. *The Link that's Fifty Years Old: Commemorating a Half Century of the Post Office Ship – Shore Service.* London: HMSO.

Grove, E J. 2005. *The Royal Navy since 1815: A New Short History.* London: Palgrave Macmillan.

Handley, C. 2001. *Maritime Activities of the Somerset and Dorset Railway.* Bath: Millstream Books.

Hawkins, M. 1988. *Somerset at War 1939–1945.* Cossington: Hawk Editions, 2nd edition.

Hinsley, F H. 1979. *British Intelligence in the Second World War, Volume 2: Its Influence on Strategy and Operations.* London: HMSO.

Hinsley, F H and Simkins, C A G. 1990. *British Intelligence in the Second World War, Volume 4: Security and Counter Intelligence.* London: HMSO.

Hinsley, F H, Thomas, E E, Simkins, C A G and Ransom, C F G. 1988. *British Intelligence in the Second World War, Volume 3, Part 1: Its Influence on Strategy and Operations.* London: HMSO.

Hogg, I V. 1974. *Coast Defences of England and Wales, 1856–1956.* Newton Abbot: David and Charles.

Bibliography

Hurley, J. 1978. *Exmoor in Wartime*. Dulverton: Exmoor Press.

Jentz, T L. 1998. *Die Deutsche Panzertruppe 1933–1942, Band 1*. Eggolsheim: Podzun-Pallas.

Jones, R V. 1978. *Most Secret War: British Scientific Intelligence 1939–1945*. London: Hamish Hamilton.

Jory, B. 1995. *Flat Holm: Bristol Channel Island*. Wincanton: Wincanton Press.

Kell, C. 1955. *Flight Tests at Transonic Speeds on Freely Falling Models*. Online at http://naca.central.cranfield.ac.uk/reports/arc/rm/2902.pdf Accessed 25 September 2008.

Lavery, B. 2006. *Churchill's Navy: The Ships, Men and Organisation*. London: Conway Maritime Press.

Legg, R. 1991. *Steep Holm at War*. London: Wincanton Press.

Mackenzie, S P. 1995. *The Home Guard: A Political and Military History*. Oxford: Oxford University Press.

Mote, G. 1986. *The Westcountrymen: Ketches and Trows of the Bristol Channel*. Bideford: Badger Books.

Parsons, R. 1988. *The Story of Kings: CJ King and Sons 1850 to the Present Day*. Bristol: Redcliffe Press.

Parsons, R M. 1982. *The White Ships: The Banana Trade at the Port of Bristol*. Bristol: City of Bristol Museum and Art Gallery.

Passmore, M and Passmore, A. 2008. *Royal Air Force Air-Defence Radar Stations in Devon: The Second World War and Beyond*. Exeter: MJ Passmore.

Pawle, G. 2009. *The Wheezers & Dodgers: The Inside Story of Clandestine Weapon Development in World War II*. Barnsley: Seaforth Publishing. Originally published in 1956 as *The Secret War 1939–1945*.

Pile, F. 1949. *Ack-Ack: Britain's Defence against Air Attack during the Second World War*. London: Panther Books. 1956 paperback reprint.

Price, A. 1977. *Blitz on Britain: The Bomber Attacks on the United Kingdom 1939–1945*. Hinckley: Ian Allan. Reprinted Sutton 2000.

PRO. 2001. *The Rise and Fall of the German Air Force (1933 to 1945)*. Richmond: Public Record Office. Reprint of 1948 Air Historical Branch document, original in TNA AIR 41/10.

Rendell, S D. 1981. Military history: a summary. In *Steep Holm: A Survey*, 37–46. Taunton: Somerset Archaeological and Natural History Society.

Rich, J. 1996. *The Bristol Pilots: A Treatise on the Bristol Pilots from their Origination to their Amalgamation including a List of Pilots' Names, Dates and some of the Boats, for almost 500 years*. Pill: Atlantis 33.

Richards, D. 1953. *Royal Air Force 1939–1945. Vol. I: The Fight at Odds*. London: HMSO. Available online at http://www.ibiblio.org/hyperwar/UN/UK/UK-RAF-I/index.html Accessed 5/9/2010.

Riley, H. 2006. *The Historic Landscape of the Quantock Hills*. London: English Heritage.

Roskill, S W. 1954. *The War at Sea 1939–45: Volume 1, The Defensive*. London: HMSO.

Roskill, S W. 1960. *The Navy at War 1939–1945*. London: Collins.

Roskill, S W. 1961. *The War at Sea 1939-45: Volume 3, Part 2, The Offensive*. London: HMSO.

Roskill, S W. 1977. *Churchill and the Admirals.* London: Collins.

Roskill, S W. 1978. *Naval Policy Between the Wars.* NMM Maritime Monographs and Reports 29. London: Trustees of the National Maritime Museum.

Saunders, A, Spurgeon, C J, Thomas, H J and Roberts, D J. 2001. *Guns across the Severn: The Victorian Fortifications of Glamorgan.* Aberystwyth: Royal Commission on the Ancient and Historical Monuments of Wales.

Schofield, A J, Webster, C J and Anderton, M J. 1998. Second World War remains on Black Down: a reinterpretation. *Somerset Archaeology and Natural History,* **142**, 271–286.

Slade, W J. 1959. *Out of Appledore.* London: Conway Maritime Press.

Smith, D J. 1989. *British Military Airfields, 1939–45.* Wellingborough: Patrick Stephens.

Stafford, D. 2006. *The Book of St Audries and West Quantoxhead: An Amble Through History.* Tiverton: Halsgrove.

Trevor-Roper, H R. 1964. *Blitzkrieg to Defeat: Hitler's War Directives 1939–1945.* Edinburgh: Birlinn. Pan Books reprint 1983.

van der Bijl, N. 2000. *Brean Down Fort: Its History and the Defence of the Bristol Channel.* Cossington: Hawk Editions.

Wakefield, K. 1994. *Operation Bolero: The Americans in Bristol and the West Country 1942–45.* Manchester: Crecy Books.

War Office. 1914. *Musketry Regulations, Part II: Rifle Ranges and Musketry Appliances.* London: HMSO. Unpublished manual: amendment I of 1910 edition.

War Office. 1938. *Signal Training (All Arms).* London: HMSO. Unpublished manual.

Warlow, B. 2000. *Shore Establishments of the Royal Navy.* Liskeard: Maritime Books.

Webster, C J. 2001. The Victorian and Second World War artillery batteries on Brean Down. *Somerset Archaeology and Natural History,* **145**, 89–115.

Webster, C J (ed). 2007. *The Archaeology of South West England: A Resource Assessment and Research Agenda.* Taunton: Somerset County Council.

Wheeler, R and Matthews, A. 2007. *German Invasion Plans for the British Isles, 1940.* Oxford: Bodleian Library. Translation of *Militärgeographische Angaben Uber England, 1940.*

Wilson, J. 2004. *The Somerset Home Guard: A Pictorial Role-Call.* Hersham: Ian Allan.

Wilson, J. 2005. *The Somerset Home Guard: a Pictorial Roll Call Update October 2005.* Hersham: Ian Allen. Four page update to Wilson (2004).

Wilson, N. 1996. The Washford transmitting station. *Somerset Industrial Archaeology Society Bulletin,* **73**, 2–9.

Winser, J de S. 2009. *Coasters go to War: Military Sailings to the Continent, 1939–1945.* Preston: Ships in Focus Publications.

Winter, M T. 2005. *The Portishead Coal Boats: A History of Osborn and Wallis Ltd of Bristol.* Lydney: Black Dwarf.

Wood, D. 1976. *Attack Warning Red: The Royal Observer Corps and the Defence of Britain 1925 to 1975.* London: MacDonald and Janes.

Index

8 Corps
    Defence Scheme March 1941, 29
    mobile reserve at Berrow, 37
    ordered RAF dawn patrols, 27
    responsible for defence of SW, 20
    reviewed defence plans, 46
    use of Minehead hotels, 78
    warned of threat to Bristol Channel, 21

A

Admiralty
    communications, 91
    control of Fleet Air Arm, 18
    experimental site, 88
    instructions to merchant shipping, 6
    need for AA defences of Flat Holm, 53
    plans for protection of trade, 5
    provision of ex-naval guns, 47
    radio beacons, 73
    responsible for coastguards, 23
aerodromes
    coastal, 94
    Naval Air Stations, 18
    targets for attack, 28, 31
air defences, 57–76
airborne attacks
    blitzkrieg tactics, 23
    by Ju-52, 24, 25, 27
    on airfields, 26
    on Dorset, 21
    on Exmoor, 21, 33–36
    on Mendip, 25, 37
    on Somerset, 21
    on the Brendon Hills, 21
    on the Quantocks, 25
Allerford, anti-tank roadblock, 35
Alstone
    possible telemetry station, 90
    RCM sites, 92, 94
anti-aircraft guns
    3-inch gun, **56**, **80**
    4.5-inch gun, **58**
    deployment, 58, 59
    Flat Holm, 53
    guns to move to Berrow, 37
    practice camp at Doniford, 37, 41, 80, 81
    radar controlled, 65
    ranges, 80–82
    rockets, 51
    US forces, 79
anti-aircraft rockets, 81, 82
anti-submarine forces
    strength in 1940, 7, **8**
    strength in 1941, 7
    strength in 1942, **13**
Appledore (Devon)
    Coast Artillery battery, 48
    experimental establishment, 88
    RN Sub-Command, 12
Ashford, threat of seaplanes on reservoir, 26
Auxiliary Patrols (RN), 11–13
Auxiliary Units, *see* GHQ Auxiliary Units
Avebury (Wiltshire)
    GCI radar, 67
Avonmouth
    alleged coast battery, 51
    bombed, 57
    defended by balloons, 59
    degaussing mobile wiping units, 13
    identified as Vulnerable Point, 38
    port denial measures, 30
    protected by bombing decoys, 74
    radar equipped AA deployed, 65
    smoke screens, 75, 76
    supply base for BEF, 5
    target for German attacks, 28, 52
Axe, river
    forming Taunton Stop Line, 22
    possible seaplane landing site, 26
Axminster (Devon)
    anti-tank island, 22

B

balloons, *see* barrage balloons
Bampton (Devon), anti-tank island, 22
Banwell, radar equipped AA deployed, 65
barrage balloons
    deployment, 59
    experimental, 38, 86, 88–90, **89**
    gas production at Weston-super-Mare, 94
    ships requisitioned, 7

Barry (Glamorgan)
    base for RAF rescue group, 13
    coal trade, 1
    defended by balloons, 59
    docks closed by mines, 57
    Naval Control Service, 5
    supply base for BEF, 5
Bason Bridge, defence of river Brue crossing, 37
Bath
    radar equipped AA deployed, 65
BBC transmitters
    controlled by RAF, 72, 73
    vulnerable to sabotage, 38
Beer Head (Devon), CHL radar station, 68
Beetle warning broadcasts, 45
Berrow
    holiday camp requisitioned, 77
    pillboxes, 37
    rifle range, 79
Berrow Flats, **38**
    beach barrages, 37, 56
    beach landing obstructions, 24
    experimental site, 87
    threat of landing, 24, 37
Berwick Wood (Gloucestershire)
    identified as Vulnerable Point, 38
HMS *Birnbeck*, **86**
    commissioned, 14
    experimental site, 85–88
Blagdon, threat of seaplanes on reservoir, 26
Bleadon, bombing decoy site, 74
blitzkrieg tactics, 23, 24
Blue Anchor
    Auxiliary Units, 42
    beach defence gun, 14, 32
    beach defences, 32, 33, 41
    beach landing obstructions, 24
    Langbury Hotel, 14, **15**, 78
    pillboxes, 32, **34**
    rifle range, 79
    SD wireless out-station, 42
    threat of landing, 24, 36
Bolero (operation)
    role of Bristol Channel ports, 15
Bolt Tail (Devon), mobile CHEL radar, 69
bombing decoys, 73–75
Box (Rudlow, Wiltshire), RAF 10 Group HQ, 59, **60**
Branscombe (Devon), CH radar station, 68
Breaksea lightship, 5
Brean
    smoke screen trials, 90
    US forces stationed, 79
Brean Down
    battery, **50**
        armament, 53
        established, 53
        Fort Record Book missing, 3, 54
        plastic armour roof, 54
        run-down, 56
        surviving remains, **52**, 54
    bombing range target arrow, 84
    experimental site, 85–88, **93**, 94
    surviving remains, 79
    undefended and requiring patrols, 40
Brendon Common (Devon)
    chemical warfare trials, 90
    potential site for CH radar, 64
Brent Knoll
    'centre of resistance', 28
    SD wireless out-station, 42
    slit trenches, **29**
Brest (France)
    base for German navy, **16**
    German airbases, 57
    navigation beam transmitters, 71
    port for supply of BEF, 5
Bridgwater
    anti-tank island, 22, 28
    'centre of resistance', 28
    coastal fuel depot, 31
    Home Guard, 79, 88
    Port of Bridgwater, extent, 5
    potential use to invader, 23
    strategic significance, 28
    telephone cable balancing house, 38
    tidal wharf, 5
Bridgwater and Taunton canal, forming Taunton Stop Line, 22, **33**
Bristol
    anti-tank island, 22
    bombed, 12, 57, 65, 71, 72
    defended by AA guns, 58, 61
    defended by balloons, 59
    low-power BBC transmitter, 73
    Mass Observation reports, 26, 32, 77
    Observer Corps 23 Group HQ, 60
    Outer Defence Line, 22, 37
    Port of Bristol, *see also* Avonmouth and Portishead
        imports 1938, 5
        signal station at Walton Bay, 5, **7**
        tonnages, 12
    protected by bombing decoys, 74
    radar equipped AA deployed, 65
    RAF Filton, 59
    target for German attacks, 21, 28, 37, 52
    target for V1 missiles, 61
    US forces stationed, 79
    Z batteries, 81, 82
Bristol Aeroplane Company, 59

104

Index

Bristol Channel
    Auxiliary Patrols, 11
    British forces 1940, **8**
    British forces 1942, **13**
    Coast Artillery, 47–56
    minefields, 13, **14**
    passenger steamers, 1, 5
    ranges, **84**, 90
    role in Operation Neptune, 15
    strategic significance, 1, 5, 20, 21, 23, 52
    submarine activity, 7, 57
'British Resistance Organisation', *see* GHQ Auxiliary Units
Brookman's Park (Hertfordshire), BBC transmitters
    use for radio counter measures, 73
Brue, river
    crossings defended, 37
    possible seaplane landing site, 26
Burnett near Keynsham, magazine guarded, 31
Burnham-on-Sea
    beach landing obstructions, 24
    'centre of resistance', 28
    east end of GHQ Line, 22
    hotels requisitioned, 78
    north end of Taunton Stop Line, 22
    ship-shore radio station, 38, 91

C

camouflage and concealment, 75, 76
Cannington
    Home Guard rifle rage, 79
    roadblock, 36
    threat of seaplanes on reservoir, 26
SS *Carare*, mined and sunk, 8
Cardiff
    bombed, 12, 57, 72
    coal trade, 1
    dealing with convoys, 52
    defended by AA guns, 53, 58
    defended by balloons, 59
    degaussing mobile wiping units, 13
    Flag Officer in Command, 5, 17
    protected by bombing decoys, 74
    RN sub-command
        established, 5
        reorganised, 12
    target for German attacks, 52
Carhampton, pillboxes, 32
Casement, JM
    appointed RNO Watchet, 13, 48
    moved to HMS *Birnbeck*, Weston-super-Mare, 14
    office nearly destroyed by experiment, 86
Castle Neroche, secret radio station, 42
SS *Cato*, mined and sunk, 8
Chain Home, *see* radar
Chard
    anti-tank island, 22

canal used for Taunton Stop Line, 22
    railway used for Taunton Stop Line, 22
Charlton Horethorne, tender to HMS *Heron*, 18
Cheddar, threat of seaplanes on reservoir, 26
Cherbourg (France)
    base for E-boats, **16**
    German airbases, 57
    launch sites for V1, 61
    navigation beam transmitters, 71
    port for supply of BEF, 5
Churchstanton, *see* Culmhead
Clevedon
    anti-aircraft range at Wains Hill, 81
    BBC transmitter, 73
        vulnerable to sabotage, 38
    beach defences authorised, 28
    pier, 1, **2**, 5, 30
    smoke screen trials, 90
Coast Artillery (RA), **8**, **13**, **50**, 47–56
    20 Coast Artillery Group at Instow (Devon), 48
    400 Coast Battery at Minehead, 48
    558 Coast Regiment
        at Instow (Devon), 48
        radar at Minehead, 68
    batteries, *see* Brean Down, Flat Holm, Minehead, Portishead and Steep Holm
    co-ordinated by RNO Watchet, 13, 14
    emergency batteries established, 47, 48
    Severn Defences, 51–56
Coastal Command (RAF)
    15 Group at Plymouth, **6**, 20
    sorties westward, 27
coastal defence troops, 40–42
    communications, 42–45
Coastguard
    assessment of beaches for landings, 23
    consulted by Coast Artillery, 49
    co-ordinated by RNO Watchet, 13
    dawn patrols for enemy agent landings, 40
    identification of friendly shipping, 50
    links to Observer Corps, 60
    stations, **8**, 27
coast-watchers
    co-ordinated by RNO Watchet, 13, 14
    limited effectiveness at night, 39
    watch along coast, 27
Colerne (Wiltshire), RAF sector station, 60, 65
Combwich
    potential use to invader, 23
    tidal wharf, 5
convoys, 5, 6, 12, 14, 52, 53, 55, 60, 91
Countisbury Hill (Devon), CHL radar proposed, 64
Coverack (Cornwall), 'watcher station', 70
Creech St Michael, anti-tank island, 22
Crewkerne, anti-tank island, 22
Crowcombe, ammunition supply point, 45

105

Culmhead, RAF station, 60, 89
Customs & Excise, gathering intelligence, 27

D

D-Day, *see* Overlord and Neptune
decoys, *see* bombing decoys
Delabole (Cornwall), RCM jamming station, 70
Department of Miscellaneous Weapons Development (RN), 14, 54, 85–88
HMS *Dipper*, RNAS Henstridge, **17**, 18
Doniford, AA range, **56**, **58**, **80**, **81**, **82**
    AA guns in anti-shipping role, 33, 56
    AA rockets, 82
    School of AA Defence, 38, 41
Dorchester (Dorset), anti-tank island, 22
SS *Downleaze*, collier's role in operation Overlord, 15
Dunball
    harbour for coastal traffic, 1
    potential use to invader, 23
    SD wireless out-station, 42
    tidal wharf, 5
Dunster
    anti-tank roadblock, 35
    coastal fuel depot, 31
    Home Guard coast defences, 45
    Observer Corps post, 61
    pillboxes, 32
Dunster Beach
    Army camp, 77, **78**, **83**, 90
    holiday camp requisitioned, 77
    pillboxes, **34**
    rocket tests, 90
SS *Durdham*, steam dredger, mined, 12
Durleigh, threat of seaplanes on reservoir, 26
Durston, anti-tank island, 22

E

East Huntspill, *see* RAF Huntspill
E-boats, 38, 52, 55
Eire, *see* Ireland
Emergency Licences, 32
enemy agents, 31, 32, 39, 40, 92
evacuation of children to Somerset, 57
Examination Service, 5, 13, 51, 53
Exe Plain, Simonsbath, CH radar station proposed, 64
Exeter (Devon)
    anti-tank island, 22
    GCI radar, 67
    low-power BBC transmitter, 73
    Observer Corps 21 Group HQ, 60
    RAF sector station, 59, **60**
Exford, HQ 540 Searchlight Battery, 62
Exminster (Devon), GCI radar, 67
Exmoor
    artillery ranges, 83
    roadblocks, 35
    threat of landings, 21, 25, 30, 33–36

F

Fairmile (Devon)
    'Meaconing' station, 72
    RCM jamming station, 70
Fairwood Common (Glamorgan), RAF sector station, **60**
'Fifth Column', 31
Fighting Vehicle Proving Establishment, mud trials, 88
Filton
    identified as Vulnerable Point, 38
    RAF sector station, 59, **60**
Fixed Defences Severn, **50**, 51–56
    survival of military records, 54
    surviving remains, 54
    under Western Command, 48
Flat Holm (Glamorgan), **50**, **86**
    armament, 53
    batteries established, 53
    Fort Record Book, 54
    surviving remains, 54
Flat Point (Devon), mobile CHEL radar, 69
Frome, anti-tank island, 22
fuel denial measures, 30, 31

G

Garlandstone, ketch, 10, **11**
GHQ Auxiliary Units, 42
    in Blue Anchor area, 36
    Special Duties Branch, 42, **43**
GHQ stop line, 21, 22, 37
Glastonbury
    RCM jamming station, 69, 70
    SD wireless out-station, 42
Glenthorne, undefended and requiring patrols, 40
GPO
    providing military communications, 43
    Radio Security Service run for MI5, 92
    ship-shore radio stations, 91
    telephone repeater stations, 38
    transmitters controlled by RAF, 73
Greenaleigh, undefended and requiring patrols, 40

H

Henstridge RNAS, HMS *Dipper*, **17**, 18
HMS *Heron*, RNAS Yeovilton, 18
Highbridge
    'Meaconing' station, 72
    'centre of resistance', 28
    coal handled by wharf, 12
    defence of river Brue crossing, 37
    DF station, *see* Alstone
    harbour for coastal traffic, 1
    Observer Corps post, 60
    tidal wharf, 5
Holford, Observer Corps post, 60
holiday accommodation, use by military, 77–79
Home Defence Units (RAF), 71

Home Guard
- beach defence guns, 83
- coast guns at Minehead, 48
- coast guns at Portishead, 51, 56
- coast defence role, 40, 41
- communications, 43, 44
- conscription introduced, 42
- false invasion alert, 45
- fuel denial measures, 30
- harbour defence guns at Watchet, 33, 51
- manpower and equipment, 41, 45
- membership of Auxiliary Units, 42
- observation posts, 27
- rifle ranges, 79
- roadblocks and checkpoints, 32
- role in Operation Overlord, 45
- states of readiness, **40**
- stood down, 45, 56
- trials of Great Panjandrum, 88
- Z batteries, 82

Home Intelligence Department, *see* Mass Observation

Honiton (Devon)
- 'Meaconing' station, 72
- anti-tank island, 22

Hope Cove (Devon), GCI radar, 67

Huntspill River, water storage for ROF, 75

Hydrographic Department (RN)
- Creechbarrow House, Taunton
  - camouflage, 75
  - protected by bombing decoy, 74

I

Ilfracombe (Devon), Coast Artillery battery, 48

HMS *Iliad* (Watchet)
- disbanded 1942, 14
- established, 11
- lack of memories, 4

Ilminster, anti-tank island, 22

immobilisation parks, 32

Instow (Devon), Coast Artillery battery, 48

internment camps, 31

invasion, preparations against
- aircraft landing obstructions, 24–27, **25, 26**
- airfield defence, 26
- ammunition supplies, 45
- anti-tank islands, 22, 22, 23, 28
- centres of resistance, 22, 28
- coast defences, 23–42, **33, 34, 39**
- guards on key points, 31
- inland defences, 21–23
- minefields in Bristol Channel, 7–11, **14**
- movement controls, 32
- national strategy, 19, 20
- naval Auxiliary Patrols, 11, 12
- stop lines and anti-tank islands, 21–23
- tank landing threat thought minimal, 28–30
- threat of 'Fifth Column', 31
- threat of seaborne landings, 23
- threat to Exmoor and the Brendons, 21, 33–36
- threat to north Somerset coast, 37
- threat to the South West, 20, 21, 37, 46
- threat to upper Bristol Channel ports, 52
- warning systems, 42–45

Ireland, potential base for German attacks, 21

Ivybridge (Devon), RCM jamming station, 70, 72

J

MT *John King*, strafed, 8, **9**

K

Kilmington (Wiltshire), radar equipped AA deployed, 65

Kilton, anti-tank range, 83

King, IHL, appointed to command HMS *Iliad*, 14

Kingsdown (Kent), Y-Service 'Home Defence Unit', 71

Kingston Seymour, tank mud trials, 88

Kington Magna (Dorset), 'Meaconing' station, 72

Knickbein, *see* radio counter measures

L

Lavernock Point (Glamorgan)
- Coast Artillery battery, **50**
  - defences run-down, 56
  - established, 53
  - Fort Record Book, 54
  - rebuilt, 53
  - surviving remains, 54
  - examination anchorage, 5

Liddymore Camp, 37, 41, 80

Lilstock
- bombing range, 84, 85
- experimental site, 88
- range target arrow, **85**
- rifle range, 79
- undefended and requiring patrols, 40

Lodge Farm, Bristol, AA guns in anti-shipping role, 56

Long Load, GCI radar, 67

Lord, LR
- appointed to command HMS *Iliad*, 11
- relieved of command HMS *Iliad*, 14

Luckott Moor, potential site for CH radar, 64

Lympsham
- 'Meaconing' station, 72
- tidal wharf, **2**, 5

M

Mass Observation, reports of public opinion, 21, 26, 31, 32

medium frequency direction finding (MFDF), 72, 94

Mendip Hills
- potential landing grounds, 25

MI5
- direction finding (DF) station, 38, 92
- monitoring enemy signals, 91, 92

Middle Hope Cove
    experimental site, 85, 86, 88
    threat of landing in bay, 24
Middle Wallop (Hampshire), RAF sector station, 59, **60**
Milford Haven (Pembrokeshire), protected by bombing decoys, 74
minefields
    aerial, 89
    anti-submarine, 16
    laid across St George's Channel, 1940, 8
    laid in Bristol Channel 1941, **14**
    laid in Bristol Channel, 1941, 13
    voyage of *Garlandstone*, 10
Minehead
    'centre of resistance', 28
    Coast Artillery battery, 30, 47–51, **47**, **49**, **50**
        abandoned, 33
        myths about, 4
    coastal fuel depot, 31
    concern about effect of war on tourism, 77
    harbour for small coasters, 5
    Home guard rifle range, 79
    hotels requisitioned, 78
    lifeboat, 8
    North Hill
        CD/CHL radar, 55, 68
        tank ranges, 82, 83
    pier, 1, 5, 30, **47**
    pillboxes, 32
    port berthing capacity, 33
    port denial measures, 30
    potential use to invader, 23
    priority for defence, 28
minelaying, by U-boats, 8
minesweepers
    based at Swansea, 12
    formation of minesweeper groups, 7
    P & A Campbell's fleet requisitioned, 7
Ministry of Information (MOI), *see* Mass Observation
movement controls, 32
Murdock, Andrew, sailed *Garlandstone* over minefields, 10, **11**

N
Nantes (France), port for supply of BEF, 5
Naval Control Service, at Barry, 5
Naval Port Service, at Bristol and Cardiff, 5
Naval Shore Wireless Station (HMS *Flowerdown*), staff move to Burnham-on-Sea, 91
Nells Point (Glamorgan)
    examination battery, 53
    proposed battery, 55
Neptune (operation)
    role of Bristol Channel ports, 15
Nether Stowey, roadblock, 36
Newport (Monmouthshire)
    coal trade, 1
    defended by AA guns, 58
    defended by balloons, 59
    protected by bombing decoys, 74
    supply base for BEF, 5
    target for German attacks, 52
Newton Abbot (Devon), RCM jamming station, 70
North Hill, *see* Minehead
North Petherton, roadblock, 36
Norton Fitzwarren
    Norton Manor Camp
        Searchlight Training Regiment, 41
        Supply Reserve Depot, 45, **75**
            camouflage, 75
            protected by bombing decoys, 74

O
observation posts (Army), 27
Observer Corps, 60, 61
    coast watching, 27
    communications, 43
    granted Royal title, 61
    links to Coastguard, 60
    tracking aircraft, 58, 59, 65
    tracking V1 missiles, 61
oil facilities, identified as Vulnerable Point, 38
Overlord (operation), **16**
    American preparations, 79, 83, 90
    DMWD experimental work, 86–88
    need for additional ranges, 84
    role of Bristol Channel ports, 15
SS *Overton*, ignored fire from Coast Artillery, 53

P
Paignton (Devon)
    internment camp, 31
Parrett, river
    difficulty of navigation, 23
    forming Taunton Stop Line, 22
    possible seaplane landing site, 26
    tidal wharfs, 5
Pawlett
    balloon experimental station, 38, 88–90, **89**
    ranges, 89, 90
    rocket battery, 82
Pembrey (Carmarthenshire), RAF sector station, 59, **60**
Penarth (Glamorgan)
    base for Auxiliary Patrol, 11
    coal trade, 1
    supply base for operation Overlord, 16
    target for German attacks, 52
Periton, anti-tank roadblock, 35
Perry Bridge, telephone cable balancing house, 38
pigeons, 44

Index

pillboxes, **33**
    at Berrow, 37
    at Blue Anchor, 32, **34**
    at Dunster Beach, **34**
    at Raleigh's Cross, 35
    at Roadwater, **35**
    at Uphill, **39**
    use in anti-tank islands, 28
    use on beaches, 19, 27
    use on stop lines, 22
Pilning, Bristol, AA guns in anti-shipping role, 56
'Pink Area' for fuel denial measures, 30, **31**
plastic armour, **52**, 54, **55**, 85
Plymouth (Devon)
    bombed, 72
    protected by bombing decoys, 74
    RAF Coastal Command, **6**, 20
    RN Western Approaches Command, 5, **6**, 20
    target for German invasion, 20, 21
    target for V1 missiles, 61
Police
    gathering intelligence, 27
    Glastonbury police station used for RCM, 69
    manning vehicle check points, 32
    power to close roads, 28
    Williton police station name removed, **31**
Porlock
    chemical warfare units, 90
    Home Guard coast defences, 45
    Observer Corps post, 60
    RCM jamming station, 70, 72
    threat of landing in bay, 24
    undefended and requiring patrols, 40
Porlock Common, potential site for CH radar, 64
Porlock Weir
    harbour for small coasters, 5
Port Talbot (Glamorgan)
    base for Auxiliary Patrol, 11
    defended by balloons, 59
    supply base for operation Overlord, 16
Porthcawl (Glamorgan)
    base for RAF rescue group, 13
    CHL radar station, 64
Portishead
    anti-tank defences, 30
    battery, 48, **50**, 51, 56
    'centre of resistance', 28
    coal and timber, 5
    defence plans, 28
    defended by balloons, 59
    harbour for coastal traffic, 1
    port denial measures, 30
    potential use to invader, 23
    power station, 15
    rocket battery range, 82
    ship-shore radio station, 38, 91
    supply base for operation Overlord, 15
    target for German attacks, 52
Portishead Point, undefended and requiring patrols, 40
Portland (Dorset), 'watcher station', 70
Portreath (Cornwall), RAF sector station, **60**
ports, harbours and piers, **2**, 5
Prawl Point (Devon), CH radar station, 63
SS *Protesilaus*, mined off Swansea, 7
Puckington, SD wireless out-station, 42
Puriton, *see* Royal Ordnance Factory

Q

Quantock Hills
    potential landing grounds, 25, 28, 35
    roadblocks, 36
'Queen Bee' radio-controlled target aircraft, 80, **81**

R

radar
    air defence, 63–68
    Aircraft Interception (AI), 65, 67
    Chain Home (CH), 57, 63
    Chain Home Low (CHL), 64, 68
    Coast Defence (CD/CHL), 53, 68, 69
    Ground Controlled Interception (GCI), 66–68, **67**
    Gun Laying (GL), 65, **66**
    searchlight control (Elsie), 62, **65**
radio counter measures, 69–73
    Knickebein, 69–71
    medium frequency beacons, 72
    X-Gerät, 71, 72
    Y-Gerät, 72
Radio Security Service, *see* MI5
RAF
    10 Group at Box (Rudlow), 59
    80 (Signals) Wing, 69
    air navigation training, 80, 94
    Army Co-operation Squadron, 27
    barrage balloons, 59
    bombing ranges, 84, 85
    Coastal Command, based at Plymouth, **6**, 20
    control of CD/CHL radars, 69
    DF stations, 92, 93
    Fighter Command, organisation, 59, 60
    flying training, 94
    Home Defence Units, 71
    radio counter measures, 69–73
    RAF Cheadle, 71
    RAF Chivenor, 72
    RAF Churchstanton (Culmhead), 60, 89
    RAF Colerne, 60
    RAF Exeter, 59, 89
    RAF Filton, 59
    RAF Huntspill (radar), 67
    RAF Middle Wallop, 59
    RAF Pembrey, 59
    RAF Regiment LAA Gunnery School, 81

RAF (cont)
    RAF St Eval, 59
    RAF Weston Zoyland, 80, 84, 90, 94
    Rescue Service, 13
    running Observer Corps, 60
    Y-Service, *see* Y-Service
raids, on coastal installations, 37–39
Raleigh's Cross, anti-tank roadblock and pillbox, 35
ranges, coastal, 79–85, **84**
PS *Ravenswood*, ferry service withdrawn, 8
River Bridge, defence of river Brue crossing, 37
roadblocks
    around Exmoor and the Brendons, 35
    closure to civilian traffic, 28
    forbidden on certain main roads, 28
    movement controls and check points, 32
Roadwater, roadblock and surviving pillbox, 35
Rockingham, Bristol
    AA guns in anti-shipping role, 56
    beach barrages, 56
SS *Rockleaze*, collier's role in operation Overlord, 15
Rode, radar equipped AA deployed, 65
Rooks Bridge, telephone repeater station, 38
Royal Aircraft Establishment, at Pawlett, 88–90, **89**
Royal Artillery
    51 Heavy Regiment at Minehead battery, 48
    58 Medium Regiment at Dunster Camp, 83
    Coast Artillery, *see* Coast Artillery
Royal Engineers
    chemical warfare units at Dunster Beach, 90
    chemical warfare units at Porlock, 90
Royal Observer Corps, *see* Observer Corps
Royal Ordnance Factory (Puriton)
    camouflaged water-storage, 75
    identified as Vulnerable Point, 38
    protected by bombing decoys, 74
Royal Signals, manning secret radio station, 42

S
St Audries
    army camp, 77
    holiday camp requisitioned, 77
    possible range site, 81
    Somerset Light Infantry deployed, 41
    undefended and requiring patrols, 40
    US forces stationed, 79
St Eval (Cornwall), RAF sector station, 59, **60**
St George's wharf (now Royal Portbury Docks)
    AA guns in anti-shipping role, 56
    beach barrages, 56
    tank mud trials, 88
St Nazaire (France), port for supply of BEF, 5
Sand Bay
    air gunnery range, 85
    beach landing obstructions, 24
    rifle range, 79
    threat of landing, 24

SD, *see* GHQ Auxiliary Units
seaborne landing threat
    to Bristol Channel ports, 52
    to Dorset or East Devon, 21
    to Somerset, 23, 27–42, **33**
Searchlight Training Regiment
    ad-hoc infantry battalions raised, 41
    based at Norton Manor Camp, 41
searchlights (Army), 61–63, **64**, **65**
    coast watching, 27
    coastal defence zone, **62**
    communications, 43
searchlights (Coast Artillery)
    Brean Down, **87**
    liaison with Navy, 48
    Minehead, 48–50
    Portishead, 51
    Steep Holm, 54
    use against E-boats, 55
seaside holiday accommodation, use by military, 77–79
Seaton (Devon)
    internment camp, 31
    south end of Taunton Stop Line, 22
Secret Service, 39, 40
Selworthy, undefended and requiring patrols, 40
Severn defences
    Coast Artillery, *see* Fixed Defences Severn
    improved by radar at Minehead, 55
Severn Sub Area Defence Scheme, December 1940, 21
SF, *see* Starfish bombing decoy
Shaftesbury (Dorset), Y-Service 'Home Defence Unit', 71
Shepton Mallet
    anti-tank island, 22
Sherford Camp, Taunton
    Infantry Training Centre, 41
Shipham, RCM jamming station, 70, 72
signpost and nameboard removal, **31**, 32
Slocomslade (Devon), hutted camp for ranges, 90
smoke screens
    deployed to protect Avonmouth, 75, 76
    trials at Clevedon, 90
Somerset and Bristol Sub Area Defence Scheme, April 1943, 30, 37
Somerset Light Infantry
    battalions raised, 41
    deployed to St Audries, 41
    deployed to Weston-super-Mare, 41
    Exmoor patrols, 35
Somerset Sub Area Coast Defence Scheme, August 1940, 12, 21–24, 27, 28
Somerset Sub Area Defence Scheme, December 1940, 23, 26–28, 35
Somerton, radio station, 91
Sopley (Hampshire), GCI radar, 67
South Brewham, radar equipped AA deployed, 65

Index

South Wales, *see* Wales
Southern Command (Army)
    airfield defence plans, 26
    beach defence plans, **33**
    Chemical Warfare Reserve, 90
    defence plans, 20, 22
    defence works no longer needed, 39, 45
    stop line junction defence plans, 37
Spaxton
    roadblock, 36
    SD wireless out-station, 42
Special Duties Branch, *see* GHQ Auxiliary Units
Starfish bombing decoy, 74
Steart
    beach unsuitable for landing, 24
    ranges, 82, 85
Steep Holm, **50**, **86**
    armament, 53
    batteries established, 53, 54
    beach barrages, 37, 56
    Coast Artillery searchlight, 54
    defences run-down, 56
    Fort Record Book missing, 3, 54
    North Battery, 53
    plastic armour roof, 54, **55**
    problem of tides, 54
    South Battery, 53
    surviving remains, 54
Stert, ranges, 84, 85
Sticklepath, anti-tank roadblock, 35
Stockland Bristol DF station, 92
    vulnerable to sabotage, 38
stop lines, **22**
    Bristol Outer Defence Line, *see* Bristol
    GHQ Line, *see* GHQ Stop Line
    policy abandoned, 22
    six-pounder guns, 83
    Taunton Stop Line, *see* Taunton Stop Line
Strete (Devon), Y-Service 'Home Defence Unit', 71
Sturminster Marshall (Dorset), GCI radar, 67
Swansea
    ammunition sent to Normandy beaches, 15
    bombed, 57, 72
    defended by AA guns, 58
    defended by balloons, 59
    defended by searchlights, 62
    HMS *Lucifer*
        base for RAF rescue group, 13
        closed, 17
        degaussing mobile wiping units, 13
        established, 5
        problems communicating with Somerset coast units, 14, 48
    protected by bombing decoys, 74
    seaborne radio beacon, 73
    supply base for BEF, 5

T
Taunton
    anti-tank island, 22
    Hydrographic Office, *see* Hydrographic Office
    low-power BBC transmitter, 73
    protected by bombing decoy, 74
    radar equipped AA deployed, 65
    training units, 28, 41
Taunton Stop Line, **22**
    anti-tank islands, 22, 28
    design and construction, 22
    relationship with GHQ Line, 37
Templecombe
    'Meaconing' station, 72
    RCM jamming station, 70, 72
Tiverton (Devon), anti-tank island, 22
torpedo development unit, 90

U
U-28, lays mines off Swansea, 7
U-29, lays mines off Bull Point, 8
U-1169, sunk in St George's Channel, 17
U-boats, 8, 12, 16, 17
Uphill
    AA guns in anti-shipping role, 56
    beach barrages, 56
    pillbox on beach, **39**
    rifle range, 79

V
V1, German missile, 61
vehicle check points, 32
Volis Hill, secret radio station, 42

W
Wales
    Blorenge, SD wireless out-station, 42
    coal and metal industries, 5
    coal transport by sea, 12
    defences in west Wales, 21
    rail transport problems, 12
    target for bombers, 58
Walton Bay, Port of Bristol Authority signal station, 5, **7**
Washford, BBC transmitters, **73**
    use for enemy navigation, 73
    use for radio counter measures, 73
    vulnerable to sabotage, 38
Watchet
    anti-tank defences, 30, 36
    base for Auxiliary Patrol, 11
    beach defences authorised, 28
    'centre of resistance', 28
    harbour defence guns, 33, 51
    harbour for coastal traffic, 1, **2**, 5
    port berthing capacity, 33
    port denial measures, 30
    potential use to invader, 23

Watchet (cont)
    priority for defence, 28
    rocket battery, 82
    Royal Navy at, *see* HMS *Iliad*
Watchet ranges, *see* Doniford
Wells, radar equipped AA deployed, 65
West Prawl (Devon), 'watcher station', 70
Western Approaches Command (RN)
    based at Plymouth, 5, **6**, 20
    moved to Liverpool, 12
Western Area Defence Scheme, June 1941, 28, 30
Western Command (Army), Coast Artillery, 48, 55
Westhay, defence of river Brue crossing, 37
Westland, *see* Yeovil
Weston Zoyland (RAF)
    aerodrome guarded, 31
    anti-invasion dawn patrols, 27
    parenting Lilstock range, 84
    target towing, 80, 94
    torpedo development unit, 90
Weston-super-Mare
    aerodrome
        air navigation school, 94
        balloon barrage, **59**
        decoy site at Bleadon, 74
        defended by balloons, 59
        HAA guns deployed, 59
        key points guarded, 31
        origins, 94
        torpedo development unit, 90
    aircraft factory
        decoy site at Bleadon, 74
        defended by balloons, 59
        identified as Vulnerable Point, 38
    'centre of resistance', 28
    coastal fuel depot, 31
    gas works producing balloon gas, 94
    GCI radar planned, 67
    pier, 1
    pier (Birnbeck), **2**, 5, 30, 38, **86**, *see* HMS *Birnbeck*
    radar equipped AA deployed, 65
    Somerset Light Infantry deployed, 41
    threat of landing in bay, 24, 37
    US forces HQs at, 79
Whiteball railway tunnel, guarded, 31
Whitechurch, aerodrome guarded, 31
Wick St Lawrence, tidal wharf, **2**, 5
Williton, police station name removed, **31**
Wimborne Minster (Dorset), RCM site, 70
Winscombe, ammunition supply point, 45
wireless stations, 90–94
Withycombe, anti-tank roadblock, 35
Wiveliscombe, SD wireless out-station, 42
Wotan, *see* Y-Gerät
Wrafton (Devon), GCI radar, 67

Y

Yeo, river, possible seaplane landing site, 26
Yeovil
    anti-tank island, 22
    Observer Corps 22 Group HQ, 60
    radar equipped AA deployed, 65
    Westland aircraft factory
        aerodrome guarded, 31
        camouflage scheme, 75
        protected by bombing decoys, 74
Yeovilton RNAS, HMS *Heron*, 18
Y-Gerät or Wotan
    German air-navigation system stations, 72
Y-Service (RAF)
    control of BBC transmitters, 73
    liaison with bombing decoy sites, 74
    monitoring German airborne radio, 70, 71

Z

Z batteries, 81